Bicycle Citizens

ASIA: LOCAL STUDIES/GLOBAL THEMES

Hue-Tam Ho Tai, Jeffrey N. Wasserstrom, and Kären Wigen, Editors

1. *Bicycle Citizens: The Political World of the Japanese Housewife,*
   by Robin M. LeBlanc

Bicycle Citizens

The Political World of the
Japanese Housewife

Robin M. LeBlanc

WITH A FOREWORD BY
SASKIA SASSEN

UNIVERSITY OF CALIFORNIA PRESS

Berkeley / Los Angeles / London

A Study of the East Asian Institute, Columbia University

The East Asian Institute is Columbia University's center for research, publication, and teaching on modern East Asia. The Studies of the East Asian Institute were inaugurated in 1962 to bring to a wider public the results of significant new research on modern and contemporary East Asia.

University of California Press
Berkeley and Los Angeles, California

University of California Press, Ltd.
London, England

Library of Congress Cataloging-in-Publication Data

LeBlanc, Robin M.
    Bicycle citizens : the political world of the Japanese housewife /
Robin M. LeBlanc : foreword by Saskia Sassen.
        p.   cm. — (Asia—Local studies/Global themes)
    Includes bibliographical references and index.
    ISBN 0-520-21290-8 (alk. paper). — ISBN 0-520-21291-6 (alk.
paper)
        1. Women in politics—Japan.   2. Housewives—Japan—Political
activity.   3. Housewives—Japan—Social conditions.   4. Political
participation—Japan.   I. Title.   II. Series.
HQ1236.5.J3L43   1999
305.42'0952—dc21   98-46632
                                                                          CIP

Printed in the United States of America
9   8   7   6   5   4   3   2   1

To
Jim McNamee
Eddie Anderson
Kay Moss
Julie Dodd
and
John Shedd
all public high school teachers
who made a difference

Contents

FOREWORD by Saskia Sassen   ix

ACKNOWLEDGMENTS   xv

NOTE ON NAMES   xvii

1. "Supposing Truth Is a Woman—What Then?"   1

2. The Identity of the "Regular Housewife"   28

3. Housewives and Citizenship   61

4. Volunteering against Politics:
   Housewives, Citizenship, and Community Service   89

5. Toward a "Housewifely" Movement:
   The Seikatsu Club Co-op's Daily Life Politics   121

6. The Ono Campaign:
   A "Regular" Housewife in Elite Politics   164

CONCLUSION   195

NOTES   205

REFERENCES   227

INDEX   239

Foreword

How do citizens not involved in high-level politics experience their citizenship? Robin LeBlanc asks this question by studying a particular subject: housewives in Japan today. Beyond the substantive interest of the question, there is the fact that in Japan we are looking at a liberal democratic political system located in a markedly different culture from that of the United States (and the West generally). Hence an answer to LeBlanc's question may contribute to our understanding of liberal democracy generally. LeBlanc is, in many ways, after the same big questions that political theorists are after, but she takes a very distinct and unusual analytic and empirical pathway. This is not so much because her focus is on Japan but rather because of how she constructs her inquiry on citizenship: by locating it in a subject — Japanese housewives — whose very identity is customarily that of a particularistic, non-political actor.

LeBlanc's work is in keeping with one of the major aims of the "Asia: Local Studies / Global Themes" series — although focused on Asia, her study is of relevance to a broad community of scholars, including non-Asia specialists. I interpret her study as making two contributions. One has to do with questions of method: how to study what is rarely represented because it is excluded from the analytic categories organizing a field of study, and further, how to advance the study of macrolevel processes through site-specific foci and through techniques, such as ethnography, not usually associated with the study of these processes. A second contribution has to do with questions of substance: how to re-read the frequently confined worlds in which women often enact their political projects or, alternatively, enact projects coded as "domestic" or "particularistic" that are de facto political.

In choosing housewives as the lens through which she studies Japanese politics, LeBlanc has to challenge the methodological and substantive boundaries of her discipline. Intellectually, the world of the housewife is not considered part of political life and, in the end, of political science. As LeBlanc explains, the typical political science study would require a table of "indicators" of Japanese housewife-ness, ask a set of questions seeking standard information (on education and family income, for example), and prepare a series of scales that would elicit a measure of the individual's political participation. This process of standardization has the effect of flattening the subjects LeBlanc aims to study—Japanese housewives, who "understand their differences from others in terms of the degree to which they are determined by particularistic, privatized relationships." Such "flattening" is more than a limitation: "It is an un-seeing." To understand and to enter into the experience of citizenship of the Japanese housewife, LeBlanc has to find a new way of seeing—what she names the *bicycle* view of politics. As LeBlanc explains, what we see depends on the social transportation we use, and for Japanese housewives that social transportation is a bicycle.

LeBlanc contrasts a "bicycle" view of politics with an elite-centered view of politics she characterizes as "taxi" politics, and she points to a disjuncture between the housewives' and the elite's views of politics that parallels the difference between bicycles and taxis as forms of transportation. There is little resonance, and often tension, between the world of politics formally understood and the political life of housewives.

In this effort at understanding, LeBlanc uses methods—participant observation and other ethnographic techniques—that do not fit comfortably with the standard methods in political science. She focuses on dimensions that do not fit the indicators and categories of political science. And she focuses on subjects—housewives—who do not fit those categories and indicators. Feminist scholarship in all the social sciences has had to deal with a set of similar or equivalent difficulties and tensions in its effort to constitute its subject or to reconfigure a subject that has been flattened. The theoretical and empirical distance that LeBlanc had to bridge between the recognized world of politics and the as yet unmapped citizenship experience of the housewife—not of women as such, but of women as housewives—is a distance we encounter in many types of inquiry. Bridging this distance entails both an empirical research strategy and a theorization. LeBlanc began her fieldwork with the presumption that she did not know who exactly was her subject or where exactly she would be located. "I saw my primary . . . task as a researcher as the learning of the vocabulary by which my subject would 'indicate' herself to another who could hear her in her own terms." LeBlanc uses a bicycle rather than a taxi to travel the bridge between research strategy and theorization.

I have often had to use what LeBlanc would describe as a bicycle rather than a taxi to bridge conceptual and empirical distances in my own research about economic globalization. Of course, LeBlanc does not focus specifically on the theme of economic globalization, but because she wants her research on Japanese housewives to speak to those outside her field, I will take the liberty of elaborating some of the parallels in my own work.

It strikes me that LeBlanc's effort to recover a neglected or excluded research site (the Japanese housewife's experience of citizenship) for the study of a broad subject (liberal democracy) resonates strongly with my effort to recover a similarly neglected or excluded site (place, in the form of cities) to study another broad subject (the global economy). And it resonates with the research practices of a growing number of scholars doing work on transnational processes, which require, perhaps to an extreme, the negotiation of macro and micro levels of analysis if we are to go beyond very broad generalizations.[1]

My concern to recover place in our understanding of a global economic system does not fit comfortably with mainstream accounts. These accounts are increasingly centered on telecommunications that neutralize geography and on dematerialized economic activities that supposedly are confined to digital spaces. Nor does my research on the international financial industry fit these accounts, given my concern to understand how the industry works from the ground up, including the many different types of workers needed to produce the final product—the clerical workers, the immigrant cleaners, the truckers, the blue-collar workers maintaining the machines.

The efforts of LeBlanc and many other scholars to resist mainstream categories and methods matter enormously. She shows us how housewives' experience of citizenship is excluded from mainstream narratives about the political system. Similarly, in my research I have tried to show that the mainstream account of economic globalization can be seen as a narrative of eviction. Key concepts in that account—globalization, information economy, and telematics—all suggest that place no longer matters and that the only type of worker who matters is the highly educated professional. The mainstream account of economic globalization privileges the capability for global transmission over the material infrastructure that makes such transmission possible; information outputs over the workers producing those outputs, from specialists to secretaries; and the new transnational corporate culture over the multiplicity of work cultures, including immigrant cultures, within which many of the "other" jobs of the global information economy take place. In brief, the dominant narrative concerns itself with the hypermobility of capital rather than with that which is place-bound.

Why does it matter to recover place in analyses of the global economy, particularly place as constituted in major cities? Because it allows us to see the multiplicity of economies and work cultures in which the global information economy is embedded.[2] It also allows us to recover the concrete, localized processes through which globalization exists and to argue that, to a great extent, the multiculturalism in large cities is as much a part of globalization as international finance is. Further, focusing on cities allows us to specify a geography of strategic places at the global scale, places bound to each other by the dynamics of economic globalization. Finally, the centrality of place in a context of global processes engenders a transnational economic and political opening for the formation of new claims and hence for the constitution of entitlements, notably rights to place, and, at the limit, in the constitution of the notion of membership and "citizenship." By expanding the analytic terrain within which we understand the global economy, we render visible what is now evicted from the account. LeBlanc's concern with the housewife as citizen parallels mine with place in a global information economy.

With respect to the substance of LeBlanc's findings, I also see some very important resonances with a broader research community. LeBlanc shows us how being a housewife restricts a Japanese woman's public life in many important ways. Yet, paradoxically, it is also a situation that provides a woman with a unique vehicle for other forms of public participation, ones in which being a housewife is an advantage. Specifically, LeBlanc documents how, in the eyes of many, a housewife can be trusted precisely because she is a housewife, and when she builds networks with other housewives, the group of women is seen as expressing desirable public concern. Their critique of mainstream politics gains power because of the women's believability.

This situation is comparable to that of women in other cultures, vis-à-vis different issues. For instance, in a very different way, women emerged as a certain type of political actor during the brutal dictatorships of the 1970s and 1980s in several Latin American countries. It was precisely their situation as mothers and wives that gave them the clarity and the courage to demand justice and to do so while confronting armed soldiers and policemen. Mothers in the barrios of Santiago during Pinochet's dictatorship, mothers at the Plaza de Mayo in Buenos Aires, mothers regularly demonstrating in front of the major prisons in Salvador during the civil war—all were driven to political action by their despair at the loss of children and husbands.

There is also an interesting parallel between the political aspect LeBlanc captures in the Japanese housewife's situation and the seemingly very different situation of immigrant women in the United States. Research suggests that immigrant women's regular wage work and increased access to other public realms have had an impact on their culturally specified subordinate role to men in the household. These women are gaining more control over budgeting and other domestic decisions, as well as greater leverage in requesting help from men in domestic chores. They are gaining greater personal autonomy and independence while immigrant men lose ground relative to their previous condition in their cultures of origin.

Besides their relatively greater empowerment in the household associated with waged employment, immigrant women—because they are the mediators between their households and various public services—have a greater participation in the public sphere and the potential to emerge as public actors. Hondagneu-Sotelo, for instance, has found that immigrant women are assuming more active public and social roles and that this reinforces their status in the household and the settlement process.[3] Immigrant women are more active in community building and community activism, and they are positioned differently from men in relation to the broader economy and the state. They are the ones who are more likely to seek public and social services for their families and consequently to have to handle any legal vulnerabilities. This greater participation by women suggests that they may emerge as more forceful and visible actors.[4]

These cases and others—such as the formation of women's voluntary associations in India—signal the possibility of a new politics of traditionally disadvantaged actors. To detect this new politics, it is necessary to develop new categories for analysis and identify new sites for research. LeBlanc's bicycle citizenship is a great illustration of this type of effort.

If we were to extricate a methodological insight or challenge from these instances of a new possible politics, it might have to do with understanding how we study specific localities and local dynamics in a context of globalization and transnationalization. Does it make a difference to the local political situation that this situation may resonate with other situations in very different places and cultures? And does it make a difference that it resonates thusly in a context of growing transnationalization in systemic dynamics and cultural practices/awareness? In her fine book LeBlanc is not simply recovering the role of women as housewives in politics but specifying a different type of politics. In this effort she joins a growing world of scholars, each studying in great detail what may well turn out to be the multiple localizations of an as yet only dimly recognized strategic instantiation of the political.

Saskia Sassen
Professor of Sociology
University of Chicago

Acknowledgments

I know of no appropriate means of discharging the debts I incurred in the process of researching and writing this book. This project would never have reached completion without the persistent encouragement and aid of friends, relatives, teachers, and most especially, the women about whom this book is written. Though I am afraid I have written a very imperfect book, I hope that in some small way the sincerity of my effort might honor the countless and irreplaceable contributions of those who have come in contact with me along the way.

I cannot mention every participant in my research here by name. I hope many will find their admirable spirits in the people and ideas on the pages that follow. However, I would like to make note of some people and institutions that have made key differences in the process. Ron Peters, Allen Hertzke, Sidney Brown, Don Maletz, Larry Hill, David Wilsford, and LaDonna Sullivan are responsible for, among many other things, encouraging me to pursue my unconventional ideas and giving me the support I needed to do so. I owe Keith Vincent for his faith in my intelligence, Sasaki Yasushi for his courageous intellect, and Megumi Ikeda for listening to me, Keith, and Yasushi, among others. Ōgai Tokuko has led me through ideas, meals, and interviews—all central to this research. Morita Nanae taught me as much about Japanese women as she did about the Japanese language. Abe Yumiko and her husband Abe Takematsu provided absolutely essential assistance in establishing my connections with the field site. Igarashi Akio has been a true mentor. Ono Kiyoko, Kakizawa Kōji, the Hasegawas, and many, many others have all taken time from demanding lives to open the doors to Liberal Democratic Party politics for me. Tsukurikko is a home to me. Morita Itsuko and Takada Chieko have also opened political doors again and again.

I owe much to the careful comments on drafts of this work by Anne Imamura, Robert Angel, Glenda Roberts, Michael A. Schneider, Michael F. McClure, and one anonymous reviewer. Madge Huntington, at the East Asia Institute of Columbia University, shepherded the manuscript (and me) through the important early stages of the publishing process. Naomi Black's kind but insistent e-mail missives kept me in hot pursuit of a publisher even when I doubted myself. Joe Knippenberg and Peter A. Lawler stood behind me (and before me) at crucial times. The enthusiasm and hard work of Laura Driussi, Sue Heinemann, and others at the University of California Press have made the last part of the work unexpectedly easy.

Institutional support has been invaluable to me at every step. The Carl Albert Center for Congressional Studies at the University of Oklahoma, a Fulbright Graduate Research Grant administered by the saints (especially Kuramoto Teruyo) at the United States-Japan Educational Commission, the School of Law at Nihon University, the Northeast Asia Council of the Association for Asian Studies, the Carrie Chapman Catt Center for the Study of Women and Politics, the Women and Politics Section of the American Political Science Association, Seigakuin University, the East Asia Institute of Columbia University, and Oglethorpe University have all contributed funds and other tangible forms of support important to this project. Individuals at each of these institutions have been important in the administrative work required in putting my book together. In particular, I would like to remember Kellye Walker, LaDonna Sullivan, and Donna Whitehead for their efforts. While all of my students have in some sense marked this work, two Oglethorpe University students have been of particular help: Karen Beach and Valerie Holshouser.

My parents, Charlotte B. LeBlanc and Robert G. LeBlanc, and my siblings, Beverly, Billy, and Lizzy, cheered for me unconditionally. Bernard Christopher believed I would triumph. And finally, in the long nights when I was afraid that this book would never get done and the stories I wanted to tell would never get told, two things kept me going: Michael McClure's faith in speaking truths, and the strength I was shown by the smart, inventive, honorable women whom I try to capture here. Writing this book changed my life.

All of the mistakes are mine, and the credit for any of my successes must, without a doubt, be shared with others.

Note on Names

With the exception of elected officials whose names and political behavior are a matter of public record, all of the participants in this study are here referred to by pseudonyms. In some cases, I have also changed place names or personal details to protect the privacy of the people who so willingly told me their stories. All Japanese names are written according to the Japanese practice, surname first, except where the person commonly uses the American style herself.

CHAPTER ONE

"Supposing Truth Is a Woman — What Then?"

For a long time now, there has been a little something about a bicycle inside my head that I have been meaning to write down somewhere; only recently did I come to understand that here is where I should write it. In December 1991, two months after I moved to Japan to do the field study for this book, I received the loan of a bicycle from a woman who had hired me to tutor her sixteen-year-old daughter in English for an hour once a week. The woman's home was a bit inconveniently located, and the family did not have a car. She loaned me the bicycle so that I could travel to and from her house for the Friday evening tutoring sessions, but she let me store it at my apartment building and use it at my liberty during the rest of the week.

The bike was old and green, and it had the low-slung woman's crossbar, the large seat, and the upright handles that had ceased to be popular with Americans before I was born (although these days such old-fashioned bikes are enjoying a "retro" vogue among a certain twenty-something crowd). Large metal baskets had been welded to the front and back of the bike. The handles were covered with tie-on vinyl cuffs lined with fake fur to keep the cold from the rider's hands, and a rusty bell adorned the right handle bar. The brakes were "iffy" on a dry day.

My feet, and more especially my shoes, had been ill-used by all the walking I had done in my first weeks in Tokyo. I welcomed the chance to zip about the neighborhood on my new acquisition, but I soon found that I was not prepared for the packed, narrow roads. When I loaded the baskets, the bike was hard to balance, and the shaky steering scared

me. If I took downhills too fast, I found that I could not stop at inter-
sections without dragging my feet in a bumping desperation. I had to
remind myself that the Japanese drive British-style, that I must stay on
the "opposite" side of the road so as not to confuse traffic, and on the
well-traveled roads, I was constantly brushed back against cement garden walls, scraping a knee or knuckle as I tried to avoid a taxi blazing
past. I was a preposterous white woman—zooming and weaving,
screaming and praying, and yelling out awkward apologies as I cycled
through Ōizumi, the section of the Tokyo ward, Nerima, where I conducted most of this study.

My predicament was not lost on the housewives whom I had come
to study. Shortly after I acquired the bicycle, I started to get a wealth
of soft-spoken instruction: how to secure packages in the basket, how
to keep the seat dry in the rain, how to hold an umbrella while pedaling,
and why it is important to dismount on the left side with your right leg
out behind you and your left foot still on the pedal. Most important of
all, I was taught which roads to choose as I moved about from an interview to a volunteer field site, to a co-op meeting, to the grocery store.
I had known the area by its train station, its shopping streets, and its
car-traveled roads, but cycling behind housewives, I came to avoid those
paths for less-traveled residential streets and back alleyways, which were
safer for the cyclist.

At first I merely added the routes that housewives showed me to my
store of knowledge about the main thoroughfares, but sometime during
my eighteen-month stay, I started to think in a wholly new manner
about the streets of Ōizumi. To the housewives' routes, I began to add
my own. My psychology about getting to places changed. In my mind,
I no longer visualized Ōizumi according to the train station, bus stops,
and commercial centers. Instead, I saw it as a collection of paths to places
I had been, and I gradually found myself talking like housewives I had
heard, saying things like, "Go up behind the co-op center toward the
'school road' near where Tanaka-san lives."

What I really learned through the housewives' lessons in bicycle nav-
igation was an alternative means of seeing Ōizumi. A garden gate, a tiny
playground, a smaller bakery, and the other cyclists—mostly women—
took a prominent place in my bicycle view, but in a bus or train, or even
my professor-sponsor's car, I would never have seen those things—or,
even if I had, they would not have come to *make sense* to me, to be part
of my daily, useful knowledge about how the world around me operated. I have lived in the United States at times without a car, and I have

heard both myself and others who do not own cars lament that "when you don't drive, you don't know how to get anywhere." But, on a bike in Tokyo, I learned that when one drives one knows only how to get some places. Without a bike, and a housewife to teach me how to ride it, I never would have seen certain places in Ōizumi.

The "bicycle Ōizumi" was important for me to see when I lived in Tokyo because it eased my everyday survival. But the idea of a "bicycle Ōizumi" is important for this book, too. In essence, "bicycle Ōizumi" is a suggestion that many worlds may be layered on each other in a single spot. The world we see at a given time is chosen for us by the transportation we use to get there. Before my bicycle, Ōizumi seemed full of taxis and smoking, suited men. After I began to bike my way around, Ōizumi seemed more like the sound of piano lessons leaking from living room windows; I seldom saw suited men, and take-out food delivery boys on mopeds unquestionably outnumbered the taxis. These are prosaic examples of the connection of "seen worlds" and "transportation," but I do not think we have to stretch very far in order to speculate that a similar phenomenon occurs in a social sense. Besides, strictly speaking, whether one takes a taxi or a bicycle to one's destination is a social phenomenon in itself.[1]

Like the Ōizumi streets, politics is also a many-layered world, and what we see there depends on the social "transportation" that we have. Our social "transportation" is who we are, or our identity—as a cyclist or taxi-taker, for example—when we enter the political system. I have chosen a particular social identity, the housewife, as the "transportation" through which I want to study Japanese politics. By employing participant-observer methods borrowed from anthropology, I have tried to "follow" the paths the housewife uses when she confronts the political system, so that, in the end, I may begin to the see the political world that she sees.

The reasons why I wanted to see Japanese politics in a housewife's eyes are several—some of them peculiar and personal. However, my particular reasons for choosing to study housewives reveal tensions in political and intellectual worlds that are larger than my individual experiences. Taking a moment to explore these tensions is important because the questions such an exploration provokes help to explain why housewives in Japan should be a concern of literate students of politics everywhere.

In part, my interest in Japan was piqued by the special characteristics of the historical moment in which I happened to be beginning my

formal study of politics. When I was filling out graduate school applications in the spring of 1988, we Americans were still living in the Cold
War with a presidency that had prided itself on bringing our defenses
up to speed, seeking even to extend the power of our weaponry to the
reaches of space. But before I had finished my second year of graduate
course work, the Berlin Wall had tumbled, and, instead of new weaponry, some political leaders began to talk of a "peace dividend." The
division of the world between communist and non-communist that I
had known my entire life was gone—leaving, if for but an instant, the
possibility that the American sort of democracy would spread everywhere.

Through that instant of possibility, however, rose a tremendous
cloud of doubt. It seemed that, practically simultaneous with the early,
unsuspected removal of the first stones in the political Berlin Wall, had
come some rather ugly revelations about the American liberal democratic alternative. In our generalized sense of insecurity we look for alternatives (or reassurances that our path is, after all, the right one) in
our competitors. Until very recently Japan dipped and bobbed before
the United States as a contrast marker—a buoy marking enviable stability, harmony, and peace in social life that the American version of
liberal democracy seemed unable to provide. Around Japan we have
developed a sort of mythology that both explains and explains away its
buoy status. In *Outnation,* journalist Jonathan Rauch attempts to probe
the nature of Japan and the source of our fascination with it. He writes:
"One day in the library browsing among the books on Japan, I began
to see a pattern among the titles. *Queer Things about Japan. A Fantasy
of Far Japan* (nonfiction). *Unfathomed Japan. Secrets of Japan. Oddities in
Modern Japan.* I plucked out *The Enigma of Japanese Power,* by Karl van
Wolferen, and noticed that on the back cover was written only this
sentence: 'Inside Japan, nothing is quite as it seems.' Good for literary
business, this queer, fantastic, unfathomed, secretive, odd, enigmatic
Japan where nothing is quite as it seems."[2]

I suppose my initial desire to study Japanese politics was not much
more than the sort of fascination with the "enigmatic and unfathomable"
of the imagined literary Japan that Rauch described. It was mere coin-
cidence that, the same summer I had begun to study Japanese, the Liberal Democratic Party lost its majority in the 1989 elections for the upper
house of the Diet, and a record number of women won seats in a sudden
burst of women's political power that came to be called the "Madonna
Boom."[3] However, one day, looking at a striking photograph of the

1989 campaign period in a news magazine whose name I cannot recall, I moved from a fascination with the "Enigma of Japanese Power" to a more scholarly desire to put the puzzle together.

According to the caption, the photo showed a group of "housewives" who were yelling at Liberal Democratic Party (LDP) candidates. The housewives were upset about a new consumption tax that had been passed under the most recent, LDP-controlled government. Either the photographer had been very good or the scene rather stunning, or both. At any rate I was duly impressed by what seemed to be such a large number of women, and I was even more impressed by the evident intensity on their faces. A woman in the foreground stood out especially well; anger had completely distorted her features.

The angry women and the election results told stories that defied common notions that Japan was a buoy marking calm (if slightly corrupt) political waters. Nearly every available English account of Japanese political culture had suggested that Japan was a model for the continuity of traditional culture despite sweeping changes in the structure of political institutions.[4] Furthermore, Japan has been widely characterized as a "spectator" political culture in which citizens do not perceive it their place to be involved in politics, presumably because such involvement is not encouraged in traditional culture.[5] Nevertheless, the disgruntled housewife voters of the 1989 elections did not look like obedient spectators.

Following the election in 1989, the split in the Liberal Democratic Party that occurred in the summer of 1993, the continuance of previously unheard of coalition government, and the concomitant move among a majority of the electorate to define themselves as disaffected, "nonparty" (*mutōha*) voters all indicate that our understanding of Japanese politics should permit more complex discussions than it has.[6] In retrospect, we might perceive the anger during the House of Councilors elections of 1989 as a sort of "Berlin Wall" for Japan. Yet our fascination with the past success of LDP elites has not prepared us to see beyond them. Our commitment to the study of a politics in which voters had an unvarying set of political choices has not encouraged us to examine what might happen in an altered setting. The housewives in the photograph of 1989 were precursors of a larger wave of public disillusionment with political leadership, but hardly any of us has paid their case the attention that a cool-headed application of our scientific methods would suggest it is due.[7]

In 1990, I spent a month in Japan, where I tried to learn more about political change, the "Madonna Boom," and the angry housewives. That summer I met a Tokyo ward assemblywoman, a representative of the Seikatsu Club Co-op's political network and a self-declared "housewife" in politics. In her discussion of politics, I noticed the assemblywoman's conviction that she and other housewife members of her movement had a unique political perspective. I was drawn to that idea both because I wanted to understand the source of her conviction and because I found something attractive in her conception of how politics ought to be.

The assemblywoman's perspective was compelling to me as a political scientist because it was rich with information about politics and citizenship that had meaning not only for Japan but for anyone who studied liberal democratic citizenship—even for Americans who were beginning to despair of their own system. If the Japanese housewife did see politics a different way, then as scholars we had better know as much. We needed to have our facts straight about Japan, but we also needed the opportunity to see new worlds as we debated the best way for men and women to live. The seething confusion of current Japanese politics notwithstanding, such information seemed, and still seems, vital in the wake of the real Berlin Wall's collapse.

To speak honestly, however, I must admit that even without the demise of Eastern Bloc communism and the beginnings of the breakdown of the Liberal Democratic Party domination of Japanese politics at the end of the 1980s, my awakening to the nature of the (my) profession of political science during my years of graduate school might have driven me from the taxis to the bicycles anyway. Those who have not met me do not know (perhaps they imagine) that I am a woman. I am small in stature—five feet, three inches tall—and I look many years younger than I am. When I smile, I look younger still. I have round cheeks; my nose turns up.

People who *do* know me probably soon forget the smallness of my physical presence. I know how to make myself heard. I can make my acquaintances forget that I look more like a nice, suburban coed and hopeful housewife than a scholar with the "terminal" degree in her field. I, myself, have a harder time forgetting my exterior, however, and the structure of my profession—the demographics of its members, the subjects of its study, and the methods it employs—all have the power of reminding me as much of who I look like as of who I really am.

Back in 1988, just before I started my first graduate seminar, I went to my first national meeting of the American Political Science Association. Reflecting on his own introduction to the convention, one of my professors mused about looking at the scholars all about him and thinking, "Finally, I have found a place where I fit in." My experience of my first meeting could not have been more different. Never in my life had I seen so many middle-aged men gathered in one place at the same time. I felt like a misfit. After a badge-wearing, tipsy conventioneer tried to pick me up while I waited in the lobby to meet a friend, I considered ditching my plans for my future altogether.[8]

My fit with political science was not nearly so bad as it first *appeared*, but I never entirely overcame the shock of that initial meeting either. I could not find myself at ease with the fact that in our broad-ranging study of political phenomena I seldom if ever encountered anyone with whom I could easily identify. Our discussions of everything from the structure of political parties to the effects of the strategic thinking of political actors on the incumbency reelection rate hovered around the elite. Of course, large voting behavior surveys and the rare crossover work actually focused on citizens. But even here, I did not hear much from voices I recognized. Where were the children of two-, three-, and four-bedroom suburban homes? Where were the women who were not in the seats of legislatures and cabinets? Where were the huge numbers of people who never bothered to vote? Of *indicators*, of *mass political behavior*, I heard quite a bit, but I could not escape the conviction that few citizens of democratic nations thought of their behavior as "mass." We use our theories to construct broad characterizations about the processes of individual political behavior. We spend relatively little time checking the dimensions in which our "indicators" and our "categories" fail to fit the people we want to study.

The Unstudied Housewife Citizens of Japan

Few scholars have studied how Japanese citizens perceive their citizenship. As I will explain again in later chapters, most studies of Japanese politics are studies of elite-level politics. The most recent English-language study of Japanese citizens, *The Japanese Voter*, is a mass opinion study modeled explicitly on *The American Voter*. The huge proportion of its data is from a *1976* survey (although the publication date is 1991), and the structure of the study is dominated by a behavioralist perspective that was called into question for its conservative, elite, white American cultural biases as early as 1969.[9]

Japanese women are frequently studied, but their political life is not. This book is the only attempt, in Japanese or English, to capture the nature of the relationship between politics and the daily lives of non-elite and Japanese homemakers in the postwar era. While certainly path-breaking, Susan Pharr's *Political Women in Japan: The Search for a Place in Political Life* (1981) focused on the political socialization of women activists.[10] Very little systematic English-language study of women in Japanese politics has occurred since the publication of Pharr's book, and indigenous research on Japanese women and politics has also tended to concentrate on activists.[11]

Studies of Japanese women in daily life have seldom included more than a cursory discussion of their political experiences because "political" is interpreted as "elite politics." Anne Imamura does find that house-wives have some specific opportunities for community participation that descend from their housewife roles. Some activities outside the home, such as the parent-teacher association (PTA), are almost unavoidable. But the purposes of Imamura's research do not allow her to probe the implications of her findings for citizenship.[12] Most English-language scholarship of Japanese women focuses on their exclusion from social participation, making assumptions about their constraint by Japanese traditions.[13]

The study of housewives has useful new information to offer specialists, but it should also be of as much interest to political generalists. Despite the neglect that she has experienced at the hands of political scientists, the Japanese housewife is a marvelous subject for an investigation of modern political life. She is at once a member of a political system that challenges our tendency to think about liberalism in solely American terms and a representative of a gender role that seems to throw a shadow on the liberal idea of the democratic individual. Taking up the housewife in Japan's post-postwar liberal political atmosphere can be a means of readjusting our sights as democratic theorists. We replicate the work of Alexis de Tocqueville, if we do so at the price of turning his project on its head. He went to America to see democracy so that he could understand the "American" future of France.[14] We look at democracy in Japan to see what that "American" future looks like, but also so that we might see truths about democracy that the powerful American example might otherwise obscure. We go to Japan to get a bicycle for political theory.

Liberalism: Its Women, Its Problems

That we require a new vehicle for seeing in liberalism is readily apparent. Like the chorus in a Greek drama, American students of liberal democracy have hailed its doom. Turning to Nietzsche, they proclaim that we have reached the age of the "last man." At best our lives are full of material comforts, but they are without the greater human excellences of spirit.[15] Scholars decry the American regime for failing to allow its citizens an enriching relationship with the political community.[16] Our politics provides a degree of individual choice, but it offers no explanation of what purpose one's choice should serve. Our politics permits us to present our interests, but it gives us little guidance for choosing among interests when we cannot address them all or address them all equally well. Our politics claims to base itself on individualism, but few citizens feel that it really adjusts itself to the exigencies in their lives. The bureaucratic systems that we build to serve the lonely and the weak are so impersonal that they accentuate the problems of individuals as much as they might solve them, and our adherence to the logic of interested individualism leaves us unable to color our politics persuasively with shades of other important motivations such as love, compassion, and a desire for caring relationships.

In his study of contemporary American populist movements, Allen Hertzke suggests that liberalism is a "crucible," and that we must "struggle through . . . its potentially corrosive individualism, its hollow moral core, its atomizing influence on communities, its disposition to cast the young adrift, and its ready abandonment of those unprepared for international competition."[17] Among traditional liberal democratic thinkers there has developed a growing consensus that liberalism is in crisis because, as the authors of *Habits of the Heart* put it, we need a means to "preserve or create a morally coherent life."[18] That moral coherence cannot survive if it is not somehow embedded in our political life. So long as morality is merely a "private" concern, we cannot make the institutions that are more and more powerful in our lives respond to the priorities that motivate us. Unfortunately, in liberalism, forging a connection between moral and political life is extremely difficult, if not impossible.

As if the unease about its seemingly empty moral legacy were not troubling enough, a yet more fundamental critique of liberalism has

come out of a growing body of feminist political theory. Feminist theorists claim to have found a paradox in liberalism's citizenship ideal.
Citizenship in a liberal worldview is supposed to be universal because it
is a mastery of an abstract understanding of basic principles of social
contract. As the principles are abstract, so, liberals would have it, is the
liberal citizen. Liberal citizenship ought to be a one-size-fits-all concept.
However, feminists thinkers point out that, precisely because the liberal
citizenship ideal attempts to be universal in its application, it cannot be
universal in content. Women especially confound the liberal citizenship
ideal because they embody a complexity in human relations that is not
well described by the model of "individual" contracting to form political
society that we have inherited from liberal philosophers such as John
Locke.

The reasons different theorists have given for the poor fit between
women and our philosophical model of the social contract individual
are various. What the explanations all have in common is an emphasis
on the connection between women and motherhood. In bringing forth
and nurturing young life, the woman (or, in the case of some theorists,
the gender role of woman qua woman) defies liberalism's picture of the
radically free, self-sufficient individual, making apparent the fact that
liberalism cannot be generally applied. The relationship between mother
and child—from the womb until the child's maturity—is not contrac-
tual, equal, or free. The fact that the mother's health cannot be separated
from that of her fetus demonstrates that the relationship extends beyond
the temporary dependence of minors on their guardians.[19] Moreover
men and women can never equally experience this heightened degree of
obligation. Women, to the extent that they represent their gender role,
must be excluded from the social contract. If not, the contract's validity
as a universal principle to which anyone in logic may accede will be
irrevocably disturbed.

Feminist theorist Carole Pateman argues that, at base, liberalism is a
patriarchal mode of social organization; the idea of equal, contracting
individuals is an incomplete picture of liberalism because the ideal of
abstract individualism does not depict the fact that women are necessarily below men in status. Women's inclusion in the social contract is
unequal because they are submitted, through marriage, to a sexual contract that comes prior to and as the basis for the social contract. Marriage, viewed as a form of "contract" in the era of liberalism, replaces
the coverture of women in marriage that existed prior to liberalism.
Locke argues that the conjugal relationship would occur even in a state

of nature where no "social" contract existed.[20] Therefore, Pateman concludes that, while the liberal marriage seems to allow women an equal status with their mates, it actually preserves the effect of excluding women from political society because the world of "family" is deemed a "private" issue, and a woman's sexuality—the very reason for her tie to a man—also remains natural and private. By placing women within a conjugal relationship that is determined to be natural, liberal thinking assures that, to the extent that women act *as women,* they cannot partake of the *political existence* that men get when they surrender their ties to the state of nature and form an alternative context for their behaviors— the social contract.[21]

Pateman's is but one feminist perspective on women's exclusion from the social contract. Working from Hobbes, Kathleen Jones argues that although women are naturally free and the natural masters of children, they are necessarily subjected to men with the formation of political society. When men covenant to form political authority, their "plurality of voices" is reduced into the "one will" of the sovereign. Jones explains: "Participation in this kind of authority amounted to the annihilation of difference because difference was understood to be divisive and destructive. In fact, Hobbes' point was that the sovereign was to make the multitude into one by overcoming their differences."[22] Women could not participate *as women* in the authorship of the sovereign because their nature as bearers of children meant that they had bodies that were "divided and dividing" and, thus, defied the "univocal" nature of the sovereign.[23]

Jones's argument that women violate the univocality principle of the idea of social contract necessary for liberal democracy is echoed in the work of other feminist theorists as well. Iris Marion Young suggests that liberalism assumes a certain "homogeneity" in its idea of "universal" citizenship.[24] Because society contains structured inequality, even when citizenship is universally extended, the idea of citizenship will be more representative of societal elites—dominant white males—than others. Those who in actuality differ from the "homogeneous citizen" are forced to transform their differences into "neutral" categories that reinforce social inequality.

A concrete example of how this works in social policy is maternity leave. "Equal" treatment in a system that views citizens as constructed on a general, homogeneous model forces an interruption of work due to pregnancy into the "neutral" category of "disability."[25] Of course, becoming pregnant signals not that a woman is disabled, but quite the opposite. The pressure to reclassify the woman's *ability* to be pregnant as a *dis*ability demonstrates the impossibility of incorporating women as they really are into liberalism's "universal" public sphere.

Other feminist theorists, such as Jean Bethke Elshtain, also emphasize the unsatisfactory manner in which maternity, an issue of tremendous *human* importance, is dismissed from the public sphere, and they call for a renewed politics in which the special contributions that women make in the family, for example, may be revalued.[26] However, even a broader inclusion of the maternal woman in public spaces cannot save liberalism for feminists. As Mary Dietz argues in "Citizenship with a Feminist Face," advocating the inclusion of women in the public sphere in the gender role of mother and nurturer can be a means of reinforcing a view of woman's citizenship where her voice is limited to public issues that fall within the socially defined feminine sphere.[27] To require that women define themselves by their maternal capacities is a form of "essentializing" that locks women into gender roles that were predetermined in a society which presumes women's inequality and relinquishes the possibility of restructuring those roles so that one's sex does not determine one's social capacities.[28]

Demanding that women fit themselves for a more generalized citizenship, however, seems to have similar implications. In "The Democratic Potential of Mothering," Patricia Boling points out that neither the Elshtain nor the Dietz alternative is satisfactory. On the one hand, what "maternal thinking" is, why only women can do it, and how exactly it will transform the public sphere are questions that those who advocate a new inclusion of maternal women into liberalism cannot answer. On the other hand, women's inclusion in actual politics has often been linked to their interests as mothers; a rejection of maternalism as a basis for women's citizenship may lead to a rejection of many real-life women's possibilities for making a distinctive contribution to public life.[29]

Feminists and more mainstream theorists alike are convinced that liberalism presents its citizens with utterly irresolvable dilemmas.[30] Despite their broad consensus on the desperation of liberalism's circumstances at precisely the moment in history when it seems to be the most attractive political possibility, however, the theorists have the stench of ivory tower mold about them. Surely it matters to real people if a real political alternative brings emptiness, alienation, and the devaluation of an entire gender and its human contributions. Yet the theorists who have dug up these apparently real problems do not perform extended investigations of their origins and effects among real people.

Most theorists stay locked up in the writings of a few philosophers, and they do not even talk much among readers of the same thinkers. For example, Iris Marion Young and Thomas Pangle are both desperate to unearth a basis for a more meaningful citizenship, but neither seems to notice that the other exists. Young's astute observations about power relations and "homogeneous citizenry" are not informed by Pangle's extensive understanding of the evolution of citizen ideals from ancient times; the reverse is also true. In the United States a few scholars, such as Bellah and Hertzke, have attempted to connect the theory with the people, but such undertakings have remained limited to the American example.

The dominance of the American case study is rather curious considering the generalized assumption, among the mainstream authors like Pangle, and even more so in the feminist writings, that liberalism shapes its unsatisfactory legacy through the power of *ideas*. Maybe the problems with liberalism are actually only problems with the American culture, but we cannot know as much if we do not follow what happens to different societies with similarly liberal politics. Theorists want to defend their devotion to the examination of the "great Western" texts as an undertaking with benefits universal to the most diverse populations, but they cannot make that defense if they have not looked at political life abroad. They have no standard by which to decide what "universal" means.

Moreover, the scarcity of studies of real women filling traditional gender role models and their relationship with liberal politics leaves feminist critics of liberalism with a devastating lack of evidence. Feminists may claim that women confound the liberal ideal of citizenship, but if they continue to base their arguments on rereading after rereading of the "dominant male" philosophical texts, they will have a hard time convincing either the proprietors of the dominant interpretation of those texts or the women they hope to empower that feminists really know what women's problems are.

The Nature of the Bicycle Citizens Study

In terms of thinking about politics, the liberal democratic theorists, traditional and feminist, are taking taxis. Their roads are real routes to political ideas, but they are already well-traveled. In this book, I am pedaling a bicycle by trying to record how Japanese housewives perceive their citizenship in a liberal democratic political system located in a culture vastly different from the American example. I still hope to get to some of the same destinations that the theorists in their taxis seek. I want to know, for example, what the liberal democratic citizen looks like. I want to know if women, or, more specifically, if women in their gender roles, fit that citizenship model. I want to know what that citizenship feels like. But I want to get to all of these destinations by taking routes we have yet to see.

The importance that my "bicycle approach" places on different means of seeing different political worlds extends to both my methodology and my subject matter. The pictures of housewife citizenship that I paint on the following pages are the result of my analysis of eighteen months of ethnographic fieldwork in northwest Tokyo between November 1991 and May 1993. I chose an ethnographic approach over other, more traditional political science approaches because, despite its well-documented shortcomings, ethnography seemed to present the greatest possible opportunity of avoiding being trapped in unexamined preconceptions.[31] Traditional political science methodologies such as the theory-driven mass opinion surveys are tremendously problematic for the study of women.[32]

Linda Zerilli and Diana Owen assert that political scientists have been unable to get a full view of women as citizens because "women are visible to the conceptual and empirical lens of political science only when they resemble or fail to resemble men."[33] They argue that political scientists do not "examine consciously and critically" the "facts" that correlate with biological sex. "In the absence of a meaningful critique of the social origins and maintenance of the sexual division of labor, for example, women can easily be blamed for 'choosing,' more or less freely, a muted role in political life," they explain.[34]

A similar argument has been made by Japanese sociologist Ehara Yumiko, who suggests that the best means of probing the Japanese woman's relationship with political power is the ethnographic method. Ethnomethodology offers the benefit of focusing a researcher on the consciousness of her subject. In doing so, she can begin to understand the source of a subject's actions as what Ehara calls "something midway between force and freedom." In other words, people, especially women, are often conscious of acting in a manner that is neither a complete submission to a power system that dominates them nor a fair execution of what they want to and believe that they should do.[35]

Ehara says that this in-between-power-and-values consciousness may be very strong in women as a result of the structure of ideologies of modernity such as democracy and productivity. As participants in the economy, men are encouraged to evaluate themselves according to the universal standards applied in these ideologies. But as the development of modern work patterns led to a division of labor where men worked away from home and women, because they were women, were consigned to the family sphere, a set of ideologies developed for women's work that were contrary to the universalistic standards applied to men. Women came to be seen as representatives of particularistics — individualism, emotion, and love in specific situations. Women are caught having to act in response to a social structure that does not recognize their motivations as universally valid, and they are likely to be conscious of a dissonance between what they think and how their actions appear.[36]

Ehara suggests that an already present tendency toward particularistic, or situation-specific, thinking in Japanese society exaggerates the Japanese woman's consciousness of the disparity between her reasons for her actions and the content of those actions. Moreover, standard political science tends to view political actors as creators of political structures and to ignore the web of historical and cultural forces that constrain the shape of those actors' choices. Without investigating the consciousness a subject has about her actions, we cannot see the constraints that operate within and result from her very exercise of free choice, and we can have only the simplest understanding of the nature of power in a given political system.[37]

Significantly, we cannot "see" the constraining power of gender structures easily in modern politics because modern universal ideologies do not recognize gender divisions as relevant. Because ethnomethodology does not require us to have "objective" proof of the existence of constraining structures but lets us instead begin an investigation from a person's *consciousness* of a feeling of constraint, we have a greater chance of seeing beyond the boundaries of modern ideologies. Ehara explains: "Because ethnomethodology departs on its [investigation] from the position of the ordinary person's cognition, it must direct itself to explaining that cognition. It cannot say that when one feels forced, the feeling is not power but only an individual phenomenon or something imagined. When someone senses a problem, the ethnomethodologist seeks to explain how the problem is sensed, why the problem is sensed."[38]

I share Ehara's and others' concerns about the tendency of mainstream political science methodology to constrain our perceptions of political phenomena and hamper our capacity to understand the complicated practices of citizens and the labyrinthine shape of power. These concerns have shaped my methodological approach in ways that I can best explain by returning to the images of the taxi and the bicycle. In a taxi-driven approach to the study of non-elite political behavior, we would place a high value on gathering a large amount of relatively accurate information about our subject of study with as much rapidity as possible—just as a traveler with heavy bags would probably catch a cab to the train station even in expensive Tokyo because carrying those bags by hand through overcrowded, winding streets would be arduous. The "taxi" student of Japanese housewives would develop a table of "indicators" of "housewifeness," assemble a barrage of questions seeking information such as level of education, family income, and age that had proven interesting on surveys of other political subjects, and prepare a series of "thermometers" (or scales) that would elicit the extent of a surveyed individual's "political participation" according to a generalized set of standards. From the taxi research, we would learn some important information about hundreds, perhaps thousands, of women. We could quickly and confidently make some generic observations about women. We could soon know which already established political groups they join in the highest numbers, how many vote how often, how many have ever hung a poster, if the richer were more political than the poorer, and maybe many other things as well.

In taxi research, we can make a big suitcase of data rapidly available, but in doing so we must begin with a great many presumptions about our subjects of study. Ideas that would seem to be deeply interior to a person's understanding of herself (for example, whether she called herself a housewife or not) can be understood only to the extent that our original, generalizable indicators are useful. In two ways, however, our indicators might already be compromised. First, we would have to make assumptions about the proper array of categories among which to allow our survey subjects to choose. If our understanding of the survey subject is already quite limited, we cannot be sure our definition of categories is as sensible and relevant as it should be. Second, the importance placed on the generalizability of our categories would force us to flatten out the differences in individual cases. Such flattening of differences would necessarily occur before we begin our data collection, during the construction of questions that can work for everyone in the same way. A similar flattening would also take place after we have done the data collection, in the process of our reading patterns that are statistically significant. For study subjects who—as Ehara suggests Japanese women do — understand their difference from others in terms of the degree to which they are determined by particularistic, privatized relationships, this "flattening out" becomes more than a limitation. It is an "unseeing."

My "bicycle" methodology was born of an attempt to reverse the priorities of "taxi" (mainstream/main road) political science research. Rather than determine the "indicators" I sought to test with my data, I formed only a very loose set of orienteering questions: What/who is a housewife (*shufu*)? What does she think of as "politics"? When and where does she encounter "politics"? I began my field study with the presumption that I did not know who exactly the subject of my study was or where exactly she would be located. I saw my primary — in many ways my only — task as a researcher as the learning of the vocabulary by which my subject would "indicate" herself to another who could hear her in her own terms. In taxi-bicycle terms (terms that only came to me after months and months at my field site), I presumed that knowing the main roads — for example the legitimate socioeconomic data, the names of "peak" organizations — would help me only peripherally in mapping the housewife's citizenship consciousness. Few people had studied her citizenship; the popular and scholarly images of it were marked by exclusion, impossibility. I believed that I had to be willing to step out of the mainstream in order to see what a housewife sees when she looks back at politics.

The humblest expression of my research method is to say that I moved into a neighborhood where I had one likely contact and that I spent eighteen months learning my way around the world that she and her acquaintances traversed. Put another way, my method was to model the routes that a housewife and people in her neighborhood took to politics — or took in order to avoid encounters with politics. Inevitably, despite my methodological concerns, I generalize those routes somewhat. We are always taxi-drivers to some extent when we write up research.

I took a one-room apartment in Ōizumi, a section of the Nerima ward in northwest Tokyo in November 1991. I chose Nerima because a graduate school professor of mine knew a professor at a Japanese university who introduced me to a woman, Ueda-san, who lived in Nerima and helped me find my apartment. Ueda-san happened to be a member of the same Seikatsu Club Cooperative whose related political movements I had studied in the summer of 1990. Ueda-san helped me find my apartment — about a ten-minute bicycle ride from her home. She and her husband acted as the guarantors on my lease. She made some early introductions to members of the Ōizumi branch of the cooperative and, later in my project, when I wanted to meet more women who had little or no involvement in political organizations, she even organized some luncheons with neighborhood women she knew. It was Ueda-san who introduced me to the family that loaned me my bicycle.

During four months of my field study time, I was also involved in the reelection campaign of House of Councilors member Ono Kiyoko, a woman member of the Liberal Democratic Party. I eventually met her after making a series of other connections, the first of which was with a former student of my professor-sponsor. The former student's mother was involved in the political-support organization of a Tokyo Prefectural Assembly candidate. I made some connections with the PTA of an area middle school by making a chance acquaintance of a Japanese woman who taught English there. She made important introductions to the principal for me.

The most important connections that I made to the "housewife" citizens of Ōizumi almost all, in their myriad ways, resulted from a charity bazaar that I recount in Chapter 5. At that event, I met women who introduced me to a number of others involved in many kinds of volunteer work. There I also acquired the identity "studious young girl interested in Japanese women at the grass roots" that stuck with me, for good or bad, throughout my tenure in the field. In the volunteer groups I began the friendships that led me to join a hiking club, study calligraphy, and form a weekly English conversation club (which, too often to bear any testament to my abilities as a pedagogue, devolved into heated Japanese); through the volunteer women, I was introduced to many of the women without volunteer or political action interests whom I later interviewed.

In a series of coincidences that reveal how neighborhoods and identities are constructed of interwoven relationships, I found that among the women whose acquaintance I owed to charity bazaar connections were many of Ueda-san's friends. Quite a few of them had children who met me when I spent a day in classes at the middle school where I had an entirely different connection. Many of them belonged to the cooperative; the woman who loaned me the bicycle knew a large number of them. In fact, a male friend of mine complained that he felt he was "on display" when he visited me in the neighborhood where I lived, so frequently did women stop me on the street or near the station to say hello.

My data collection consisted of a mixture of practices. Placing priority, once again, on the housewife's vehicle over the "taxis" of political science, I devoted a majority of my effort to actually participating to the fullest degree possible in the activities in which the women I studied were involved. I worked at volunteer sites, sometimes several times a week. I attended hours of cooperative branch meetings. I traveled with women I met—attended cultural events with them, ate lunch and a rare dinner here or there with them. I kept a journal in which I recorded a day's events: sometimes I would have long, interesting conversations to note down, sometimes just a bare recounting of routine activities, but later I learned that the routines were precisely what I needed to know. I also undertook lengthy interviews with women and groups of women whom I wanted to know better or who were different enough from those represented in my daily activities to warrant investigation. Many of these interviews I taped.

As I will explain in more detail in the next chapter, I could not have actually known but the tiniest fragment of even the Ōizumi area population. My efforts to expand those numbering in my acquaintance— modeling in a Western painting class for several weeks and then interviewing the students, for example—could not have begun to answer the challenge presented. The fact that many of the women knew or knew of each other might be said to "bias" my sample population in the terms of "taxi" research. However, with regard to understanding how a housewife's social, and thus political, world is constructed in her consciousness, my sampling method was perfectly appropriate because it reflected the way in which she was connected to or divorced from sociopolitical institutions, elites, and arenas of power. My "sampling method" let me replicate in my own body and consciousness how a housewife might eventually arrive at the doors of a political party function or the ward legislature or a bureaucratic office—or why she easily might never get to any of those places.

I will share two good examples of how a different research method might have prevented me from fully seeing the subjects I wanted to study. The first example is my difficulty in connecting my case study of an LDP politician, Ono Kiyoko, with my investigation of the non-elite housewife's world. Despite the fact that sometimes all of Ōizumi—even all of Nerima—seemed interlocking to me, my participation in the Ono campaign never did fit coherently into my suburban neighborhood lifestyle. I persisted for a long time in thinking that Ono should fit in somehow. Her rhetoric was full of words like "kitchen," "children," "motherhood," and "housewife's point of view," which also peppered the volunteer groups, the cooperative meetings, and even the conversations with housewives who declared themselves to be totally uninterested in politics. But I could not make the activities of the Ono campaign intelligible to the women whose volunteer meetings I skipped for speeches, political support group meetings, or dinners with politicians' aides. Nor could I find many in Ono's office who could comprehend why I would dash from the office to teach English to handicapped people in a place that was forty-five minutes by train away from the fashionable areas of Tokyo that many LDP events haunted. The mutual incomprehension of the members of the two groups was more than bemusement at the methods of an eccentric scholar.

The two groups *literally and figuratively* transported themselves differently. I have not ridden in as many taxis before or since Ono's 1992 campaign. Given the pace of events in politics at that level, taxis were absolutely necessary. We could never have gotten quickly enough from speech to luncheon to organizational meeting sites. Moreover, the image of a member of the House of Councilors walking quietly from a reception at a large downtown hotel to a train station only to stand and sweat with all of the other commuters in the packed cars was inconceivable. The loudspeaker calls for politicians' chauffeured sedans, the dark-suited arms of secretaries signaling for taxis, the orange flashlight beams waved by the campaign workers who directed parking, pick-ups, and drop-offs were not only the infrastructure of a campaign event. They were a key part of the event—symbols of power, prestige, industry, officialdom, identifiers of the "something big and important" that was surely happening.

At a cooperative meeting, a volunteer site, or most housewives' homes, however, automobiles were often impossible means of transportation. Parking was almost always nonexistent. Even bicycle storage could be problematic. Sometimes one woman would carpool with several others to a distant event, but many housewives could not drive. Grabbing a taxi to get to a club meeting would have looked bad—as if the woman were too good for the others, as if she were a spendthrift who cared little if her own enjoyment cut into her family's financial well-being. When a group was selling old clothes to raise a few thousand yen to support activities, spending the same amount of money for one's own luxurious transportation would have seemed plainly selfish. At any rate, taxis were hard to pick up on residential streets.

For Ono to fit in fully with the "unorganized housewives" that her campaign rhetoric touted, she would have had to meet them according to their own transportation—social or otherwise. Notably, a flyer of hers showed her riding a bicycle! Housewives who wanted to fit into Ono's National Assembly world would have needed more than a taxi ride to her events. They would have had to admit that a taxi was necessary for transportation and image purposes, and such an admission would have required a dismissal of the "plain folks just getting by" values that made things like their volunteer work seem like valuable social contributions. In fact, women's sections of political support groups that backed Ono often provided charter bus transportation to special events—a widely acknowledged perk of political connections.

I came to understand this through my own experiences. During the last part of Ono's campaign, the time I could spend in my ward had grown shorter and shorter. I left my apartment early in the morning and returned late at night. I ate quickly at self-serve coffee shops, and my old habit of wandering the streets of my neighborhood on slow days was curtailed. I missed events at the volunteer groups that I had joined and canceled my participation in much of the regular activities. When the campaign was over, I felt curiously out of place in Nerima for a while. When I had time to sit and talk to a volunteer group, I was shocked at how much had changed in my absence. Groups had expanded or changed some of their focal activities. Membership had changed. Conflicts I had not anticipated had arisen. But I was also a bit discomfited to see that no one of my volunteer world had experienced the mounting tension and the emotional upheaval of the campaign. They had worried about completely different things, and they hardly seemed to have noticed there had been an election. I seemed to have slipped away to a different world, and found it a bit difficult to come back.

Misfits like the simple one between Ono's campaign transportation and the housewife volunteers' transportation can be keys that help a political scientist unlock the nature of different political philosophies. But such keys will be less available to the mainstream researcher, who is oriented toward large samples. She will not learn in her very body, as I did shuttling back and forth between the bicycle and the taxi world, the concrete ways in which those political philosophies form barriers between citizens and their political representatives. I had to learn. Because I had to share my life day after day with people from these two different perspectives, I did not have any choice but to learn.

The example of the campaign misfit highlights how a participant-observer methodology such as mine might do a better job of explaining some sorts of political phenomena than a more seemingly "scientific" methodology. My second example reveals a more subtle problem with scholarly "perspective," one that was much harder for me to recognize. Negotiating the differences between Ono's campaign world and the vol- unteer world was energy consuming; more troubling was my negotia- tion of the gap between my field site and my "siting" in academic dis- courses. My immersion in the housewife world of Ōizumi did not remove me from the pressures of scholarship. I was required to report bimonthly to the United States-Japan Educational Commission office in Tokyo, which administered my Fulbright grant. Administrators there encouraged me to network with other Fulbright recipients, Japanese scholars, and other foreigners doing dissertation research in Japan. I joined a group of foreign graduate students called the Ph.D. Kenkyūkai (research club), and every few months I met with these researchers and others to talk about our work.

In these groups of scholars, the emphasis was hardly ever on "fitting in" to the field site in the sense of knowing what behaviors and expec- tations might be appropriate to our participation in a particular group, such as an LDP campaign or a volunteer association. We researchers talked, instead, of the difficulties of finding a theoretical "perspective" for our work. The search for perspectives that would transport us suc- cessfully through our careers back home often required that we tame the richness of the information our informants provided us. A striking example is a memory I have of a group discussion where a frustrated fellow researcher complained that her informants "even said things that contradicted themselves." Most of our subsequent discussion focused on how she might elicit what her informants *really thought*. Perhaps, her rapport with them was not yet good enough. They could not trust her to hear what they really believed.

Later, I realized that we had all missed the most important point about this anthropologist's finding. People *do* contradict themselves. They can be fully committed to several contradictory positions at the same time. They may need to be. Finding out why may be the most important work of any researcher. Unfortunately, the methods or ob- jectives of our scholarly programs may blind us to the value of an in- formant's contradictory or complicated experience of her position(s). The need for coherent conclusions frustrated the anthropologist who had discovered the contradictions through her long association with her research subjects. But the frustrated anthropologist was still fortunate. Another social scientist who, in the interest of a broader sample, would have spent less time with any particular informant might not have even *noticed* the contradictions.

Sasaki-san, a housewife I discuss in great depth in the next chapter, made many presentations of her feelings about her identity that were, in the strictest sense, contradictory. I was aware of her varied self presentations because I saw her once a week or more for a year and a half. Because I also knew her family, many of her friends, and a great deal about the sorts of situations in which she made her self presentations, I also came to understand something about the pressures of different contexts and the range and constraints of the housewife identity. Finally, rather than being confused about how Sasaki-san identified herself, I came to have a richer understanding of the inner logic of her position. By understanding Sasaki-san's position in something like its real complexity, I developed a more useful "perspective" from which to approach my engagement with other housewives whom I knew less well.

In order to glean this "perspective," I had to spend a lot of time with Sasaki-san — time that could not simultaneously be spent enlarging my sample of the population or networking with other academics. In order to share my perspective with readers in a rewarding manner, I will have to spend a lot of time in this book talking about Sasaki-san — time that cannot simultaneously be spent on describing other cases or elaborating my readings of other scholars' theories. Housewives are very clear in their understanding that time spent as political activists cannot be spent cooking dinner, helping children with their homework, or tending the home. Academics are sometimes less aware of similar sorts of choices that their research priorities force them to make.

The Presentation of the Study

In my fieldwork and in this book, taxis and bicycles have been crucial in many ways. As my research methods were unorthodox, this presentation of my findings will also be unorthodox. I do not expect, or want, my readers to take away a set of certainties, a collection of reliable facts by which the "subjects" here might be deciphered. Instead, I want my audience to find a field for planting questions, a rich case study that can provoke thoughtful reflection — on Japan, housewifery, liberal democracy, social science scholarship, or, hopefully, a myriad of concerns that I have not imagined.

The rest of this book is devoted to my presentation of my best picture of and "conditional reasonings"[39] about the political world of the Japanese housewife. Chapters 2 and 3 examine how and why women come to identify themselves as housewives and how, generally, they read the significance of that identification for their participation in political life. Chapters 4, 5, and 6 look at the manner in which the housewife identity is manifested in three different types of women's activism. Chapter 4 describes the connection among community welfare volunteer work, housewifery, and politics. Chapter 5 digs into the possibilities and problems of the use of housewife identity in the female-dominant electoral movement of the Seikatsu Club Consumers' Cooperative. Chapter 6 investigates the uses and limitations of "housewife" rhetoric in the re-election campaign of LDP House of Councilors member Ono Kiyoko.

In various forms in all of these cases, I found a perceived disjunction between politics and housewives. I characterize this disjunction as "bicycle citizenship." In the concept of bicycle citizenship, I am trying to capture the fact that being a housewife paradoxically restricts the expansion of a Japanese woman's public life in many important ways while, at the same time, providing her with a unique vehicle for other sorts of public participation. To put this idea in terms of my transportation metaphor, housewives, because of their identity as housewives, can move only very slowly, over short distances through those parts of public life that political scientists tend to take most seriously. Unlike "taxi citizens" (elite, educated men), housewives are not properly equipped for traveling on political highways—getting elected to the Diet, changing the minds of highly placed bureaucrats, or winning the attention of major party power holders. To begin with, most housewives are uneasy about being housewives. While they feel unable to call themselves anything other than "housewives," they tend to think that their identity carries an inescapable social stigma. A woman who is a "housewife" is a symbol of inexperience, impracticality, ignorance. She will be too distracted by trivia, by housework and babies, and by gossip to manage the affairs of the world. She will be too dainty to play hardball with her opponents when it really counts. Both housewives and others are likely to laugh at the idea of a housewife in politics, just as they would laugh at a national leader who transported himself to state dinners on a bicycle.

The unsurprising finding that the housewife identity is not the best transportation to the center of the Japanese political system is not the end of the story of housewives' citizenship. If we political scientists are willing to get out of our taxis and conceive of the study of politics in a multilayered fashion, we will find that there are some sorts of public life where the housewife identity is a very appropriate form of transportation. On the many Japanese streets that are not wide enough, direct enough, or well traveled enough for taxi drivers to use, the bicycle often is the best means of travel, and most certainly the cheapest. Similarly, housewives participate in some kinds of public activity where being a housewife is an advantage—an advantage denied to those who might have the qualifications to be "taxi" citizens.

In the world of local politics, or in the varied public life of a *chiiki* (local area), housewives garner benefits from their identity. They find it easy to build networks with other women who call themselves house-wives. The housewife identity can be used, with both housewives and non-housewives, to associate women with images of desirable public concerns—the protection of the environment, children, the weak and aged. Housewives can justify a oneness with the ethics that "ordinary" people would espouse by simply reminding others they are housewives. They can present a powerful critique of the operation of mainstream politics with very little effort. As "housewives" women are clearly not interested businessmen, arrogant officials, or self-serving politicians. As "housewives" women are, by definition, outsiders to the ugly modern world of competitive individualism and insiders to the old-fashioned world of communalism, of mutual self-sacrifice, outsiders to the world of amoral, man-crushing organizations and insiders to the world of personal creativity, moral development, and unfettered self-expression.

Because bicycle citizenship is linked to an alienation from politics and an espousal of the "plain folks" values with which many men and women in many advanced industrial democracies claim to identify, the concept of bicycle citizenship may seem to describe something other than a "housewife's" experience. Couldn't bicycle citizenship work for ordinary men, too? Does it work for housewives of all economic classes? Is the bicycle citizenship consciousness merely a class-based phenomenon? I won't claim definitive answers to these questions. The data I collected among *Japanese women* gives me little authority when speaking for others in Japan or elsewhere. And, in fact, the odd familiarity of the Japanese housewife citizen's predicament to those who are not Japanese house-wives is one reason why writing about bicycle citizenship seems valuable to me.

Nonetheless, we should be careful when equating a housewife's consciousness with a class consciousness or with the consciousness of all citizens male and female who feel distanced from political power. In the first place, when they are asked about politics, housewives frequently describe it as a "male society." No matter that *political alienation* is not a gender-specific phenomenon, Japanese women perceive *political opportunity* to be gender specific, and thus, regardless of how an outsider would label the housewife's citizen consciousness, she quite clearly sees it as located in a gender-divided world. In the second place, while her husband's membership in a relatively affluent economic class is, in fact, a prerequisite of a woman's being a full-time housewife, consciousness of economic class, per se, does not provide a distinguishing marker for bicycle citizens' experience of politics. Japanese men and women have been shown to be generally loathe to see themselves as anything other than "middle class,"[40] and the housewives among whom I conducted my study insisted that they were all "middle class," despite the obvious differences I could occasionally see in their standards of living. Moreover, how a housewife's socioeconomic status should be classified absent her own volunteering of a label is unclear. When a woman identifies herself as a "housewife," her educational and wage work backgrounds are left undifferentiated. Distinctions between housewives whose families could afford for them not to work and those who must also have employment outside the home have also receded in recent decades as a majority of women hold some sort of paid work, and a majority of those not working express the desire to be doing so. The persistence of sex discrimination in the workplace muddies the waters yet further; women are in a class marked more by gender than other attributes.[41] The politically salient social cleavages by which housewives themselves argue they should be classified are their gendered roles as caretakers and the fact that they are not members of the tiny group of people nationally recognized for their power to alter the circumstances of their fellow countrymen and women.

The Japanese housewife is a special case, but she is still a case that should be suggestive for non-housewife readers. After all, most of us, men or women, feel somehow closer to the housewife's bicycle than the Diet member's taxi seat. And, despite the peculiar advantages we may learn to see in the housewife's vehicle, most of us who could choose taxi citizenship probably would. The skewed ratio of the books on the Liberal Democratic Party to the smattering of writings on Japanese housewives may reflect just such a wistfulness. If we could have the power of the best educated, most well-connected men in an advanced industrial society, I dare say we would not willingly decline it. Few of us have such free reign over the terms of our encounters with public life. In that sense, the chapters that follow are more than a series of sketches of the political world that the housewife as a bicycle citizen sees. These sketches are also experiments in mapping, a practice at finding a way to chart the world that most of us as just usual citizens—in Japan, or the United States, or elsewhere—see. We need to know where the housewife cannot go in politics, but, even more important, where she *does go* and the benefits and drawbacks of her form of transportation there. Mapping the housewife's "bicycle routes" will help us see not only the greater power of the taxi, but the costs that power imposes on public value systems in the "advanced nations." In most American suburbs we use neither taxis nor bicycles for our actual transportation, and we may tend to feel ourselves better situated than any Japanese housewife, yet in paying attention to the situational particularities of a Japanese housewife's citizenship, we are teaching ourselves a democrat's discipline—a rigorous unease with sets of categories that are preconceived for us in a world where so few of us are "taxi" citizens.

CHAPTER TWO

The Identity of the "Regular Housewife"

In arguing that housewives experience a "bicycle citizenship," I am claiming that their experiences of public life are crucially affected by their consciousness of themselves as housewives, that "housewife" is a label for a *public* identity. Even more important, housewives persist in using the "housewife" label even when other identities seem available and despite the women's awareness that their label comes with negative connotations. We must understand how a contemporary suburban social structure can bolster the peculiar staying power of a woman's housewife identity if we want to grasp what it means to be a bicycle citizen.

"Housewife" sometimes seems too vague a label to distinguish any particular political creed because our analysis of citizenship is driven by categories that accept the basic premises of liberal interest politics — that a citizen's identity is univocally abstracted to any member of the political system regardless of sex, and reflective of a coherent response to the array of concerns (usually economic) recognized as "real" in decision-making arenas such as legislatures and government agencies. Given such premises, the "housewife" is theoretically and politically invisible. However, the housewife identity is *not* invisible to women who call themselves housewives. Rather, housewives are often painfully aware that the same label that makes them recognizable to the public seems to disqualify them from participation in much of public life.

I was compelled once to describe my research to a Japanese banker at a breakfast briefing on U.S. and Japanese trade. As if revealing the secret formula for a world-famous soft drink, the man smirked and said, "I'm afraid you'll find that our housewives have little interest in or knowledge about politics." I wasn't surprised by what he said. Not only had many other men—Japanese and American—shared similar "fears," Japanese housewives themselves were constantly cautioning me that I could hardly come to understand the Japanese political system by studying them. Just like the banker they would tell me, "Housewives aren't interested in politics," and as we will see in the stories of women in Chapter 3, even housewives doubt that a housewife possesses the necessary training or credentials to be successful in politics. "Her point of view is too narrow," some explained.

The ironic pairing of exclusion and opportunity that define a housewife's bicycle citizenship begins in her strained but somehow necessary housewife identity. By describing herself as a housewife, a Japanese woman places herself in a paradoxical position—a paradox of which most self-described housewives are quite aware. A housewife is a specialized expert in certain sorts of human arts. She may feel she has chosen the gender role that "society" thinks is most becoming to her. But a housewife is also clearly not a full-fledged member of the work world outside the home. She may visit there as a part-time or temporary worker. When the home and family are her priorities, however, she is defined as being outside most of the economic structures in which other citizens come to know their interests and form their sociopolitical identities. In her identity the housewife has a ready-made vehicle for certain kinds of social approbation; yet by using that vehicle, she places herself clearly beyond the mainstream of socioeconomic and political life—despite the fact that housewife is a "mainstream" occupation for women. Perhaps all citizens of advanced industrial representative democracies possess only tentative ties to meaningful citizenship, but the housewife's sense of distance from the realm of politics is increased by her ambivalence with regard to her position as a housewife. In Japanese, we could say that the problems of gender identity and citizen identity are *tsumi-kasaneteiru*—piled one on top of the other.

Some of the complications of the housewife identity are modeled in the problem of translating the Japanese term. The Japanese word for housewife is *shufu*. "Housewife" is not the only possible rendering of *shufu*; it just seems to be the best word in American English for conveying what Japanese women understand they are saying about themselves when they call themselves *shufu*. In American English, a "housewife" is a married woman who is occupied full-time with the maintenance of home and family. Of course, along with its more positive connotations of unselfishness, nurturing qualities, and loving obligation to others, "housewife" can also convey a sense of dowdiness, of empty-headed devotion to daytime television dramas, shopping, and trivial gossip. Therefore, when we want to express a positive view of home-centered women in contemporary American usage, we usually employ the subtly more high-status "homemaker."

The term *shufu* contains a bit of both American words for the home-centered woman. A literal translation of the sense of the characters that make up the Japanese word would be something like "master woman." One might argue that neither housewife nor homemaker is an adequate translation of *shufu* because in feudal Japan, *shufu* often referred to the wives of aristocrats whose household management was more like a sort of "mastery" over other workers than is the case for contemporary *shufu*.[1] However, the consciousness that women in contemporary Japan who describe themselves as housewives share about the terms for their identity focuses at least as much on the negative images attached to the word *shufu* as its origin in noble society. Japanese housewives often claim that housewives are viewed as shallow, unambitious people who can be completely fulfilled merely by doing housework. As a Japanese woman friend of mine interested in studying at a culinary school said about her ambitions, "I'm not interested in studying cooking just to be someone's cute *shufu*. I really want to be involved with food as work." In fact, a clear awareness of the ignoble social position of a *shufu* seems to make many women, even women who are quite satisfied with their actual lives, profoundly ambivalent about presenting themselves as *shufu*. "Housewife," in both its attractive and ugly shades, best represents in English the meaning that Japanese *shufu* think is attributed to their identities by societies at large.

Of course, housewives with political interests do appear in the mass media. Letters to the editor signed "housewife" urge political action such as demanding a more outspoken prime minister or hanging signs on garden walls calling for the resignation of a corrupt Diet member.[2] Some opinion pieces make explicit connections between a housewife identity and political perception. For example, calling herself a "house-wife and writer," essayist and novelist Yoshinaga Michiko criticized the media for focusing too much on elites and failing to cover politics from the "daily life" perspective of people such as housewives like herself.[3] However, even when a housewife writes a letter, we hesitate to believe that it was her "housewifeness" that drove her to her conclusions. Furthermore, there is equal evidence that the segment of Japanese society known by the housewife identity would choose to be presented differently in the mass media if it could. *Shufu to seikatsu* (The Housewife and Daily Living), a popular woman's magazine for forty-seven years, ceased publication because its readership has all but disappeared, and *Shufu no tomo* (The Housewife's Friend), the last remaining of what were once known as the "giant four" of women's magazines, has altered its format and content to appeal to the ever-increasing number of women who work outside the home and have to squeeze traditional homemaking tasks into their increasingly busy schedules.[4] The fates of these housewife magazines seem to underline housewives' ambivalent assessment of the value of the housewife identity. The end of *Shufu to seikatsu* suggests that "housewife" is no longer a fashionable identity, while the continuing publication of *Shufu no tomo* in a format that attempts to take greater notice of the variety in a "typical housewife's" daily work suggests that many busy women for whom there is no other title but "housewife" do exist. Even publishers, wordsmiths, struggle to find a satisfactory label for women who take primary responsibility for the home—as if, although the housewife role still exists, making a direct reference to it is a bit unseemly.

Despite the fact that the bearers of the housewife identity are undergoing a process of change, the housewife identity is still one of the most powerful frames on many Japanese women's social experiences. Japanese social psychologist Kunihiro Yōko explains that, although the contents of women's daily lives have changed considerably in the postwar period, the label of *shufu* remains inescapable for most married women because the basic sexual division of labor undergirding society's view of women as home-centered has not changed.[5] Even women who devote most of each day to employment outside the home are not likely to forsake a housewife identity. The pronounced M-curve in women's employment rates caused by the large number of women who drop out of the workforce while their children are young continues to demonstrate the primacy placed on a woman's duties in the home. Women who persevere in working through childbearing or return to work after their children are older are likely to discuss their work in terms of the financial contributions it allows them to make to family expenses. Work outside the home is thus usually presented inside a "good wife, wise mother" perspective that tends to reinforce a woman's identification with a housewife role, despite the decreased significance of in-the-home activities in her daily schedule.[6]

We should not assume that many Japanese women uncritically view paid work as an extension of their housewife role because they are unaware of the restrictive aspects of the identity. Instead, as we can hear in the voices of the women who follow, the real question about the housewife identity is why women who are coolly rational about its downsides continue to use it. The answer lies in the fact that "housewife" is a useful label for the very women who chafe under its negative dimensions. Especially in their interactions beyond the home as representatives of the family, women use "housewife" to make short-cut references to their commitments and expertise, to the quality of their contributions to a truly human life. The low status of the housewife identity, and the housewife's awareness of the status problem, reveal as much about the hierarchy of values in the larger society as they do about women's "oppression" within it.

A Community of Housewives

Surprisingly, considering its low status, the housewife identity remains a hallmark of community membership in a place where few other symbols of community are available. The housewife identity's usefulness in public settings may be one reason why the identity survives despite the negative dimensions that housewife-women feel are attached to the label. The practicality of being a housewife in the community I studied is an educative example. When I first consulted statistics charts to learn the population density in the area around my apartment in Ōizumi, a section of the Nerima ward where I did my field study, I was unsettled. I suppose I had thought that my familiarity with the area's residents was far greater than it possibly could have been. Nor was such a familiarity possible for my informants. Furthermore, a prevalent perception that Nerima was an alien place, a place that stood in contrast to the "tradition" of one's rural origins, one's "countryside," meant that the identity of Nerima took on a dubious quality. I had hoped to enter the "community" of Ōizumi, but for many of my informants, the existence of that "community" is perpetually in question. Instead of a community, one might have a collection of friends or activities, a series of experiences that never quite assume the shape of a permanent community in the minds of most of their participants.

In one strange sense, the Nerima in which my informants lived was an immigrant culture of women. From just after sunrise until well after sunset, their husbands were away. The women came from different regions and different families. They had different educations and different work experiences, and they lived in a crowded, ceaselessly changing corner of a monstrously huge and bustling city. But, as women, they almost all had two things in common. They almost all lived in Nerima because their husbands (who all had different kinds of jobs) had come here to be able to commute to downtown Tokyo for work, and they almost all had or had had children in the local school system. They first met each other and could find similarities in each other in their capacities as wives and mothers. While certainly the distinctions among close friends and acquaintances were wrought by more personal characteristics, sharing the housewife identity was a means by which my informants could establish a threshold of commonality among themselves and their "wife and mother" experiences.

I would argue that among the most important political acts in my informants' lives were the unnoticed moments in which they described their community to themselves. Inextricably woven into their description of their community is their sense of identity as a housewife, however ambiguously carved, and in both their housewife identity and their community definition is an overlapping of their values and the concrete, unalterable conditions of their lives. Presenting themselves through a particular identity allowed my informants to mentally condense and organize their "community" in Nerima and arrive at an ethic for proper public behavior.

Nerima must be experienced in this condensed way because Nerima, without such selective perception, is, in an infinite number of ways, simply too vast for comprehension. For example, it is the fifth largest of Tokyo's twenty-three wards in area; it is the fourth largest in population; it encompasses approximately 48 square kilometers of land, 258,000 households, and 630,000 people; the average population density is 12,893 people per square kilometer.[7] Ōizumi, where I lived, was in the westernmost, least densely populated section of Nerima. The name Ōizumi is a shortened form of the name of the nearest train station, Ōizumi Gakuen. But even there, in most neighborhoods, the population density was still over 10,000 per square kilometer.[8]

More impressive than the sheer numerical vastness of Nerima might be the enormity of development and change that the area experiences.

In Ōizumi, the wave of change that has engulfed the ward ever since the war was clearly evident. A history of Ōizumi sponsored by a farmers' cooperative shows the area as transformed from the "country" that it was just over thirty-five years ago. In aerial photographs of one location in Ōizumi, what were once agricultural fields have been turned into residential neighborhoods. In the most recent photograph, it is hard to discern any free space where one rooftop leaves off and another begins. A new portion of a recently opened subway line, the widening of the major train line through the ward, and freeway expansion projects stretching across the Ōizumi horizon all suggest that the torrent of development is not yet over.[9]

The flavor of ever-deepening urbanization is especially thick in the Ōizumi area. The streets near the Ōizumi Gakuen Station are lined with shops and the majority of the area's banks. Parked bicycles make passage on the sidewalk a near impossibility, and taxis and buses seem to loom incessantly toward collision. On rainy days, it can be difficult to exit the station even on foot. Umbrellas bump up against each other; their owners sway and duck to avoid the umbrellas' pointed rib ends. Traffic is so bad on the south side of the station that buses that are supposed to stop near the south entrance often let their passengers off much earlier. It is faster to walk, wending one's way among the automobiles, the motorcycles, the trucks and cyclists. Above the din, a traffic cop constantly blows his whistle — unobeyed.

In Ōizumi, the major thoroughfares are not the models of "tradition meets modernity" that some guidebooks have pictured in Tokyo. Ōizumi streets look new. Shiny car dealerships, fast food restaurants, and boutiques fill the lower floors of new buildings. *Mansions,* Japanese condominiums, are upstairs. The old, dank noodle shops and bars that are a famous characteristic of Tokyo are actually hard to find on the most well-traveled roads. But new bakeries, franchised family restaurants (like Denny's) and other types of chain stores — take-out sushi, convenience stores, Baskin Robbins — abound. When one ventures off the main roads, it is usually to enter a quiet residential neighborhood, some combination of single-family homes and apartments. The age of the buildings is varied, but construction that was ongoing or completed during my stay tended to be on apartment or *mansion* buildings.

In the eighteen months of my stay, huge new apartment buildings suddenly appeared on the skyline. On the traditional shopping street of lower, older buildings, several new multistoried buildings reared their heads out of the scaffolding before I was quite conscious that construction had been undertaken. The small fields to the south of my apartment building were paved into parking lots. The aging house and garden that my window overlooked was demolished in the course of a weekend. The calligraphy shop on the corner was closed down and its owners, who had lived upstairs, moved away. The same happened to the commercial laundering service next door to it. Just a bare minute around the corner, a new restaurant sprang up, where there had once been a bar. Down that street and around the comer, a new Korean restaurant opened up. A little further down my own street, a vacant lot was suddenly filled with cluster homes that were, in turn, suddenly filled with families.

The women in the neighborhood were themselves proof of the surging "newness" of Nerima. Hardly any of them had been born in the area. Most had moved there after marrying. Very few had lived more than twenty-five years in the ward. Many of the women I knew in Ōizumi had been there just long enough to see their neighborhoods metamorphose from a rather rural to an urban atmosphere. Therefore, my informants carried with them a consciousness of having come to Nerima from elsewhere as well as relatively recent memories of a Nerima that was much different from what it is today. Consequently, they perceived their Nerima neighborhoods and social networks as living contrasts to "tradition."

Proof of this perspective was the concern many housewives expressed that, in Nerima, I could not get to know the "real" Japan. The "real" Japan was embodied in a tradition that was not to be found near my Ōizumi home and, in fact, not anywhere in Nerima. The real Japan, the housewives explained, exists out in the countryside—or, more precisely stated, *uchi no inaka* (my countryside). Each woman possessed her own "countryside," the more rural place where she was born and raised at least until adolescence, when she might move to Tokyo for work or education. Of course, some of the women had been raised in other sections of Tokyo, but even those areas were proposed as more "Japanese" than Nerima. In downtown Tokyo, the old ways still exist, I was assured.[10]

One's countryside acted as a cultural and historical reference book. Conversations could be strung around the participants' differing countrysides of origin, and those habits of speech gave the odd impression that the speakers were only temporarily in Nerima—as if they were camping out or had come on a sort of cultural exchange. "In the countryside where I come from, we make that food a different way," one might say to provide some new topic of discussion. Another might refer to the countryside to diffuse confusion over etiquette in a hazy situation: "In the countryside where you are from, did you do it this way, too? We always had to." Or yet another might explain her initial hesitancy toward some new activity by saying, "In the countryside where I grew up, women did not do those things." The countryside formed an explanatory background for questions as diverse as why an informant had an arranged marriage to why she knew no local politicians. In fact, even those who had come of age in some section of Tokyo tended to present "country" politics as more "real" than those in their own communities. When their sense of their community was already this temporary and uncertain, the importance of their identities as housewives was deepened. Other traditional justifications of common interests were weak or nonexistent.

Most informants talked about their first years in Nerima as lonely. Busy with infants, or recently moved from a husband's transfer, they did not get out much or found it difficult to meet people. When they did meet others, it was often through organizations like the PTA, grocery cooperatives, or block associations. Mothers of very young children said that they met other women in the parks where they took their children to play. The women joined the PTA, purchased cooperative groceries, or went to the park in order to fulfill obligations as wives and mothers, and so it seemed automatic to view other women and to present themselves as housewives.

Even those who resented being categorized as housewives might be likely to generalize that other women were housewives. One woman with elementary school-age children said that she found it difficult to meet people when she first moved to Ōizumi. The people in the area seemed busy, even cold, and the women in the parks where she took her children seemed too housewifey to her. She did eventually make friends when her children entered school by joining a group of parents that led an after-school program for the elementary school.

Like this woman, the after-school group's active members were primarily women who did not work outside the home. The woman said that after meeting the after-school group leaders, she at last came to feel involved in the community, and her sense of incompatibility with "housewifey" women declined. In fact, she said that she now thought of herself as a housewife. This woman seemed to reflect the group's emphasis on the housewife role as a source of common identity. The members' educational and work backgrounds, families and incomes were all different. One woman had been a journalist and lived in Australia with her husband. Another, the wife of a conservative politician's aide, had studied to be a pianist, but quit work as a research assistant to a music scholar in order to have children. Another said she had never done anything but be a housewife. Despite—or maybe because of—their obvious differences, all of the group members said that they called themselves housewives.

Because housewives often meet each other in a context involving their children or defined by their residence in a particular geographic location, they may find themselves involved in social networks that cut across what might otherwise be expected to be barriers. Erecting the "housewife" identity as a focus for the similarities among disparate members of a group, my informants promulgated an unwritten ethic of appropriate behavior among themselves. Distinctions in family background, education, one's husband's work or status, even political views were presented as "unimportant" in their housewife's ethic.[11]

Ueda-san interpreted the housewife's socializing credo for me when she explained why retired men found it so difficult to feel comfortable spending time at home. Men, she explained, relate to each other according to their position in a particular career. Their names are always attached to a business card that says just who they are and what they do. When they retire, they lose the distinction of their career position and thus lose the only method of determining their relationship to others. Housewives, in contrast, do not have such positions. They have no business cards. They relate to each other as "friends in the neighborhood," and the social networks they build are not subject to shocks of the type men experience as their careers change or come to an end.

On a certain level, there was a lot of truth in Ueda-san's argument. Being "housewives together" could override other differences among women. For example, Ueda-san's friend, Hashimoto-san, was the wife of a self-employed man who was somewhat active in conservative party politics. Hashimoto-san was much older than Ueda-san and many of her other friends because she had children late, and her friends were women she had met in the PTA. She herself expressed conservative political views.

Many conservatives I met in other circumstances described volunteer activity enthusiasts in general as "socialist," but Hashimoto-san spoke highly of the volunteer work of PTA co-worker Satō-san, a political progressive whose husband was a civil servant in the local social welfare bureaucracy. Tanaka-san, another self-expressed conservative and the wife of an executive in a large chemical company, worked alongside Satō-san in volunteer activities and grew quite close to another political progressive in the group, Kawashima-san, the wife of a ward accountant who also knew Hashimoto-san from PTA activities.

None-of-the-Above Narratives of the Housewife Label

Most of my informants had been describing themselves as housewives long before I met them, but one, Keiko, the daughter of Sasaki-san, another of my housewife informants, was a young, single, working woman when I first moved to Nerima. Before I completed my fieldwork, Keiko married. Keiko's fiancé was to be transferred to another town just after the marriage, so she quit her job at a stock and securities brokerage in order to move with him. She expressed some interest in finding part-time work after her marriage and move. However, as both she and her mother pointed out, her most important new responsibilities would be those she took on as *shufu,* or housewife. In fact, the older Sasaki went to great lengths to impress the weight of this new role on both her daughter and me (I was also single and nearly the same age as her daughter).

Life as single people was all the two of us knew, Sasaki-san said. Those twenty-odd years seemed long to us, but our (she implied that I, too, would inevitably marry and become a housewife) time as housewives would be much, much longer—the rest of our lives. Sasaki-san teased her daughter that she was ill-prepared for this big step. Keiko must work hard to improve her cooking and cleaning skills, Sasaki-san complained. She joked that Keiko had not been at all attentive to her mother's admonitions about the proper maintenance of a home and had actually shown her future husband discourtesies, allowing him, for instance, to refill his own rice bowl when they were eating together.

Sasaki-san made us all laugh because we knew she was really only touching the tip of the iceberg. It was hard to imagine that Keiko would become a housewife. She spent her weekends on road trips and wore tattered jeans. She had educated me on the single woman's advantage at pachinko parlors: go alone, wear a short skirt, and you can expect the old men sitting next to you to give you some of the metal balls they win. Only a little more than a year earlier, I had heard Keiko tell her mother that she was considering studying abroad in Australia. When Sasaki-san protested that, if her daughter did to go to Australia, she would return to Japan too old to find a decent husband, Keiko had laughed at what she called her mother's old-fashioned views. Over the year between her announcement of her Australia dreams and her marriage, Keiko had changed, but we could all see that she had a much larger change coming if she were going to be the sort of housewife whom her mother described.

Keiko's mother insisted that her daughter's move from her single twenties to the world of the housewife had implications that required disciplined commitment and would shape the rest of her life. In a similar vein, Keiko's new housewife identity will also significantly condition the development of her lifetime relationship with the political world. Statistically speaking, chances are that Keiko's experience of her housewife identity will be intermingled with experience in one or more work situations as she moves among, perhaps, several communities in various areas of Japan.[12] She may acquire more and different education and develop a wide array of new skills.[13] She will raise her children in a society in which fewer and fewer women call themselves or are considered to be housewives.

Nevertheless, for better or worse, among other possible identities, Keiko will carry a housewife's identity with her. As a result of its symbolic and concrete nature, this housewife identity will have the power to structure her social experiences in crucial ways. In doing so, the housewife's identity will also mark the ground on which Keiko will, from time to time, meet politics. The political world Keiko knows will always be in part a housewife's world. Because that is true, if we will understand Keiko's political life, we must first understand her housewife's life.

The housewife identity becomes a form of social transportation that marks the status and possibilities of Keiko's future experience of her citizenship because classifying herself in terms of a simple, broadly understood category is necessary for establishing the context that defines her position in public life. Scholars find it useful to think of the Japanese self as relational.[14] In other words, one's understanding of one's position, obligations, and actions will vary greatly depending on one's relationship to a given group.[15] Moreover, one's relationship to a group is not a matter of purely personal choice. The possibilities of groups to which one may belong are usually delimited by social consensus on the appropriate fit between certain kinds of individuals and various groups.

Characteristics such as age and sex are important determinants of possible group identifications. Individual identification within a group is further mediated by a broader, ritualistic understanding of roles and the behavior appropriate to them. As we can see even in her interactions with her mother, women like Keiko cannot be said to simply have "chosen" a housewife identity. "Housewife" is an identity because there is broad social agreement on its appropriateness as a ritual marker of the woman who bears it.

An individual might have several "appropriate" identities, each brought to the fore depending on the context in which she wanted to present herself. Keiko is a daughter with her parents, a housewife with the PTA. Both the contexts in which a woman might claim an identity and much of the content of the identity she claims are already specified by socially shared understandings of relative appropriateness.[16] We can understand that appropriate behavior for a mother would be socially specified, because we can easily think of examples of appropriate and inappropriate mothers in our own context. We might have a harder time believing that a woman's role in political life would be similarly elaborated because "political life" is a boundless, vaguely determined context; examples of acceptable and unacceptable citizen behavior are harder to bring to mind. Paradoxically, however, the vagueness of public space can exaggerate the importance of a person's primary social identity.

The housewife identity becomes important to a woman in public life, even if she amends it or disavows it in private life, because perceptions of "people in general" or "society in general" can be powerful influences on an individual's perception of social obligation. Takie Lebra's analysis of the Japanese construction of self explains why this is so. She suggests that beyond the relationship of an individual to various groups there exists a relationship of different types of selves within a single individual. These selves are distinguished from each other by the different degrees of constraint of expression one shows when dealing with another person in a variety of contexts.[17]

Of course, the ways in which a woman might conceive of and present herself differ when she is with her father or with her best friend. In both cases, however, appropriate self-presentation is probably relatively easy to determine because the relationships are specific and well known. When a woman attempts to conceive of the appropriate self-presentation in a more generalized, less known (or knowable) set of relationships such as that between a woman and political power in a modern state, she faces a more daunting set of demands. As Lebra explains, a person

succeeds in developing a conception of self for generalized social relationships when she can satisfy her need for both status and empathy in
the vague "world audience" or *seken* of relationships in broad social
contexts.[18] Drawing metaphors from idiomatic Japanese, Lebra describes the status-seeking aspect of the self as the "face" of the self's body
and explains the relationship of *seken* and the self this way:

While the *seken* has something in common with the Western concept of
"reference group," or with the "generalized other" of Mead, I identify it as
the generalized audience or jury surrounding the self in an inescapable way.
Two features of the *seken* make the self especially vulnerable to its sanction.
In parallel with the "face"-focused self, the *seken*-other is equipped with its
own "eyes," "ears," and "mouth," watching, hearing, and gossiping about
the self. This body metaphor contributes to the sense of immediacy and
inescapability of the *seken*'s presence. On the other hand, the *seken* itself is
immediately invisible and ill-defined and thus can make the self defenseless.[19]

Under the felt pressure of the *seken,* a woman becomes extremely
conscious of her social status, leading sometimes to a sense of compet-
itiveness with others. Yet, contrary to this competitive spirit, she is also
"intimacy-seeking." As Lebra explains, the status-oriented and empathy-
oriented aspects of the self are tied together. A poor self-presentation
can reduce one's chances to develop intimacy. "Being isolated, being
excluded from a group, lacking a friend whose support one can count
on or who counts on one's support — all these can result in one's loss of
face vis-à-vis the ubiquitous audience," says Lebra.[20] She offers the example of an elderly couple that resides with children even though neither
the couple nor the children like the arrangement: "The family care of
the aged, which superficially may indicate a strong bonding between
generations, in fact turns out to involve the presentational self to be kept
up in good standing."[21]

The Housewife as the Presentational Self

When we describe a non-elite housewife's political experience, we are talking about her relationship with a generalized reference
other, or, as Lebra would say, the *seken*. In any mass democracy, the
world of politics is always imaginable as infinitely expandable. Even
when one thinks only of one's own actions or the actions of a favorite

few, it is impossible to assume that others, currently unknown, will not take action in a similar vein. The generalizable rights of a modern democratic nation offer the possibility that one's own political experience is generalizable. Like Lebra's *seken* (general society), politics has faces and voices but is "ill-defined." The more a woman feels herself vulnerable to the amorphous "general society" in her interactions with others, the more likely it becomes that she will seek to shore herself up with a presentation that both assures status and elicits empathy. Therefore, we may suppose that, when an individual places herself in relationship to politics, she seeks a self-presentation, or, in other words, an *identity,* that promises security of status and a possibility for acquiring the understanding of others.[22] The most convenient status and empathy-eliciting identity for many women—housewife—is, however, also the most inconvenient in terms of securing their political presence.

Housewives seemed to take on their identity as if they were checking a none-of-the-above box on a survey. Most expressed little confidence that a housewife was highly regarded in society and even less confidence that the label was a fitting description for the mixed palette of attitudes and activities that characterized their daily lives. When I used interview questions borrowed from Japanese social psychologist Kunihiro Yōko's own research on the housewife identity, my results almost exactly mirrored hers; housewives called themselves housewives only because they thought no other label was available to them.[23] Despite the profound uneasiness with which they employed housewife identities, my informants also resisted giving up those identities. These "housewives" experienced a dilemma about their identity that eventually produced the effect of bicycle citizenship. They were not bereft of a public identity, thus not bereft of a means for seeing politics, but something about the public identity of housewife made the *public housewife* seem anomalous, much like a bicycle is real transportation—but not on a major freeway.

When I asked an informant if she considered herself to be a house-wife, she often hesitated before replying, and the reply would usually go something like this: "I guess I am a housewife because I am responsible for the cooking and cleaning and the home." But, if I asked her if she were a typical housewife, or, in the Japanese phrasing a "housewife-like housewife" *(shufu rashii shufu),* she would be more likely to demur.[24] She could not be considered a "housewife-like housewife" because she failed to devote herself fully to things like cooking and cleaning that were a housewife's mark, my informant would explain. She might say that she worked part-time and was deficient in her housekeeping. Or she might "confess" that she did not achieve fulfillment from doing housework even when she did it well.

Takezono-san, a middle-aged woman who had not been employed outside the home since her marriage, described herself as a housewife. But, the more she talked, the more qualifications she added to her self-presentation. For example, when I asked, "Are you a housewife?" she quickly replied, "Yes, that's so," in a strongly affirmative tone. Then she paused with a humming "but. . . ." After hesitating a bit, she went on, expressing her dissonance with the housewife image.

Housewife—really, I've always thought that it would have been better if I had kept working. [She had trained as an architect in college and had been employed in a design firm before marriage.] To come to the end as "just a housewife," it's terribly—you resist it—it's empty. That's why I've always kept doing something, you see—studying painting, or the PTA, or the co-op—as a sort of sense of purpose. I'm not suited for being a housewife. Being a housewife doesn't give me a sense of purpose.

Takezono-san thought that to be a housewife in society was a form of nonexistence, and she had a hard time explaining exactly what function the "housewife" label filled. "Basically, 'housewife' is like an occupation," she said, but she was not satisfied. "You write 'housewife' in the occupation column [on forms], but it's not an occupation."

"Housewife" seemed to describe something that both was and was not an occupation, and that troubled informants. In part, the problem seemed to be that the "work" in "housework" was unappreciated by society. Another woman, Tashiro-san, labeled herself "housewife" despite the fact that she taught painting to children on a regular basis. Perhaps she chose the label instead of "art teacher" because, by her own assessment, she spent a great deal of time on housework. But Tashiro-san felt frustrated with the way society viewed that time.

A housewife's work is a very important thing, but somehow—it is not that I want to be acknowledged, but anyone has that feeling where they want somebody to see what they do. So anyway, if you go out and work, and you do something, you get some recognition for it, right? But nobody recognizes a housewife's work. They don't say, "Oh, this is clean," or, "That is well done."

When I was younger I thought if I went outside the home and used this same amount of energy, how would it be? But now, gradually I've gotten older, and I have my own free time, and I have started to think recently that there's no luxury like that. Now I think this [being a housewife] is okay.

Although she stressed the importance of the unrecognized work that housewives perform, Tashiro-san was reluctant to go all the way and say that she used the housewife label as a sort of job title. Using one of Kunihiro's questions, I asked Tashiro-san how she would describe herself in a letter to the editor. She said that she could write "housewife" but that it seemed strange to her since "housewife" was not really an occupation. She wanted her housework to earn the recognition that other work might, but she was reluctant to call housework "work" when pressed. That may be because, like many other housewives, Tashiro-san did not want to identify herself too closely with work that had an image of being low-skilled and unfulfilling. Takezono-san may have also summed up Tashiro-san's feelings when she claimed that, although she did like cooking, she did not "get all that happy from doing housewives' things."

Younger women also found themselves in the dilemma of struggling to express frustration with the status of a housewife identity that they assumed while simultaneously distancing themselves from its image. One mid-thirties member of a young mothers' support group put it this way:

I hate the word "full-time housewife." I get upset when people call me that. The reason I hate it is that inside the word "full-time housewife" is the image that housewives are idle, and that it's easy. It is not as if a housewife's work is easy or as if her time is totally free. In one way, I feel like resisting those people by saying a housewife's work is pretty tough. Besides, even though I am living right now as a full-time housewife, I am not fulfilled. I also hate the "housewives' perspective" or the "housewives' way of thinking."

This woman expressed more anger about her image than most women. The phrases "housewives' perspective" or "housewives' way of thinking" that she says she hates are common in the media and even used by many other housewives who are not as negative about their image.[25] However, it was not unusual for even "satisfied" housewives to see the housewife's image as negative and to explain that negativity by employing popular phrases. One such phrase to which informants referred was "stinking of *nukamiso,*" a strong-smelling agent for making a type of homemade pickled vegetable. Another common saying described the daily work of the housewife as "three meals and a nap."

Even those who showed a strong affinity for the arrangement of their daily lives as housewives tended to be equivocal about accepting the title "housewife." Another member of the young mothers' support group qualified her expression of contentment with the conditions of her life as a full-time housewife by highlighting her own initial unease at taking on such a role.

Right now I think I'm really having a good time. If I am called a housewife, well, looking at it, for the most part, I am doing what a housewife does, so there's not really much I can say to deny it. But, of course, from that [housewife's life] I want to get my own enjoyment. I am afraid I wouldn't be able to see things I see now if I was [hesitation] working now—working in the kind of work there is in Japan.

The things given to me now [that I am a housewife] are children, raising children in this world—what I have is time. Being a full-time housewife you have more time than most people. I really want to treat this time as important. And I guess I thought there were parts of me that I hadn't seen, and I wanted to use those parts.

She [the woman quoted earlier] said that being called a housewife irritates her. I thought being called a full-time housewife was awful, too, but, now, being a housewife while raising children—that particular enjoyment—in that I want to find something . . . and I haven't completely found it. But lately if I am told I am a housewife, I say, "Yes, you're right. I am."

This mix of dissatisfaction with the housewife identity and insistence on its applicability came across intriguingly in my conversation with Sakurai-san, a well-educated woman in her sixties who teaches Japanese to foreigners part-time in a ward program. She explained that part of the impetus behind her studying to get a language teacher's certificate had been a disparaging comment her daughter made about Sakurai-san's housewife life.

You know there were some other reasons why I decided to teach Japanese. I was a perfectionist. At first I was a perfectionist about housework. I even made all of my children's clothes—I was really busy.

Then one day when my daughter was in her freshman year of high school, she came to me and said, "Mama, don't you feel purposeless?" So, when I said, "Why?" she told me, "If I thought I had to become a housewife like you, Mama, I would just never get married."

Well, housework has no end, right. So, every day from morning to night, I was doing housework. Of course, I did work on my own, too,[26] but the majority of what I did was housework. Then my daughter comes to me and says, "I don't want to live like you." It was a shock. It was really a shock for my daughter to say such a thing.

Sakurai-san admitted that she had originally intended to be a working woman. In fact, she had gotten her master's degree at an elite university and had hoped to have a career before meeting the man who became her husband. Soon after marrying, however, Sakurai-san had children, and she decided she could not work. She says that she did not think much about becoming a housewife because she had no other choices. Sakurai-san's connection of her efforts to get into teaching with her daughter's negative comments about housewives seems to suggest that she accepts her daughter's characterization of a housewife's life as purposeless. Yet, even now that she has certification and a job as a language instructor, Sakurai-san clings to her housewife identity.

I have written "housewife" in the "occupation" blank [on forms]. Now I am doing part-time work, and I get a salary. But I don't really have a feeling of resistance toward writing "housewife." After all, there is something of value to being a housewife. Besides, as far as my actual life goes, I'm not working to support myself, you see. My children tell me that I just work for enjoyment, not money.

Sakurai-san seems to be saying that, although she could claim another occupational title—teacher, for example—she feels that she is still really a housewife. Because she still depends on her husband's salary to pay part of her expenses, Sakurai-san says she feels that she does not meet a sort of economic criterion that would justify her calling her teaching job an occupation. Moreover, some aspect of being a housewife, daughter's criticisms aside, remains attractive to her: "After all, there is something of value to being a housewife." The identity that, for Sakurai-san, had been the inevitable delivery of fate is eventually preserved by choice.

Pushing her daughter Keiko to become a good housewife in her upcoming marriage, Sasaki-san seemed less ambivalent toward the housewife identity than many of my informants. However, her expression of what "housewife" meant changed from day to day in a manner suggesting that she, too, experienced the uneven coming-to-terms with her housewife self that Sakurai-san and others described. In fact, Sasaki-san's case is especially informative because it reveals how necessary a housewife identity is to its bearers even when they are ambivalent about the label, and it demonstrates to what a great degree social context is responsible for the content and value of the housewife label.

Near the end of my fieldwork Sasaki-san asked me to tell her some of my interesting findings. I chose a simple one—the unwillingness of some of the women I interviewed who had worked to emphasize work experiences as valuable. I explained that some women who held a job had been reluctant to mention it when I asked whether they were employed because they said they worked "only part-time" or "just to have a little money." Her friend Satō-san listened to my reply with interest.

Satō-san suggested that maybe women who found their work boring or somehow unfulfilling did not think that they were really working. Sasaki-san, however, disagreed. She worked mornings at a small shop. The work was not particularly fulfilling, but she knew it was work, Sasaki-san said. She said that she could not understand why women were reluctant to classify their jobs as work. We discussed the issue for a while, but none of us had a satisfactory resolution.

Our inability to resolve the uncertain status of work in the self-portrayals of some of my informants may have only reflected the dilemma that Sasaki-san herself exhibited. It is true that Sasaki-san openly described her job as work. In fact, she was vocal about working. Nearly all of us who saw her with any frequency knew her work schedule. We were the audience to her comparisons between herself and unemployed housewives. But over time, I came to hear contradictions in Sasaki-san's description of the relationship between working and her life as a housewife.

The source of those contradictions seemed to be Sasaki-san's attempt to juggle acceptance of definitions of her housewife identity that were, if not mutually exclusive, at least largely incompatible. Sasaki-san emphasized her belief in the importance of the rightness of a woman's role as a "traditional" housewife, dedicated first and foremost to maintenance of the home and family.[27] Yet, with similar clarity, she at times presented the housewife's role as an artifact of old-fashioned ideas about women, something that had largely outgrown its usefulness. In other ways, Sasaki-san viewed the housewife as only one of many roles that women might shoulder in a larger attempt to be a whole person. The meaning and purpose that Sasaki-san accorded her work varied with the qualities of the housewife identity toward which she leaned at a particular time.

I joined her once-a-month hiking club for a spring trek. As we walked, we talked about my life in Ōizumi. We were talking about another woman who also lived in the neighborhood when Sasaki-san commented that that woman was unemployed. She is lucky because she can be a full-time housewife, Sasaki-san said. Sasaki-san pointed out that she and another woman friend in the hiking club had to work because they did not have powerful, rich husbands. Sasaki-san said that she was jealous of women who could be full-time housewives, but her tone toward the neighborhood woman was condescending. "What does she do with all her time?" Sasaki-san asked me.

Sasaki-san was habitually quick to make comments about the loose time that full-time housewives whom she knew had, and her comments usually contained the same flavor of mixed envy and condescension that was revealed in her remarks about our neighborhood acquaintance. One of the women Sasaki-san knew from a volunteer group devoted her free time to outdoor activities like hiking that Sasaki-san also enjoyed. When she heard that the woman had been showing pictures of a trip to the mountains to see the autumn leaves, Sasaki-san said, "It must be nice to be a full-time housewife and still have money to travel all the time."

She made similar teasing comments to unemployed Tanaka-san, another participant in the volunteer group. When Tanaka-san complained of continuing fatigue, Sasaki-san told her that she had no excuse to be tired because she was a full-time housewife and could nap during the day whenever she pleased. Tanaka-san protested that volunteer work and her hobbies, studying English and painting, absorbed her free time. Sasaki-san laughed. "I wish I had time to really study English between classes, but I never do," she said. She often teased Tanaka-san for having a rich husband and not having to work.

Sasaki-san sometimes tended to go so far as to argue that full-time housewives were a dying breed. Her teasing and frustrated comments seemed to suggest that she thought household chores were simply not demanding enough to absorb a person's entire day or that, at least, few people could luxuriate in sole attendance to household duties. In her snips at "full-time" housewives, her picture of unemployed women was one of lazy or pleasure-seeking privileged women. But if her views had really been thus one-sided, it is doubtless that she would have had far fewer friends who were full-time housewives. Her condescension toward full-time housewives was tempered with a mixture of acceptance of the existence of limitations on the choices of many of the women who were full-time housewives and, in a sort of self-contradiction, acceptance of the full-time housewife role as the truly proper one for women.

Sasaki-san sympathized with Tanaka-san and was always quick to point out to me and Keiko, also a member of the group, that at the time she and Tanaka-san had each married, the ideas of what was proper for a woman to do had been very constrained. "I never went into a coffee shop until I joined the PTA, and we had a meeting there," said Sasaki-san. "I did not think that was the sort of place young girls should go." She and Tanaka-san often told us how rare it was then for women to hold a career and lead an independent life.

Sasaki-san and Tanaka-san agreed that their husbands placed great demands on their time, and Sasaki-san pointed out that she was freer than Tanaka-san because her husband was away on the weekdays. He had been transferred to a work site a few hours away and was living apart from his family—a practice so common in Japan that it has its own special vocabulary. Sasaki-san sympathized when Tanaka-san said that her husband criticized her for leaving the home at night or being busy with volunteer activities too often on weekends.

When her own husband was home, she could never get out, Sasaki-san explained. He wanted her around just in case he needed something. Sasaki-san told me that when she had first started working at the shop, she had hidden the information from her husband. When he found out about her job from something one of the children had said, he was angry that his wife worked for money and at a menial task. At first he made her quit. It had taken time to make him accept the situation. Sasaki-san understood that it was difficult for some women to work without upsetting their families.

Sometimes, however, Sasaki-san's acceptance of the housewife's role went beyond resignation to existing limitations. On occasion she could be a promoter of the very construction of women's identities that led to the limitations about which Tanaka-san complained and Sasaki-san sympathized. Sasaki-san said that she accepted the label "housewife" for herself, and while she acknowledged that some people felt the label was demeaning, she insisted that she did not. "I manage a whole house. I put the house and family first. I think that is important," she explained. Despite the fact that she sometimes distinguished herself from unemployed housewives, when I asked Sasaki-san if she was a typical housewife, she said definitely, "Yes."

Sasaki-san's discussions with me and her daughter, Keiko, about marriage were even more revealing of Sasaki-san's promotion of an accepting version of the housewife's role. A few months after the two women recounted their argument about Keiko's desire to study in Australia, the topic of marriage again took the floor in our conversation.

Slightly younger than Sasaki-san, Satō-san remarked that her husband had been cranky lately because she had been absorbed during the day with her growing volunteer tasks while at night she often had meetings or phone calls related to the daytime activities. He had complained that he was tired when he returned from work and needed his wife's time and attention in the evening. Sasaki-san's daughter took Satō-san's part. "You're tired, too," Keiko said. "Your husband should understand that and help out." But Sasaki-san, despite her own frequent complaints about a tight schedule, thought her daughter was wrong. She told Satō-san to be more careful, suggesting that she should refuse to take part in evening activities outside the home and ask friends and other volunteers to refrain from telephoning her home after dinner.

Keiko complained that her mother's ideas of marriage were out of date. She would not live the same way herself; her husband would have to help out at home because she wanted a fun life, too. She said that her mother's generation might have been able to sacrifice everything to move their family up in the world, but today's young people wanted comfortable lives. Given the high cost of land, they could not count on ever being able to buy a nice home unless both worked—maybe even then all they could hope for would be a small condominium. They had to make up for such a situation by enjoying their free time.

Keiko said that she thought her mother's ways of thinking about women made Japanese women's lives more difficult. She used her own job as a salesperson for a large firm as an example. "You said I didn't need to go to a four-year college because I was a girl," Keiko complained. "So I went to a junior college, and now look at the job I have. It's so boring, and they work you three years. And then when you're not a cute little girl anymore, they want you out of there. Then you feel like you might as well get married."

Certainly, there is a generational difference between Keiko's and her mother's views. Despite the generation gap, however, Keiko found herself on a path to be a housewife. More women of Keiko's generation than her mother's avoid housewifery, but in a recent letter written from her new home, Keiko told me that she found plenty of other young women at home with children with whom to socialize. I cannot foretell what will become of housewives. Perhaps they will disappear, but social change is slow.

Keiko's engagement many months after the debate about Satō-san's volunteer work was to a professor whom Sasaki-san had met by chance several years earlier and introduced to her daughter a few months before the engagement and marriage. Since Keiko had few job prospects in the town where she and her new husband were going to live, and since her husband made a good salary as a professor, it was likely that she would not work, at least at first. She was about to become the very sort of woman her mother had referred to almost condescendingly, a full-time housewife. But Sasaki-san did not seem disturbed by this.

Sometimes Sasaki-san could seem more conservative than almost any of her contemporaries. A young housewife in the neighborhood wanted to hire a French exchange student staying at the Sasakis' to teach her French conversation, and she asked that he come to her apartment for the weekly sessions because she had trouble getting out with her pre-school daughter. Sasaki-san was scandalized. How could a young married woman allow a young single man into her home when her husband was at work? Didn't the young woman care what other people thought? But Sasaki-san was not consistently conservative in her views. For example, unlike many of the women I interviewed, Sasaki-san said that she believed that even women who were full-time housewives could achieve independence if they were spiritually, or psychologically, self-supporting.

Like the women she claimed not to understand when we talked about women's discomfort with assigning their work a status in their daily lives, Sasaki-san was also ambivalent about the final position of her working/housewife self. When I went to her home to interview her, I had already known her for over a year, and when she leaned over and quietly told me that, although she was loathe to admit it, her family needed the money that she took in by working, I was surprised. I had already heard her refer to her work in front of so many people as something she did because she was not a privileged, rich housewife that I could hardly think she found it difficult to admit that she worked for economic reasons. In fact, I had assumed that she worked primarily for the money.

But as I reconsidered the interview much later, I realized that Sasaki-san had offered more than one reason for working. She had talked about her loneliness when she first moved to Ōizumi and how she came to know the people at the shop when she was a customer there. She had now worked there over thirteen years, and I knew that she socialized with her co-workers, not just at the hiking club, but elsewhere. As much as Sasaki-san complained that having to work kept her out of the home, she filled her time when she was not working with volunteer activities, teaching arts and crafts at ward facilities for disabled persons, driving for facilities that were short on transportation, selling cakes made with tofu to benefit local volunteer groups, and helping a singer friend of hers do promotion and ticket sales for benefit concerts.

Sasaki-san spent a great deal of time away from home—not all of it was spent making money. I wonder whether the work did not provide as much human sustenance as economic. One of the reasons Sasaki-san gave for staying with the shop over so many years was that it was a job where she found it easy to take time off. But when a health problem of her husband's coincided with health problems of some of his aging relatives, forcing her to lay off work and her volunteer activities, Sasaki-san was dismayed by the ease with which she could free up her time. "I know that I am not doing anything valuable at all, because even though I took time off from everything in the past few weeks, no one has needed me," she said glumly. It seemed that Sasaki-san reaped benefits from the human ties of her workplace, and her volunteer work, as much as she increased her income. But the human aspect of her working benefits was more difficult for her to admit than her family's tight finances. A human need put Sasaki-san in tension with the image of her as a housewife who was supposed to fulfill those needs in the family.

Moreover, Sasaki-san downplayed work she did that was probably dearer to her heart — after-school art teaching for middle school children. When she said she worked, she referred usually to the shop clerk job, but the truth was that she had also acted as an after-school art teacher in her home since her children were in middle school. Sasaki-san describes her art teaching as a carryover from a stop-gap measure designed to support her own children. Some problem had developed with the art teacher at the local middle school, and she wanted to send her children to an after-school program. Unfortunately, the company where her husband worked was having difficulties, and family finances were not as good as they might have been.

Sasaki-san said that she was forced to tutor her children at home, and when word got around that she was teaching children at home, other mothers asked her to take on their children, too. Because she still has some old contacts in the area who have asked her to teach their children, she continues to teach even though her own children are now grown, Sasaki-san explained. She supposes that she will quit teaching soon, but neither her interest nor the number of students shows signs of waning.

It is interesting that the shop's unspecialized labor is what Sasaki-san most commonly refers to as "work." She obviously has a serious commitment to her home tutoring and to her pupils. She holds parties for her students, worries about their development and social lives outside her teaching time, and takes a large number of them along on her hiking club trips. Sasaki-san talks about her students often and follows their progress through the educational system as well as observing the way the stresses and strain of the system can affect her students. She takes her own teaching duties seriously, making a concerted effort to maintain and improve her own skills. Finally, art education is the work that Sasaki-san trained for in her years at junior college. One would expect that she would prize any opportunity to employ her skills.

Sasaki-san's framing of her teaching is as a task she "happened" to pick up in the line of her regular duties as a *housewife and mother*.[28] Prevailed on by others, she expanded the range of the task as a sort of favor.[29] Possibly, in the frame of the "housewife's favor" conducted at home and at times that are convenient to her own schedule, the teaching does not appear as "work." I noticed a similar framing occurring when other women placed different tasks in relationship to their "housewife" identity. In fact, Sasaki-san's continued use of the housewife identity is really no different from Sakurai-san's insistence on it even after getting a job partially as a means to escape her "housewife's emptiness."

Sasaki-san's presentation of the housewife identity varied in response to her reading of the milieu in which she made the presentation. Hearing the shift in Sasaki-san's presentation of her housewifery is crucial to our understanding of her experience of political life because, in learning how different social contexts affect her view of herself as a housewife, we are also learning a great deal about how she conceives of the community to which she belongs. For example, most of her more conservative statements were made when other housewives, such as full-time housewife Tanaka-san, were present. This is important. The shifting tone of Sasaki-san's housewife self-presentation did not vary arbitrarily; it changed in accordance with a shift in social context. The fact that a group of other housewives seemed to be the context most likely to elicit an accepting or sympathetic rendition of the housewife identity from Sasaki-san points to "housewife" as something more than an ill-fitting label for use in general society, on bank forms or surveys. This "something more" is the reason that, unsatisfactory as they find the image, housewives continue to identify as housewives.

My research method allowed me to trace the development of friendships among informants, and by doing so, I could see why a woman might continue to carry the banner of a housewife's identity. Although calling oneself a housewife might not be attractive in terms of status or even quite correct in terms of one's daily activities, it could be tremendously convenient, perhaps even necessary, in a social sense. "Housewife" worked as a short-cut self-presentation that let others know how they might establish common ground in a situation where other indicators were too divisive, complex, or simply indiscernible. "Housewife" operated as one means of imposing social intelligibility on the challenging urban landscape.

Among Friends:
Maintaining the Housewife Identity

As I have claimed already, housewife is a weighty political category because it is a necessarily public category. The fact that nearly all of the self-identified Japanese housewives I interviewed described feeling that the housewife label only partially suited them suggests that "being a housewife" is not merely an indicator of one's role within a family. These women admitted to filling their families' housewife roles — cooking, cleaning, and caring for children, the elderly, the sick. However, they did not accept the housewife label merely because they performed those tasks. They needed the category in order to describe themselves to the outside world. In fact, the housewife identity probably got its real meaning when women used it *outside of the home* as a means of establishing or explaining a social presence.

When I vacationed with three women I knew from Ōizumi volunteer activities, I realized that they enforced the housewife identity among themselves — even when, as individuals, they may have felt discontented with the light that the housewife label cast on their lives. The housewife comes to be *because* a woman has a social role beyond her role in the home that requires her to organize and present herself in a way she thinks a "generalized other" will understand. Politics is just such a generalized other. Thus when a housewife confronts what she perceives as "politics," she feels the pressure of presenting herself in a manner acceptable to an only vaguely understood social order; she is pressured to rely on her housewife identity to make who she is clear to the social audience. Politics as a social context reinforces housewifery.

On the vacation, the power of social context beyond the family in defining the housewife identity was obvious. Kawashima-san, the ward accountant's wife, invited me, Tanaka-san, and one other woman whom she worked with at a benefit second-hand shop to spend three days at an apartment she and her husband had recently purchased in a vacation home development not far from the popular resort town Karuizawa. From the start, our trip was hemmed in by potential conflicts. These conflicts stemmed directly from the women's sense of obligation to friends and family, obligation which, in turn, was inseparable from their housewife identities.

The first difficulty, originating out of a housewife's credo of equality, was making the trip without offending those in Kawashima-san's circle who had not been invited. A greater potential area of conflict was the possibility of exerting pressure on one of the women to violate the home-first priorities of her housewife identity. These priorities existed in terms of the concrete conditions of their daily lives. Yet the home-first attitude was a means of defining oneself in relation to other house-wives, as well. A home-first attitude provided a backdrop for a house-wife's self-portrayal that allowed her to remind her friends of their common and uniting experiences.

Family needs provided the concrete conditions that demanded home-first priorities. The trip had to be scheduled after peak vacation times in order to ensure that it did not conflict with anyone's time with her husband or relatives; in fact, each of the women had already vacationed with her entire family when we took the trip. When the calligraphy teacher could not participate, Kawashima-san did not openly press her, but rather insisted that the friend share a travel opportunity with her husband. Each of the women had sticky arrangements to make to ensure that cooking and household chores would get done while she was away or that her husband and children could eat meals out at restaurants. The woman with the youngest children, who were in elementary and middle school, had to ask her mother in downtown Tokyo to take the children for the trip's duration, and she called home often to make sure every-thing was going well.

Making sure that household duties were covered while the housewife was away was not the only home-first task confronting the women, however. It seemed important that my informants demonstrate to fellow housewives that they had not left their families in the lurch. In fact, most home-first issues seemed to be of a dual nature; one must deal success-fully with a concrete problem at home and present oneself appropriately to one's friends. As always with an activity that took place away from the home during mealtimes, the housewives explained to each other how the members of their families would get fed. They told various stories about managing their previous absences and, in their narratives, usually portrayed husbands and older children as virtually unable to care for themselves. The women remarked again and again how infrequently they were able to get away from home overnight, although they all did so with the volunteer groups from time to time.

The housewives also emphasized that they were taking the vacation without placing a financial burden on each other's families. The women insisted that they could not eat food that Kawashima-san had stocked in her family's vacation apartment because she must save it for her family. In the grocery store, selecting food for the first evening meal, they engaged in a sort of competition of bargain hunting, each woman demonstrating her knowledge of innovative ways to simplify the making of or reduce the cost of a good family meal. A similar competition existed regarding household chores. Each woman insisted that she did not mind cleaning the bath or whipping up a meal. I was not allowed to participate in cleaning or cooking—in part because they could not stop seeing me as a foreign guest. I realized as we talked about everything from childbearing to international relations, they also perceived me as young and inexperienced, without a house and thus without any certification of my ability to efficiently manage meals or cleaning. "It's okay, we do this every day; it's easy," I was told when I protested that I should not be allowed to sit idle.

In general conversation the home played a prominent part. When I spoke about the United States, the mother of the young children spoke about "internationalizing" her children's education. Much of the "shop talk" about volunteer work centered on the difficulty of managing to be of real assistance to people in need without sacrificing the time and energy one's own family required. Even seeing the sights elicited references to a housewife's context. Stories of and plans for family vacations were shared. Tanaka-san talked nostalgically about her "schoolgirl days" and about trips she had made "back when she was single," and a general atmosphere of irony about a group of housewives acting girlishly pervaded some of the remarks.

One home issue nearly threatened to ruin the entire trip. Kawashima-san had originally intended to make the trip with just her friends, but she lived with aging parents, her own mother and her father-in-law, and, at the last minute, she decided that she could not leave them at home alone. She never made clear exactly why she felt it necessary to bring them and a friend, one of the parents' contemporaries, but it may have been because she knew of no one to care for her father-in-law, who could no longer walk unassisted, in her absence. She told her friends that the parents just wanted to breathe the mountain air and really took care of themselves.

The other two women did not accept her excuse, however, and when they met me at the train station on the first day of the trip, they whispered that they thought we ought to cut our visit short. We cannot impose on Kawashima-san's parents, they reasoned. If Kawashima-san has to play hostess to us, she will be forced to neglect her parents, they said, and we made quiet plans in the apartment's spare bedroom to offer the excuse that we were called back to Tokyo to our own daily responsibilities and had to leave quite early the next morning.

Kawashima-san would not hear of it. She seemed almost angry. The parents do not need our interference, she insisted. She pointed out that she had looked forward to hiking with her friends for a long time. She would not have brought the parents if she thought she would be overrun attending to them. But, unfortunately for Kawashima-san, it was well known among the Ōizumi volunteers that Kawashima-san devoted an ever-increasing amount of time to caring for the parents. I had heard more than one person remark on Kawashima-san's fortitude as her days were eaten away driving her father-in-law to the doctor. In the end, we compromised. We stayed and hiked with Kawashima-san the next day and left the following day, ostensibly so that the other two women could show me around a town that they had not visited since their "schoolgirl" days.

Kawashima-san protested, but it was clear that the compromise was the most workable situation for her as well. Her father-in-law needed help getting to and from the toilet and bath and getting his meals, and her mother, over ninety, could be of only limited assistance. The conflict over the aging parents demonstrates the curious duality of the housewife identity. Kawashima-san's original plans were constrained by her duties as a housewife, and her friends thought that such a constraint, while regrettable, was only natural.

The conflict was made even more complex, however, by the desire of each involved to show an appropriate picture of herself. Kawashima-san did everything she could to avoid appearing chained to her home responsibilities while at the same time meeting those responsibilities fully. Thus, as she ran in and out of the room attending to their needs, Kawashima-san insisted that the parents did not require extra work on her part.

In contrast, Tanaka-san and the younger mother, Sakurai-san, strove to demonstrate their sensitivity and devotion to the home by describing their reluctance to interfere with Kawashima-san's home obligations. I heard Tanaka-san remark on the problem of caring for aging parents on several other occasions when the conversation was about how Kawashima-san or another woman's time and energy were required to care for parents or in-laws. She was glad, Tanaka-san said, to live far from her own in-laws because otherwise her duties toward them as a housewife would be immense. Tanaka-san demonstrated her full awareness of and, indeed, acceptance, if grudgingly, of a housewife's role. As it was, a visit from her mother-in-law caused Tanaka-san to cancel all of her volunteer and study activities for two weeks. Spending even an hour away from her mother-in-law would be unfavorable, Tanaka-san had explained.

The idea of striking a balance between the needs of aging relations and one's own interests did not come up. It would have seemed an impractical demand for a housewife to make. What alternatives, after all, did a woman in Kawashima-san's position have? Although Kawashima-san stressed her desire to be with her friends, they were extremely self-conscious about disturbing Kawashima-san's home life. The tension was present throughout our vacation.

Kawashima-san and her friends use their housewife identities as a point of solidarity. When Kawashima-san has difficulties related to a housewife's life, her friends empathize and reassure her of their support by saying that they, too, would do the same thing. This sort of support paradoxically reinforces the idea that, even when being a housewife is distasteful, Kawashima-san should see her social self as a housewife self. Were she to take on a different ethic, she would be in defiance of the commonality with other housewives that has earned her empathy in difficult times. But when she accepts empathy on a housewife's terms, she is placed in the conservative and, probably, unsatisfactory position of maintaining the status quo.

The Inevitable Housewife in Politics

The summer of 1997, during a short trip to Tokyo, I visited with the women who had taken me to Karuizawa with them. A year earlier I had at last married, and since this was the first time I had returned to Tokyo since my wedding, my conversation with Kawashima-san and the others was inevitably full of questions and explanations about my husband, my wedding ceremony, my new lifestyle. Anticipating the conversation, I had brought wedding pictures, and we poured over them laughing about the differences between American and Japanese customs. Glad for me, the women were full of compliments. Perhaps because I had been away from Japan for some time and had not yet readjusted to the language, one of the compliments — a sort of cliché, really — particularly struck me: "You are *wakai okusama rashii*" (just like a young wife), one of the women said, and others agreed with her. I looked so grown up—finally, so like a woman, so changed from my Karuizawa days appearance, they assured me.

I doubt that in the American academic social circle in which I am known I would be complimented for looking like a "young wife." Yet I was pleased, really. I knew that the contrast the women made between my married appearance and my "Karuizawa days" image was intended to show that I was a successful young woman, that I was maturing as I should. By accepting that I was "just like a young wife," I felt that I was at last being included in the group of women who hadn't needed my help with the chores when we were on vacation. I also had a real sense of the urge to be known as a housewife—the urge to claim a rightful membership in a warm community.

The housewife identity is an odd one. Unlike other potentially politically important identities such as labor union leader or banker, housewife seems to become the label for a woman's social self in the *absence* of any really appropriate title. Housewife becomes a woman's identity as a combination of gender role determination and the unknitted structure of a modern suburban community. We should not assume that housewives are, therefore, without a substantive identity experience. As the vacation at Kawashima-san's summer home demonstrates, no matter why it is chosen, the housewife identity can be an important means of developing and maintaining group solidarity. As we will see much more specifically in the chapters that follow, this solidarity is accompanied by an ethic that derives from and then justifies the housewife's identity. This ethic becomes a standard of measurement that may be applied to the housewife's interaction with the social world. Mutually reinforced in a community of other housewives, the housewife identity provides an individual with the possibility of establishing feelings of esteem and intimacy in relationships with the "outside world" that works even when individuals feel that the label does not fit them perfectly. In fact, the ill fit can be useful. When I am a "young wife" I am not a professor at a foreign university halfway around the globe. When a businessman's wife and a pianist are "just housewives," they have something in common that their different backgrounds—regional, educational, and otherwise— probably couldn't provide them.

Although we may be inclined to view the housewife identity as a private one, it is ironically in public, community-oriented spaces that women are most likely to employ the unsatisfactory but inevitable housewife label. Therefore, while, on the face of it, housewifery might seem unconnected to political life, the label "housewife" is inherently political; it is the primary vehicle to a socially recognized public position for many women. The fact that "housewife" seems to be a private-world label especially when it is worn, as it most often is, in public, community spaces does not mean that housewives are not political beings, but that their transportation to citizenship may be clumsy. Housewives are public beings whom we describe with a term that is a reference to the refuges of private life. Therefore, when someone claims to be a housewife we and she are confused about how she might also claim to have a political life. When we think about it carefully, we can see she might have a justification for political expertise in some limited area, but it takes us a long time to see that. For this reason, housewifery is a bicycle to political life.

CHAPTER THREE
Housewives and Citizenship

Near the end of my longest period of fieldwork, I visited the office of Ono Kiyoko, the Liberal Democratic member of the House of Councilors whose campaign I had followed during the late spring and summer of 1992. As I was leaving, she gave me a copy of a campaign photograph collection that she had distributed to supporters.[1] When, one afternoon, I turned nostalgically through the pages of campaign scenes, I was arrested by a picture of a public appearance that Ono had made near the subway station in the Hikari-ga-oka neighborhood of Nerima-ku.

What drew me to the photograph was the manner in which it composed a scene that I had recorded so differently in my field notes. In the Nerima event pictured in the campaign photo, a group of concerned-faced political leaders gather in a tidy residential community of the sort of new high-rises that house the young families caught in the cost-of-living and poor environment troubles to which Ono's campaign rhetoric frequently made reference. Two *uguisu-jo*,[2] seven male local politicians (one of them in a wheelchair), and one woman on the party's proportional representation list stand around Ono. Ono wears a striped knit shirt with her skirt rather than a suit jacket, and, a bit unusual, the whole group stands on the pavement rather than on top of an advertising car, high above the passersby. In the photograph, the group looks sincere, friendly—open for discussion. The photo seems to have captured a moment of real political dialogue.

In the scene I saw, noon approaches on a summer morning. A few young mothers and their children stroll by, and occasionally a man or woman descends the stairs to the subway station. Others ascend the stairs and head quickly in the direction of a nearby shopping mall. Hardly anyone pauses to listen to the pleading voices coming from a sound-truck's amplifier; few take notice of the smattering of middle-aged women who have gathered to express support for a group of stageless players. Outside the edges of the photograph, Ono's rhetoric meets silence. No one is there.

As students of political processes, we are not surprised that "typical housewives" cannot be found within the margins of the campaign photographer's view. We know that most passersby would reject this campaign event as an opportunity for experiencing citizenship, because we have plenty of data demonstrating how little the average person participates in politics. What is surprising is that, despite this data, we spend far more time analyzing the political moment as it is seen within the frame of the campaign photographer's composition than we do studying the way that moment exists in the huge landscape outside the campaign lens. This has been especially true in the case of Japan, where nearly all of the political research done by foreigners has focused on elite's actions, and the majority of native research has simply followed this pattern.[3]

To answer some of the most interesting questions about Japan's political life, we must step beyond the margins of the campaign photograph. When Ono's campaign set up in Hikari-ga-oka, a seeming possibility for engagement in the political process was placed before the young mothers, the shopping women, the scattered businessmen, and the countless others who might have peered out at the scene from the windows of their apartments. However, instead of taking an opportunity to exercise their citizenship in a democratic nation by answering the invitation to a dialogue with their elected leaders, the passersby ignore the scene and go on about their business as if the political moment enacted there were of absolutely no importance to them. One way of cataloguing the scene is the campaign photographer's: a nonexistent audience is marginalized in a political moment. A more perplexing cataloguing is the would-be citizen's: *a political moment is marginalized in the space of daily life.*

During my months in Ōizumi, I tried to see the political moment as the passersby did, from outside the edges of the photographer's frame. I concluded that most of the housewives I knew would have composed the event scene much differently from the campaign photographer's. Although some of the women might have paused to listen for a few minutes out of curiosity, very few would have attached much significance to the event. Almost none would have perceived of it as a moment of political dialogue or seen it as an opportunity for citizenship.

Ōizumi housewives thought of politics (*seiji*) as something that could be edited out of their pictures of their daily lives. For most of my informants words such as *seiji* (politics), *shimin* (citizen), and *seisaku* (policy) connoted people who moved and activities that occurred in a closed sphere, somewhere outside the housewife's web of significant people and events. Politics included legislatures and their members, bureaucratic agencies and their staffs, political parties, and various support groups. Politics was something that was reported in newspapers, talked about on television, or done in official buildings where the general public was not welcome. Occasionally it could be either interesting or boring, admirable or stupid, but from the perspective of many Ōizumi housewives, the "political" was private in the sense that only specially qualified people could participate. Housewives frequently pointed out that without connections, money, maybe even a parent who had also been a politician, one could hardly expect to be permitted to enter political circles. Moreover, few housewives personally knew or expressed an interest in knowing anyone who was successful in the political world. The "political" was marginal to the housewives' world.

Behind the housewives' act of marginalizing the political was the complicated nature of the relationship between housewives' perceptions of politics and their perceptions of identity. No matter how ambivalently they may have identified themselves as housewives, their housewife identities nevertheless led these women to align themselves with a set of values and a manner of behaving that they believed was incompatible with the political world. Because they embraced the values of their identity, housewives were encouraged to interpret their instances of social activism as divorced from political significance. As we will see later in this chapter and those that follow, housewives who participated in community activities from the PTA to volunteer groups to ward advisory boards often went out of their way to distinguish their efforts to change the community from activities undertaken by those whom they considered political activists.

If we define citizenship loosely as the possession of an understanding of one's integration into both general and political society,[4] we must conclude that Ōizumi housewives tended to restrain themselves from perceiving even their most publicly oriented experiences as citizenship. When social participation is perceived as explicitly differentiated from political participation, that social participation would not seem qualified for "citizenship" in a rigorous, democratic sense. However, Japanese housewives sometimes challenged such notions. They seemed determined to employ an alternative category of citizenship for their public activities—a rich, community-spiritedness that would have been rendered feeble in the thick of "politics." Even some of the housewives who worked daily in Ono Kiyoko's campaign headquarters denied that their efforts could be accurately described as political. Housewives' determination to separate their community activity from what they called political activity made it seem as if they thought integration into "politics" actually made a significant public life unlikely.

As I explained in the first chapter, housewives frequently characterized the difference between themselves and politicians by pointing out that politicians ride around frequently in taxis while housewives seldom do. In honor of that distinction, I call the housewives' brand of community-spiritedness "bicycle citizenship" because I see it as an attempt to lead a full public life by routes other than those the political system traditionally offers. Bicycle citizenship can also be an appropriate image in the Japanese context if we picture a housewife citizen as paradoxically both encumbered and ingeniously mobile in the way that women cycling home from shopping in Tokyo often are. Pedaling a bike with baskets loaded front and back (sometimes with small children) up hilly streets is hard going, but the alternative possibility of maneuvering a car through traffic jams and full parking lots is often worse, and cycling is almost always easier than traveling on foot.

A housewife finds herself encumbered as a citizen because she believes that it is probably impossible to both enjoy a meaningful political life and maintain the home and family priorities that make one a housewife. In their narratives about their separation from the political world, housewives I met often pointed to what they saw as the physical barriers to their participation. Places where politics "was done" were too far away from home or did not offer day care. Politics took too much time for the person who must make it home each day early enough to prepare the family's supper. The demands of the political world are contrary to those of the housewife's world; in order to meet those demands, one must leave one's housewife responsibilities behind. In order to be a citizen, one must dispose of one's home. To the extent that the housewife embraces "home and family" or an ethic that demonstrates a relationship to such personalized concerns, she is unfit for politics. She may be extremely concerned for her community, and her public activity on behalf of that community may be extensive. If she is unwilling to relinquish the connections between that concern and housewifery in either ethics or behavior, however, the housewife will find herself unable to move effectively along the "highways" of a political system where that personalism is a handicap.

As a "bicycle citizen," the housewife acts as if she were a citizen, but she believes that extending the reach of her actions to what she conceives of as political spheres would be defeating. The constraints of politics would strip her actions of their real meaning for the community. The housewife might be said to see herself as a citizen, but with a citizenship that is not viable in the contemporary *political* world. Through the eyes of political theory, we might see this housewife as a citizen without a polis. We might conclude that the problem of citizenship for a Japanese housewife results from unique characteristics of the Japanese political system — that the Japanese political system is simply not open enough to the representation of a variety of interests, that Japan has failed to have a fully liberal democratic political system. But it is not the fact that her interests are not expressed in politics that turns a Japanese housewife away from the political system. Rather, she is disturbed to think that politics is nothing but "interest representation." Japan is too clearly liberal to manage the housewife citizen.

Behind the paradoxes of a housewife's bicycle citizenship lurks a more basic issue. The essence of the housewife identity is grounded in its bearer's exclusion from other possible social identities. A clear manifestation of this exclusion is the fact that, as we saw in Sasaki-san's description of her work life in the previous chapter, the housewife is not "of" the work world even when she has paid employment outside the home. Implied in this "not-of-ness" is a fundamental difference in the priorities that justify and structure a housewife's daily life and the daily lives of members of other identity groups.

Because it is structured according to priorities such as economic interest representation that seem to violate the structure of the housewife's identity, politics does not make sense according to a housewife's ethic. Thus, even more important than the fact that she is outside the margins of political event such as Ono's campaign speeches is the fact that a housewife often thrusts politics outside the margins of *her* life. If we reexamine the Ono campaign photograph in a landscape drawn from the housewife's perspective, a curious thing happens. The photograph not only gets smaller, but becomes a picture of a sort of place where most housewives do not deign to seek inclusion because they are critical

of the terms on which inclusion could occur. From the campaign photographer's seat, we might say that the political event has failed because
it has not brought the housewife in. From the housewife's seat we would
say that the political event has failed because it is irrelevant to housewives. In order to understand this curious reversal, we must know more
about the housewives who write the campaign and its photographer out
of all but the margins of their lives. But even studies that concentrate
on Japanese political culture or political participation have tended to
begin from an elite-driven perspective. The culture is assumed to be
represented by the writing and thinking of a few intellectuals, or participation is conceived and measured in terms of response to largely elite-
determined situations, such as balloting, party membership, and participation in political movements.[5] Mass opinion data, such as that collected in voting behavior and participation studies, show us how few
people seem to act as engaged citizens in Japan.

But these survey-based mass studies do not do much to illuminate
how the potential citizen-actor perceives politics in relation to his or her
daily life, because survey data do not let a citizen speak in his or her own
voice. Therefore, unless we rely on only the most circumstantial of evidence, we cannot explain why an apparent opportunity for citizenship
such as participation in Ono's campaign event is often plainly ignored.
Nor can we explain why, in some cases, the commonly ignored citizenship opportunity might be seized. We are especially bereft of explanatory
power for the political actions of Japanese women.

Statistical data demonstrate that Japanese women do not participate
in politics in the same way Japanese men do. Women are less likely than
men to report supporting a particular political party, participating in a
campaign, joining a political support group, or meeting an elected official or powerful political activist. And, even when they are highly educated, women are far less likely than men to declare themselves highly
interested in politics.[6] Nationally, women have voted consistently in
higher percentages than men since 1969. Nevertheless, in surveys the
much greater likelihood of women to explain their voting habits as a
duty rather than an expression of opinion on a political issue has led
political scientists to discount the turnout difference and continue to
perceive women as less fully integrated into the political system than
men.[7]

These studies seem to confirm many of the trends seen in studies of
women and politics worldwide. But they are not very helpful in explaining recent surges of political activity among women, mostly housewives.

For example, current theories do not fully explain women's participation in non-party grassroots organizations that have elected their members to regional and local assemblies in Japan in quite noticeable numbers since the mid 1980s.[8] According to most mass political participation data, the gradual increase in women's participation in the work force, coupled with the increase in their level of education, has led to a gradual growth in political participation. But the successful new grassroots movements are not the work of well-educated professional women. In fact, the movements have become widely known for their dependence on volunteer *shufu pawā* (housewives' power).[9]

Studies of the political sociology of non-elite Japanese women have emphasized their exclusion from politics through a combination of historical and ideological factors. Women do not participate in politics as men do because women were legally prevented from participating for so long, and because a privatizing ideology that discourages the involvement of women outside the home still lingers.[10] Privatization is a major theme of women and politics studies in the Western nations as well, and, as one might expect, housewives are considered to be the most privatized and the most handicapped in relation to politics.[11] Feminists' theoretical discussions of women's citizenship in liberal democracy array the public-private dichotomy in a variety of ways, but, generally, universal citizenship is assumed to be constructed on the model of an individual male who possesses free agency in the economic system.[12]

Privatization measures usually correlate well with standard survey items indicating low political activity. Others have argued, however, that privatization is not a very penetrating way of explaining the sociopolitical position of Japanese women. The idea of the home as a woman's appropriate sphere of action was not a traditional Japanese ideology. Prior to the Meiji Era, which began in 1868, most women were expected to be economic producers alongside men. The "women in the home" ideology was in part constructed through the efforts of the Japanese state, which intended to appropriate the woman-centered home for goals that were often very public.[13]

The construction of the Japanese housewife gender was concurrent with the state's public-spiritedness and frugality campaigns of the 1920s and 1930s, and although a few women resisted such a gender construction, many activists saw the housewife construction as a means for defending an expanded public role. Larger roles for women in local government were justified on the basis of the connection between the business of local government—garbage disposal, poor relief and health policy, for example—and the experience that women gained through the management of their homes.[14] Even when Kathleen Uno argues that women's political movements in postwar Japan are bound within the possibilities of a *ryōsai kenbo* (good wife, wise mother) ideology, she traces that ideology to the activity of the Japanese state in the prewar years of the late nineteenth and early twentieth century.[15] The "wife and mother" components of housewifery are thus markers of the definition of a *public* role for women, not their exclusion from the public sphere. True, if a woman finds it difficult to operate outside a *ryōsai kenbo* image, then her public life is severely constrained. *Constraint,* however, cannot be equated with *privatization.* Men, too, are constrained in a variety of ways when they seek to enter public life.

We may be blinded to the public quality of the Japanese housewife's identity because we insist on viewing her public experiences through theoretical lenses that cloud our vision. Relying on such measures as party affect or voting behavior as indicators of the quality of a woman's political experience means that a woman is measured by her response to what historically has been an overwhelmingly male-driven agenda. When we ask a housewife to respond to a multiple-choice survey of political activity that uses the politically active male as its model, we may be forcing her to restate herself in terms that are alien to her experiences.

Conceptualizing differences between male and female experiences along the lines of a public-private dichotomy only confuses matters. In her revisionist portrayal of today's Japanese women, Sumiko Iwao complains that the capacity for freedom and fulfillment enjoyed by Japanese women has been grossly underestimated, especially by Western scholars, whose theoretical prejudices often blind them to reality. "Dichotomous values or categories—private/public, good/bad, happy/unhappy, winner/loser, male/female—are not seen by Japanese as the only options: Between the two ends of a scale there is usually a broadly perceived zone of yet further option."[16]

The World That Is Not There: Politics in Daily Conversation

Getting housewives in Ōizumi to talk about politics was difficult, sometimes nearly impossible. At first I was wont to attribute this difficulty to the women's privatization, but housewives' reluctance to discuss politics turned out to be driven by their perceptions of their obligation to a particular ethic of appropriate and considerate behavior in public life. My sponsor's wife organized several lunches for me so that I would have the chance to meet her friends and ask them their "political opinions." But she was chagrined that, despite both my efforts and her own, maintaining a political theme in the conversation proved nearly impossible. Asking direct political opinion questions led more often than not to unwieldy silences. If an assertive woman did venture an opinion, others in the group would be quick to label her the table expert and, thus, hastily exempt themselves from speaking on the subject. The assertive woman would dominate the conversation for a bit until, most likely, it broke off into more popular channels—the menu, my Japanese skills, the hostess's lovely dishes, and so on.

Sometimes just announcing that my field was political science was enough to send a conversation whirling off on a chorus of "Oh, that must be so difficult" if not to stop talk entirely. I begged interviews by promising that most of the questions would be about a housewife's daily lifestyle and that the "political" questions would not require detailed knowledge of the political system. I always felt that I had to say, "I want to talk even to women who know nothing about politics." And, soon after I began to do interviews, I realized that I confronted a mystifying tendency of my informants to underreport their political activities.

Once, I spent three hours with twelve PTA leaders from an Ōizumi middle school. Nearly the entire time was devoted to a discussion of their PTA activities, their opinions about the school system and their daily life. In the last fifteen minutes of the session I risked a few specifically political questions. "Do you ever talk about politics with your friends?" "Have you ever attended political speeches or campaign events?" "Has anyone here ever participated in a political campaign? Hung posters? Made phone calls?" Everyone shook their heads, and I concluded that the group was amazingly apolitical. As the meeting ended, however, one of the women approached me. She had participated in a campaign, she said. In fact, she was a member of a local woman politician's support organization. Two women who overheard her also said that they knew of the politician, one had attended some functions for her support.

The woman who had been a campaign worker was sufficiently interested in my research topic to call her politician friend, and a woman from the politician's support organization office then called me and invited me by to meet the politician and some of her supporters. I remained mystified by the PTA leaders' silence when I had asked the group about political activities, however, and I recounted the anecdote to several of the women I met with regularly. When I asked other women why the politically active PTA members had been loathe to identify themselves, I expected to be told that what I had seen was the remains of the traditional privatizing ideology of Japanese women. In other words, the woman refrained from owning up to her political activities because it would be unseemly to appear interested in something as unfeminine and far from the home as politics.

But the explanation I received again and again was crucially different from the privatization hypothesis I had expected. In all likelihood, I was told, the woman had avoided disclosing her political activities while the meeting was still in session because to have done so would be to risk interjecting political tension unnecessarily into a PTA meeting. This interpretation was not meant to imply that the PTA and its concerns were not public in nature.

Two varieties of explanation were given for why discussing political interests during PTA activities could be disruptive. The PTA was not viewed as a private arena in either answer. One suggested interpretation held that the PTA's business of building a strong, open relationship between parents and schools was very important for assuring a good education to the community children, but it was also rife with the possibility for conflict. To take time in a meeting to assert one's *personal* political views about things only indirectly connected to education issues might often mean traveling beyond the level of consideration necessary for solving most controversies. It could mean risking unnecessary conflict among members and make it difficult for the PTA to operate effectively.

Another, not entirely unrelated, interpretation held that when a woman's comments or actions were perceived as unnecessarily controversial, her child could suffer from his mother's reputation for making trouble. He might also find himself in conflict with children whose mothers held opposing views. The implications of either the PTA business-centered or the child-centered interpretations of restraint from political expression are not that politics is an inherently inappropriate activity for a woman or a mother. Rather, expressing political opinions is not *useful* for PTA business. Political opinions are a *private* luxury that one should not indulge in while charged with serious community duties. The housewife identity was ultimately more public than its bearers' political party identification in the sense that the housewife identity was a form of *permission to participate* in communal discourse, whereas openly expressing political party identification was perceived as a possible *fetter* to common discussion.

But even when they were not pressed into public service, most of the women I knew did not talk about politics very often. At social gatherings or classes and clubs related to hobbies, I seldom heard any reference to politics unless I prompted it myself by making a comment or asking a question. In interviews I pressed women to tell me if they ever talked about politics with their friends, and most women said that politics was seldom a topic of conversation. The rare exceptions were shocking scandal disclosures or extremely unpopular policy changes. The unpopular policy example I was given was usually the establishment of a 3 percent consumption tax in 1989. Significantly, the upper house election following the passage of the tax bill received international attention for the unprecedented number of women who ran for and were elected to Diet seats.

What I thought of as unavoidably political phenomena were often remarked on without the slightest reference to political views. One afternoon I was at a neighborhood grocery store when a candidate for a Diet seat went by in his sound truck. He stood on the back of the truck waving at the shoppers in the produce section near the front of the store. As the truck passed on, I heard the women remarking on the candidate to each other and the store clerks. But no one said anything about his politics — which were actually rather controversial due to his support of Japanese participation in United Nations peace-keeping operations. "Look how tan he is; he must be working hard," I heard, and, "Look how serious he looks," and "He looks so young."

More than once I tried to ask members of the local branch of the Seikatsu Club Co-op about a split that had occurred among members when the co-op's political wing, the Netto, decided to enact a three-term limit system for ward assembly representatives elected on its recommendation. Prior to establishing the term limit system, the Netto had sponsored an Ōizumi woman, Katano Reiko, for three successful runs for an assembly seat. She was unwilling to give up her seat at the end of her third term and decided to run without the Netto endorsement. The Netto, meanwhile, endorsed two of its own candidates. Katano won her bid for a fourth term with the assistance of many supporters who were also co-op members. Only one of the two Netto women landed a seat. The election was reputed to have caused quite a rift among co-op women. But, except for the minority of co-op members who were active in either the Netto or Katano's support organization, women avoided committing to an opinion on the issue when I asked them about it.

At a volunteer group meeting I told one woman who was also a Seikatsu Club Co-op member that I had heard about the split but did not really understand it. She put it to me this way: "I am sure that they [the term-limit group] want to avoid corruption by keeping people from staying on in their seats forever, and I am sure that many of those who have worked hard to support Katano-san think she has worked very hard, and they don't want to let her down." The woman's explanation altogether avoided taking sides, although I knew that she was a fairly active co-op member. She had, in all probability, chosen either the previously co-op–endorsed four-termer or one of the two newly endorsed candidates when she went to the polls. She changed the subject, however, and it became impossible to ask her how she had made her own decision, without my sounding rude. Most women were slightly less opaque. Even though I could determine where they stood, they almost always phrased their comments to avoid the impression of a commitment.

I made a point of asking my informants if it was somehow rude or embarrassing to talk about politics with one's friends. Most resisted drawing such a characterization. "It just doesn't come up," I was told. "If we talk about politics, it's just emotional—who we like or don't like, not policies." "We always talk about our kids and our husbands." "Housewives' talk is just gossip, the trivia of daily life," many said. But the same women often expressed contempt for trivial talk and said they enjoyed opportunities for more "serious" discussions. Members of a child-care support group said that the group's most important function was to provide women with young children an opportunity for something more than the small talk they had with mothers they met in the parks where their children played. Serious talk was valued among housewives; but *political* serious talk was not.

Women often told me that some Japanese women probably avoided talking about politics because they wanted to avoid seeming too aggressive, always ranting about political ideology. However, the women who offered these explanations always curiously placed themselves as outsiders to the traditional image of unaggressive women. They historicized the traditional image by describing it as a holdover from "long ago" and insisting that "times have changed." Furthermore, these women usually refused to characterize their own relationship to politics in terms of the traditional feminine image. A traditional woman was always someone other than the speaker.

Nevertheless, something about politics was socially unacceptable. Political discussions moved much differently when I tried them in groups from when I attempted them in individual interviews. When I talked to a woman by herself, she was more likely to talk at length about politics than if I met her and one of her friends together. Yet two good friends were far more likely to give my political questions serious answers than were women in a bigger group. The same women were different in different situations.

One good example is a woman whose interview I solicited in a painting class. When I asked members of the class to volunteer for interviews, her classmates pointed her out as a woman with an interest in politics. But at first she declined the interview vociferously, saying she was a terrible talker and, anyway, knew nothing about politics. I had lunch with the entire class, and I noticed that, although she talked a good deal, she never mentioned politics. A friend of hers finally prevailed on her to meet me at a coffee shop for an interview a few weeks later. I dreaded the meeting, but when I met her I was surprised to find that the class was right. She had a lively interest in politics and talked freely and with enthusiasm.

What accounted for the tendency of women to avoid political conversation in not only the PTA but most other social situations as well? The answer that gender-and-politics scholars might offer us is that, as housewives, the women were enmeshed in a privatizing ideology that made politics appear as an inappropriate subject. True, politics is an inappropriate subject, but it is not made so by the housewives' unwillingness to step outside their private lives. Rather the inappropriateness of discussion of politics was a feature of their public housewife identities. Housewives were *publicly* apolitical much in the way a justice on the United States Supreme Court would resist associating her opinion with a particular partisan ideology in order to avoid making her seem more a panderer to supporters than a thoughtful, just critic of the law. It may be that, just as politics was perceived as *obstructive* or not *useful* in the case of PTA meetings, it is perceived as unhelpful in many other situations, too. Ironically, from the perspective of the Ōizumi housewives, it is sometimes politics, not the lives of housewives, that looks privatized. Politics exists apart from even the housewives' most public actions — a fortress that cannot be broached from ordinary society.

Distance: A Measure of Politics' Meaning

In the terms of Ōizumi housewives, politics and citizenship were not matters of the public or private. Instead, politics was described in terms of relative *distance*. When I first began talking to women, I was at a loss for good Japanese expressions to describe feelings about the political world. I explained my project to a friend, a woman college student. She doubted I would get any interesting findings. "At least for us college students, politics is so *far away*" (*seiji wa tōi*), she said, using *tōi*, the Japanese word for "far." Women who claimed that they were uninterested in or not knowledgeable about politics were often reluctant to answer my political questions. But I found that I could usually elicit some comment by using a version of my student friend's description as a question. Asking whether politics seemed "far" tapped into a woman's sense of politics in a way that questions about participation, parties, or policies could not.

The success of phrasing my questions in terms of distance sensitized me to the way terms of distance came up again and again in a housewife's political vocabulary. In fact, words for "close" or "close to me" were used frequently to explain political feelings, more frequently than the word for "far." "Close" was used even when I, myself, did not bring distance into the discussion. Because it was usually a negated form of "close" that was employed, it was evident that politics seemed generally distant. However, the use of "not close," and especially "not close to me," in place of "far" is interesting because it emphasizes the speaker's own position as the standard of judgment for distance. The two characters used for the word "close" (*mijika*) are especially revealing. One means "body," and the other means "near." The "body" character from "close" is also used in idiomatic expressions such as *mi ni tsukeru*, which means "to learn a new skill" but could be literally read as "attach it to one's (my) body." When a housewife says politics is *mijika ni nai* (not close), politics is far from the housewife, who is central. Politics, not the housewife, is peripheral.

A good example of the relationship between a housewife's image of politics and a judgment of political distance came out quite clearly in my discussion with Kameda-san, a thirty-three-year-old full-time housewife with a three-year-old daughter. From one perspective, Kameda-san probably exhibited all of the attributes of a typical privatized woman.

When I asked her if she had participated in politics, she said that she had not and instead talked about her husband's participation in the Democratic Socialist Party through his membership in a company union. Asked to describe her image of politics, she said only (and rather curtly), "I don't have one." I asked her to describe a political activity. "I can't think of one," she said.

Kameda-san probably felt unable to comment when asked directly about politics because she perceived the distance between herself and the political world as very great. The perceived distance was the result of her assumption that people like herself could take no meaningful role in politics. In Kameda-san's view her own opinions on politics were worthless because they had almost no chance of having any meaning in a political world that she saw as stagnant, corrupt, and dominated by men. Kameda-san's sense of being at a great distance from politics was exacerbated by her perception of the weakness of individuals, particularly women, and this was further worsened by her distrust of organizations.

Kameda-san opened up a bit when I asked her if she felt that politics was far from her. "Yes, yes. It's not that I don't have any interest, but I don't have much. Well, if I did have an interest and try to participate, I think politics would probably come closer, but as long as I don't do that, well, then, there's nothing but elections," she explained, and she added that, since the candidates for election were always equally unattractive, it made little difference whether one voted. Kameda-san's sense of distance was not merely a matter of her lack of participation, however. She thought her own and others' rate of participation was low because few avenues of meaningful participation existed "nearby," and because politics seldom touched on issues that were "close to home." Kameda-san said that environmental issues, a garbage disposal crisis, for example, might be sufficiently close to home to encourage participation, but she could not think of a single such issue around her currently.

In her assessment of participation opportunities, Kameda-san referred to a physical lack of proximity as well as a psychological distance. Like most of my informants who were not politically active, she gave the impression that she might participate more in politics if more of it were located in proximity to her residence. Women often suggested that, being in Tokyo, they had little chance of seeing politicians in person, and places for them to do socially oriented activities were far away in a physical sense. They contrasted their own experiences with those of people "in the country" who were said to be much more active in politics.[17]

"If someone would ask me, I would participate, but in Tokyo, no one comes to ask you," said one woman.

Nevertheless, the housewives' sense of distance seemed to correspond much better with their understanding of political power relations than with physical realities. Ironically, most housewives drew their picture of politics from national news media. When they spoke of politics, it was usually clear that they were referring to national-level elite politics. They admitted to knowing very little about the political leaders and policy issues in their own ward. Therefore, when housewives said that, in Tokyo, chances to get close to politics were scarce, the politics and even the physical space to which they referred were conceived of in broad terms. They seldom acknowledged the political space at lower levels of government that existed physically much closer to them.

Many women had an opportunity to participate in *chōnaikai*, residential, self-governing organizations similar to block associations. The women found *chōnaikai* activities difficult to classify. No one described the activities to me as explicitly political activities. Yet when a housewife mentioned *chōnaikai* activity, she tended to do so in a discussion of political participation, perhaps because of the *chōnaikai*'s public or administrative associations. Usually *chōnaikai* devoted themselves to tasks like earthquake preparations and neighborhood festival days, but, especially in Ōizumi neighborhoods that had sprung up during sudden development spurts, the *chōnaikai* could have weightier duties. Several women had served on *chōnaikai* that negotiated with the ward administration for infrastructure improvement projects.

One woman brought up her *chōnaikai* participation when I asked her if there was anything political that she felt was close to home.

It's not that there's nothing close to home. Well, there are things that come up in, say, the *chōnaikai*. Sometimes those are politics, aren't they. Well, I do make phone calls and think and talk about how those [*chōnaikai*] things should be, but in the big meaning of politics I really don't.

I asked her what she had done in the *chōnaikai*, and, once again, she hesitated to classify *chōnaikai* issues as politics because they did not seem "big" enough to her.

Well, I don't know if you can say that it is politics, but we decide if it would be good to widen the road or make a place for children to play—or look for the location for a little festival. There really hasn't been anything that has started in these things and led to politics.

About politics in general, she said, "There's the sense that things have already been decided. I really don't understand politics in the big sense." This woman had been invited to politicians' support group meetings, but she said she did not go because the meetings were a waste of time. She did not know how to judge what politicians said (implying a sense of distrust), and, besides, no matter what an individual did, political outcomes would never change. In this woman's view, issues close to home were not politics because politics was large, murky, and controlled by others.

Like that of the *chōnaikai* participant, Kameda-san's sense of political distance was tied to her cynical view of political power. For example, she said that she might feel closer to a woman politician who had been a housewife than to a male politician, but that no such women existed nearby. Yet, just a few doors down from her apartment on the same street, the Seikatsu Club Co-op's housewife-centered grassroots political movement maintained an office for their ward assemblywoman—a self-declared full-time housewife. Moreover, assemblywoman Katano Reiko's office was less than a ten-minute walk from Kameda-san's house, near the train station.

Kameda-san seemed to be speaking in defiance of reality. But according to her understanding of "real" politics, no "real" housewife could succeed as a politician. Like nearly every non-active woman with whom I talked, Kameda-san assumed that "housewife politicians" were not really housewives but rather symbolic fronts for larger organizations that were trying to get the woman's vote. She knew this to be true because she knew that politics was a "man's society" in which only extremely exceptional women could hope for any success. As other women explained to me, a "real" housewife was probably too burdened by home and family to have time for politics, and few housewives actually possessed the educational background and skills to make them able politicians. Furthermore, even men needed "backup" in the form of behind-the-scenes organization and money to have any power. Therefore, even if she had known that apparently "close" women politicians had offices "close by," Kameda-san was still likely to draw the conclusion that political opportunity was *not close by*. Kameda-san's reading of housewife politicians was not unique. Most of the women I knew said that they suspected the "reality" behind female politicians who campaigned as housewives.

Curiously, Kameda-san both identified with and fundamentally distrusted the concept of a housewife politician. A provocative assumption is hidden in Kameda-san's understanding of how "real" politics makes a "real" housewife politician an impossibility. The distance between housewife and politics can never be reduced; making what is close by political is to make it distant and thus, not close. This formulation claims more than that citizens are merely withdrawn from politics, a truism that could apply to men as well as women to some degree in presumably all postindustrial democracies. In the Kameda-san equation, the political distance is directly related to her perception of her gender role. She could trust and be close to what is like her; therefore, she could trust and feel close to a politician who is a housewife. But in politics no housewives can be successful politicians. Hence, Kameda-san is far from politics.

In Kameda-san's case, as in the case of many housewives, the political distance formula leads to a turning away from politics. Kameda-san would probably pass a politician's campaign event with an assumption of its irrelevance; she appears to be the 100 percent privatized housewife described in many gender-and-politics studies. But Kameda-san, whose child is still only three years old, has yet to move into public housewives' spheres. With her child home, her time for clubs, classes, and volunteer groups is severely limited. Her child has not attended school; and she has never been to a PTA meeting. Not every housewife who enters those more public spheres enjoys them or remains there. But older housewives were more likely to have many more of these public experiences, and they were quite likely to claim that such experiences had made them in some sense more socially and publicly oriented. Kameda-san's thinking could change with time.

Socially oriented housewives will manage the political distance equation less succinctly than Kameda-san did. They speak with a greater sense of obligation to their community, and they are more likely to see problems close to home all around them. They may have participated in attempts to solve those problems, and this participation tends to lead them to a paradoxical position. They are convinced of the importance of a housewife's point of view and a housewife's expertise, and they identify with it even more than did Kameda-san. But they are, if possible, more cynical about a housewife's ability to translate her skills to the political world.

My neighbor, Ueno-san, was one such socially oriented housewife. In part, her social activism was a function of her outgoing personality. She recalled having been an officer in student associations in grade school, and she had served on women's employee associations during her working years after design school and before her marriage. She had

been active in the PTA for over ten years. But part of Ueno-san's awareness of social concerns had descended from the accumulation of experiences she considered a matter of course in her role as housewife. This
was particularly true of the development of her political interest, which
could be most clearly attributed to her experiences in the PTA.

That Ueno-san is a joiner is a matter of personality. But the fact that
she joined the PTA has everything to do with her being a housewife.
Joining the PTA had not been Ueno-san's ambition, but when her children entered school and the call for PTA volunteers went out, Ueno-
san felt unable to refuse because she was a full-time housewife and lived
close to the school. PTA activities nearly always occur during work
hours on a weekday. If full-time housewives do not volunteer, it is hard
to get people to participate, Ueno-san explained. During the second year
of her PTA duty, Ueno-san was asked to edit a newsletter. She enjoyed
the opportunity to use her design skills so much that she stayed on year
after year, finally rising to the president's seat at her daughter's junior
high school PTA.[18]

As PTA president, Ueno-san bumped up against the conflict between
the political world's principles of operation and those of a housewife.
PTA presidents were expected to interact with their counterparts from
other schools and with education officials of the ward government,
which managed public junior high schools. Since PTA presidents had
traditionally been male, the setting for the interaction resembled traditional male socializing. At ward expense, PTA leaders were invited to a
rural inn where they cemented their relationships in a night of drinking
together. As a housewife and mother, however, Ueno-san felt that she
could not leave her home overnight simply to go drinking. Furthermore,
the drinking evening did not sound the least bit attractive to her. It
sounded like a waste of the ward taxpayers' money.

Ueno-san refused to go on the PTA retreat and protested to the ward
chief. She perceived herself as fighting a close-to-home example of Japan's general political rottenness. When she saw an advertisement in the
ward's newsletter soliciting applications for the ward government's
women's policy advisory board, Ueno-san's growing political consciousness meshed with her frustrations with other aspects of her housewife's
role. She saw an opportunity to suggest ways in which ward resources
could better address housewives' problems, such as the obligation to
nurse aging in-laws. She sent in an essay describing why she wanted to
serve and was selected.

Ueno-san was amazed by how few women held advisory board

positions. The female membership on the women's policy advisory board was nearly 100 percent. But women held an average of only 23 percent of the seats on all the ward's various boards, including the women's policy board. Ueno-san pointed out that it was strange that only one woman served on the disaster relief board, for example. As housewives, many women were at home in the ward far more than men, and they were more likely to know what was required for a family to maintain true disaster preparedness. Like Kameda-san and most other women, Ueno-san was convinced that politics was a male world. She was, through her PTA and advisory board experiences, also deeply convinced of the importance of a housewife's perspective in politics.

Yet Ueno-san's understanding of politics and of housewives led her to believe that it was impossible for a housewife to participate effectively in most political arenas. She claimed that she had discovered in her own life that women have choices, that they do not have to be bound by traditional views of femininity or the duties of a housewife. Regardless, Ueno-san's skepticism about how much power a "real" housewife could hold in politics demonstrated her perception of the limits of those choices.

Thatcher-san is amazing isn't she? And Carla Hills, does she have kids? Well, I think that to run a home and do politics in Japan is a terribly difficult thing. Japanese men are so spoiled that they do nothing. And, of course, Japanese women hate to stand out, and their privacy would be lost and they can't put up with that. And they would be criticized—men criticize each other, but women, even if the criticism is correct, they can't bear it.

Doi has no family, right? Women think that if everyone says bad things about them it will be hard on their children. Therefore, maybe it's better for women to do neutral things—advisory committees and such—if you are outspoken there—the public opinion that comes out of the committee is that of the whole committee with the chair acting as spokesperson. . . . If you become a politician, everybody looks at you, and you are criticized. Your face is visible. Maybe a place where a woman's face doesn't show up is better.

Ueno-san mixed several ideas together, but they could be separated into two general lines of thought. The first is that political participation is difficult for women with home and children responsibilities. The second is that women are somehow psychologically incapable of the rigors of political leadership.

We might accept Ueno-san's home and family concerns as her rather realistic assessment of the difficulties presented for women by the division of labor in most Japanese households. We would do well to look more deeply at her psychological concerns. At first it seems that Ueno-san subscribes to the belief that it is improper or difficult for women to hold strong political opinions, but, in fact, that is not the case. She holds and discusses her own opinions with fervor. When the PTA problem came up, she took her opinions to a decidedly public forum, and she expressed her desire that more PTA women do the same. Furthermore, Ueno-san held opinions not only on issues directly related to her activities as a housewife, but on much broader issues such as the cabinet makeup, the Japanese constitution, and Japan's role internationally.

At the bottom of Ueno-san's concern about a woman's political opinion seems to be politics, not the woman's psyche after all. Ueno-san believes that politics is so structured that honest, well-considered opinions are squelched. She once attended a politician's support group event during a campaign, but described the experience as worthless because she could not trust anything that she had heard.

[Politicians] can't really say what they are thinking. A scholar, for example, really writes what he wants to say. But what a politician is thinking never comes out. And, for example, with the Liberal Democratic Party, suppose there's a member who's a little different from the others — even though he's different, he just goes along and says the same thing as all the other members. I don't think that's acceptable. You should do your own thinking more properly.

Like women, most men cannot make good use of their own opinions in politics. But Ueno-san's comments about women's fear of criticism might lead us to believe that at least some men are unafraid to stick out and be leaders. However, Ueno-san was critical of the sort of men who became leaders. In fact, she thought leadership was an overrated quality in a politician and pointed to Tanaka Kakuei, a Japanese prime minister famous for his leadership capacity and the corruptness of his politics. He was "half dictator," Ueno-san explained.

The qualities that Ueno-san thought were needed in politics were a willingness to listen and a willingness to study. She gave no indication that women could not do those things if they were not as burdened with home responsibilities. Aside from the demands of the home, however, women were hampered by a lack of political experience, the intractability of the political system, and poor public opinion regarding women's political effectiveness. Ueno-san was led to believe, along with Kameda-san, that "real" housewife politicians did not exist. And she criticized the women candidates of the late 1980s who had been known widely as members of the Madonna Boom for their emphasis on "clean" housewifely and daily life viewpoints.

Do you know about the "Madonna" elections? A lot of women said they knew the kitchen and they knew about regular people and they could become legislators and reform politics. But it's not something that can be so simply reformed, is it?

If those sorts of people learn to have their own opinions, do research, participate in advisory committees or something to learn about their surroundings, and go from there, that would be good. But they didn't do that; they just jumped straight into being legislators. So I don't think they'll really be able to continue this way.

It would be good if women would do some things with results that you could see through the PTA or work at the ward level. Then everyone would realize that women do have something to offer.

A picture of the distant political world can be drawn from the words of Ueno-san, Kameda-san, and other housewives much in the way that Ono's campaign photographer created a picture of the political world. Politics is, first and foremost, elite, national-level politics, what is reported on newspaper pages and television news. Politics is male-dominated and requires special qualities of its participants that are not available to women—time, experience, money, and reputation—for them to achieve success.

For many housewives, the epitome of this combination of special qualities was the second-generation politician. In Japan there is a significant and growing trend of Diet members winning election to seats previously held by their fathers or other close relatives. This is, at least in part, a result of the importance of personal organization in the form of extensive political support organizations and contacts with other politicians.[19] One woman described the second-generation Diet member quite bitterly, pointing out that he lived in a world apart from people like herself. Her conversation highlights the difference between taxi citizenship and bicycle citizenship.

There are many second-generation politicians these days, aren't there? There are a fairly large number whose parents have been politicians, and if you look at the generations of these families, a lot of them are rich people, right? And those people who come from rich families don't know about real life, and they are becoming politicians. I think they probably can't understand the daily lives of just regular people like us, human beings. Not in the real sense. Wherever they go they ride in taxis.[20] "We'll get the taxi fare from the government," they say. "We'll get our meal paid for." "We're having a meeting at a 50,000-yen restaurant in Akasaka," you know. "We went out and drank 50,000 yen's worth." If you are satisfied living that kind of life, I think that you get to where you cannot see the level of the regular person's life. So, I think a good politician would be somebody who does not want to become one of those elites, but someone who really understood the life of regular people. The people who are politicians are the sort that don't even know what one *daikon* [Japanese radish] really costs. They don't know the real pressures of life.

There is an element of class distinction in the words just quoted, but the idea is not that being in the upper class allows one to be in the ruling class. Actually, what these women show when they talk about second-generation politicians is that being an elected elite allows the opportunity to be and place one's progeny in a more privileged position. Although a continuation of the second-generation trend could lead the development of clear class distinctions in the future, most of what these women had to say about politics was not class-based—unless, that is, one wants to consider housewifery a class.

In the housewives' understanding of politics, it does not really matter how down-to-earth the person who becomes a politician is. Politics operates on the basis of organizations in which an individual's opinions and differences are rendered unimportant. The organizations are largely inert; they respond little to stimuli from the outside, and inside operations are not transparent to outside observers. As the male disaster-preparedness board demonstrated, politics is not driven to practical problem solving. In politics things are done pretty much as they always have been, just as they were in the ward-PTA president relationship. The rules of politics are not easily bent.

Many women suggested that women politicians were far less likely to be corrupt than male politicians because they were not members of the male political culture. Women are "cleaner" about money, I was told, and "of course, women have eyes for the daily life side of things." Nevertheless, the necessity of organization outweighed a woman politician's more attractive qualities. "The election system is set up so that it costs money. Even if some people say that they won't use a lot of money [in campaigns], the others [who do spend] are too strong [to defeat]," explained one housewife.

Another housewife suggested that women would not be able to get their special perspectives heard in political organizations. "Those on top are too strong; women wouldn't be able to do anything." And one woman who said that she thought it was important for women to be more involved in politics said that she did not make particular efforts to vote for women because "if you look behind the woman, you see a big organization." According to this formula, when an outsider, especially a housewife, appears to succeed in politics, one should be suspicious. In politics, things are not always what they appear to be.

Particularly in Ueno-san's case, there is a curious lack of place for her own brand of social activism in her perceived politics. The same place-lessness was repeated in the discussions of other housewives who had been active. Several women who had interests in or had participated in political campaigns discounted their participation as being non-political. "I participated because the candidate was an acquaintance of mine; that's not democratic, is it?" said one woman. But many had similar ways of interpreting their actions. Being drawn into politics by an acquaintance is not inherently undemocratic. The woman was collapsing "democratic thinking" and ideology, which she understood as impersonal. Other women discounted political participation because their participation was not motivated by personal political ambition but by a desire to support a worthy friend's enterprise or protect a social project that they valued, such as an anti-pollution movement. They distinguished their partici-pation from what political scientists call "political participation" because they equated the democratic political world and participation in it with radically independent, interest-seeking individuals.

Earlier I suggested that women were more likely to refer to the distant political as "not close to me" than as "far from me," and that the differ-ence in terms placed priority on the position of the women as the ac-cepted standard of judgment. This is most true with housewives who are socially active in a broad sense. They value their activism and resent the inability of what they perceive as the political world to value the activism equally. Moreover, the women place tremendous importance on the *motivations* of their actions. They deem that these motivations are seldom present in the political world because people like themselves are seldom present there. They separate politics and socially concerned public behavior in their thinking. Put another way, the same action could be political if it occurred in a taxi, and public when undertaken on a bicycle.

This separation of the political and the public is not unique to socially active housewives. Those who are not active may feel more constrained by the nature of the political world. While they express concerns about public problems, they feel that they are without a means of addressing their solutions. Politics is the least likely place where the non-active housewife would turn to find those means, partly because the political is a world that she feels unable to enter, but also because she distrusts the political world's ability to operate in such broad terms. If full citizenship means engagement in a public discourse about the nature of a community, then citizenship is not possible in politics as non-active housewives see it.

One woman who had been forced to leave her Ōizumi home when the government decided to locate a highway expansion on her property said that she could recognize the effects of politics on her daily life. She was concerned with such issues as the economy and whether Japan should send civilian workers rather than its self-defense forces overseas to take part in United Nations peace-keeping operations. Political corruption also made her angry. But she would not participate in politics, she said. "Shō ga nai kara to iu kanji" (I have the feeling that there is nothing to be done), she explained. When she continued to explain herself, she pointed to the structure of political parties in Japan. The Liberal Democratic Party is corrupt, she said, and the other parties simply oppose things. They are always "spouting ideology."

Significantly, this woman and others are not unaware of or unconcerned about politics or social problems. They simply do not see the sense in attempting to act in a political manner. We must do more than see this as a low estimation of efficacy, which, of course, it is. The real question is why such low efficacy feelings come about, and the answer seems to lie in the fact that politics and housewives' daily lives are separately constructed, incompatible worlds. This incompatibility is especially startling in the case of a mother of preschool children who said that since becoming a mother, she had developed a growing understanding of the importance of politics.

When I was single I thought politics was something other people do. But now that I have kids I have come to understand that if you don't do it yourself, nothing is going to change, and it's not okay to just not be interested. I came to think this since I had children because there are things you have to do for small things to live. I used to think that I should be patient or I would say it would be nice if things were this way or that. This is true with politics, but also with other things. Since I've had children, I've learned to speak up.

Every day I worry about *seikatsu* [lifestyle, daily life] problems—environmental problems, for example—disposable things. When I was working, I would just use whatever things were around me without thinking. They made my life more comfortable. But when the children were born, I started to feel a sense of responsibility and thought, when they get older, I want to leave them something, and, so, even if it's a little, I want to do something.

This woman had obviously developed concerns about the effects of politics on public goods such as the environment. Furthermore, she felt keenly that she ought to express her concerns and make efforts for better political results on behalf of her children. When I pressed her to tell me how she had or planned to participate in improving politics, however, she made a quick turnabout. She said she "did nothing special," explaining that political action would mean joining an organization. She did not intend to go that far, she said, and stressed that her efforts to provide for posterity would be restricted to what she could accomplish through her "own daily life."

"I do feel I have been separated from the world because I can't get out," she then added. She expressed an interest in attending study groups on important social issues if day care was available. Her presentation of herself as "separated from the world" is worth consideration. She attributed her growing concern for politics and public problems such as environmental pollution to the fact that she was raising children. In fact, she contrasted her new, politically interested attitude with the attitude that she had had when she was working prior to marrying, bearing children, and becoming a housewife.

Unfortunately, now that her daily life experiences have convinced her of the importance of politics she feels that she is restricted from acting on her concerns in some ways. She will not join an organization. She does not say so explicitly, but her inference that she cannot go "that far" suggests that organizations are too extreme, somehow incompatible with her lifestyle.[21] She is interested in further study, but to pursue it she must have a means of solving daily life problems such as child care. The life conditions that give her a valuable new perspective on society and politics also prevent her from perceiving herself as capable of acting in society and politics. When she worked and presumably had fewer such barriers to action, she did not care to act. She is caught in a bind that is best described as bicycle citizenship. The impetus for her citizenship is tied to her housewife identity, but that identity seems ill-suited for action as a citizen.

Non-active housewives who had broad political concerns often explained their failure to take any political action by saying that they "had no place to go." In other words, they could not see a location, physical or ideological, for introducing themselves into the political power structure. When even more active housewives discounted voting or other forms of action that political scientists would normally count as political participation, they were probably indicating a similar perception of their

actions as not within the political power structure. This outsider thinking was important in describing the housewife's physical absence from
political organizations, but it also reflects her belief that she can not
"organize" her concerns according to the available choices in ideological
terms. Simply put, the political concerns that housewives have do not
translate to spots on the map of the Japanese political system.

The words of the women who described their apathy toward or dis-
interest in politics were laden with dissatisfaction about the choices available in political society. The feelings of distance, murkiness, and insid-
ious organizational power that seemed to shroud nearly all political
possibilities were not feelings that could be easily dispelled with a newer
image candidate or a more transparent political organization. The criticism runs deeper because the implication in these women's discussion
of politics is that the political system itself *requires* distance, murkiness,
and organizational wrangling. Eventually no participant is exempt.

It may seem odd at first, but the message that came across as my
informants described their image of *ideal* politics (as opposed to what
they already had), was that politics was doomed because it was composed of actors whose thinking was always "too close to home." At times
women sounded as if they were contradicting themselves. A good example is Totsuka-san. She attributed political apathy to the fact that
most people were involved in things close to home that politics failed
to address, but she also criticized politicians for being too absorbed in
what is close to home. She even complained that voters were remiss in
their duties because they chose candidates who provided temporary,
close-to-home benefits.

Even if we assume that Totsuka-san is self-contradictory to a degree,
we can still glean an important perspective from what she says. Two
types of "close to home" appear in her words. One is the narrowly
conceived "close to home" that can be equated with a base interest in
increased power for politicians, pork-barrel benefits for constituents.
This "close to home" makes politics the uninspiring event that it is today. The other "close to home," however, has a more universal value.
In this other sense, "close to home" is the essence of daily life, that which
really counts to "regular" people. This sense of daily-life closeness opposes itself to precisely the other closeness, what is *not* in essence important, such as a politician's personal ambition or a tax break for a
particular constituent.

When the concerned but non-active housewife says that she has "no-
where to go" to make her mark on politics, she offers both herself and

us a clue to the real problem. If we restate her words in terms of our transportation metaphor, we could say that, in the perception of the non-active housewife, politics does not occur in the places she is able to go. Politics does not exist in the community as she understands it and travels it. Politics is a specialized, faraway world, and the resources required for transport there are either unavailable or distasteful to the housewife. Hence comes one source of bicycle citizenship. Of course, if this picture of society as divided among self-serving spheres where leaders are concerned only with what is closest to themselves is correct, then there is no reason to conclude that a feeling of bicycle citizenship would not be pervasive in all spheres, making all the more compelling a housewife's belief that her sphere is especially distant from the political. She would seem to have internalized the very dividedness that she decries.

CHAPTER FOUR

Volunteering against Politics
Housewives, Citizenship, and Community Service

Given the cynicism with which most housewives viewed their potential for acting in politics, I was fascinated by the extent to which Ono Kiyoko's House of Councilor's campaign rhetoric relied on emphasizing the special public value of "housewifeliness." On an afternoon toward the end of the campaign I stopped in at Sagyōsho, one of the volunteer sites where I studied social activity among Nerima women. I asked the volunteers, all housewives themselves, why they thought a politician would find it advantageous to represent herself as a housewife. The volunteers did not hesitate to answer. Housewives are good with details, they told me. Housewives are dependable, honest, clean. Housewives are practical.

Many housewife informants were content to express general distaste for politics and be done with it. They indicated that politics was dissatisfying because it was not close to them and the women assumed that the close to home would remain neglected. Many housewives gave no thought to citizenship, and when their public concerns went unaddressed they shook their heads. *Shō ga nai:* nothing can be done.

In the world of volunteer activity, however, good citizenship was of great importance. The problems of public life were the source of daily concern, and the failures of narrow politics to reach the heart of what is nearby were keenly felt. Moreover, the housewives who were volunteers did not say "*Shō ga nai.*" They saw themselves as actors, striving to care for the world close to home that politics forgot. Volunteer housewives were immersed in a dialogue about the nature of society, and, therefore, they seemed like prime candidates for the experience of democratic citizenship.

Yet while the volunteer world was plush with props of democratic life — public concern, discussion, action, openness — the volunteer experience did not lead easily to a political citizenship. Most volunteers stopped short of accepting the political as a legitimate field for the struggle to alter society. Like Tanaka-san, a volunteer whom I will discuss again later in this chapter, volunteers had a great deal of exposure to the political world through their activity, and they developed an acute awareness of the effect of politics on the societal conditions about which they were concerned. Tanaka-san described herself as generally uninterested in and unknowledgeable about politics. What she did know, she said, came from her volunteer experiences. "After all, if you are doing volunteer activities, politicians always show up at the bazaars and things like that. So, I've been invited when politicians, especially Liberal Democratic Party politicians, have functions. I've gone to election speeches," she explained.

Volunteering had provided Tanaka-san with an opportunity to meet politicians and go to political events, and she had learned from observation that the connections between politicians and the volunteer sector were important. Powerful politicians, especially well-placed conservative leaders, could promote and protect a volunteer project; without them apathy, sometimes even opposition, in the community could undo such enterprises. Yet Tanaka-san said that volunteering had also taught her that Japanese society was getting "harder and harder on the weak." She suspected that this was the result of long-term conservative dominance in politics.

Tanaka-san finally concluded that politics offered little real hope to the volunteer world. Ties between volunteer organizations and politicians, while necessary, were "actually unacceptable" in some moral sense. Furthermore, the achievements of politics in the areas that volunteers worked were minimal. "No matter what, [politics] falls short of what you expected. By the time something gets to the Diet, and you don't get what you expected, you wonder why they even made such a fuss," she said. More and more, Tanaka-san was becoming "disinterested, turned away from" politics.

Similar to Tanaka-san, volunteers often seemed to think that, rather than "supplying . . . the defect of better motives,"[1] politics infected "better motives" with destructive interest. Volunteers suspected that, for this reason, their public-minded actions could not have taken place inside a framework that included politics. In ruling politics out of their consideration of possible solutions to social problems, volunteers shaped what might have been citizenship into something else—something that looked like energetic citizenship in nearly every aspect except its rejection of political routes to social change—bicycle citizenship. For most volunteers a determinedly apolitical bicycle citizenship was almost inevitable because their volunteer activity was permeated by the housewife identity and reliant on the housewife ethic, and that identity and ethic resist participation in spheres that could be widely considered politics.

However, because much volunteer work occurred around the margins of sectors of society managed by state agencies, housewives who were experienced volunteers inevitably became quite conscious of, indeed ambivalent about, the "apolitical" nature of their public service rhetoric. Later in this chapter, we will follow the transformation of the group Sagyōsho from a small housewives' effort to a para-public facility receiving ward subsidies for operation. Long-time volunteers saw the ethical difficulties of Sagyōsho's teaming up with the ward administration quite clearly, but they were also eager to make use of resources that would let them expand the scope of their special contribution to community life. They wagered that their work would transform the community more than administrative politics would transform them as workers. In order to defeat politics, Sagyōsho volunteers made a pact with the enemy.

Volunteer Activity and Politics

In Ōizumi, I learned that the development of a volunteer ethic can work against a citizen's desire for political integration because politics and the volunteer world seem to oppose each other. This finding is unusual. Since Alexis de Tocqueville first remarked that the United States was a nation of joiners, political scientists have assumed that voluntary civic activity has a positive connection with democratic political life.[2] Tocqueville argued that, in the process of combining to solve problems, citizens "turn from private interests," learn that they are not independent of their fellow human beings, and come to "feel the value of public goodwill." By doing this, citizens can avoid the great dangers of despotism that Tocqueville believed must otherwise lie in an equal and individually isolated population.[3] In many ways, the students of politics and voluntarism since Tocqueville have accepted his thesis without examination. Even when confronted with the puzzle that men and women seem to draw different political benefits from volunteer work, political science has devoted little effort to examining in detail the educative processes of voluntary association.

Theorists of modern American democracy have agreed with Tocqueville that voluntary activity provides crucial support for democracy. Some have argued that, in the advanced welfare state, voluntary action is even more important to democratic public discourse than Tocqueville might have suspected in the nineteenth century.[4] Deriving his argument from Tocqueville, Robert Wuthnow holds that the "voluntary sector" acts as a mediator between the state and the market, providing services that the other sectors cannot and protecting arenas for public discourse and an "example of alternative norms and values."[5] The assumption that participation in voluntary life leads to fuller participation in politics is the guiding idea of a recent thoroughgoing quantitative study of political participation in the United States, but as this "taxi" study finds out, even when women are highly active in voluntary spheres, their sort of activism leads to political participation less than that of men.[6]

In general, however, political scientists have spent scant time examining the specific effects that different types of voluntary activities have on democracy and citizenship. On the one hand, theorists such as Benjamin Barber who extol voluntarism have little empirical evidence to support their claims. Empiricists, on the other hand, have been content to document correlations between voluntary association memberships and democratic political behavior through a rather superficial process of counting. Much of the literature about voluntary associations in the United States focuses on tallying who joins which organizations or matches numbers of memberships with increases in political participation.[7]

Systematic, cross-national study of the connection of voluntarism and citizenship has been sparse, and when it has been done, cross-national comparisons are usually limited to examining a nation's volume of volunteer activity.[8] We know little about how political socialization processes work inside the voluntary associations of other nations. Early studies found that, as Tocqueville suggested, Americans joined more voluntary organizations than people of other nationalities, but these studies presented little discussion of why this would be so.[9] One study concluded that low-level voluntarism may be related to traditions of centralized, hierarchical states, but no corresponding cross-national data was presented as support to the claim that differences in state traditions and voluntarism levels are significantly correlated.[10]

In general, studies of levels of voluntarism do a poor job of connecting variations in association membership with variations in democratic experiences. Most studies have been done in the United States; the models of voluntarism are dominated by our cultural peculiarities. Furthermore, even American studies are a failure when it comes to understanding the internal dynamics of voluntarism. Scholars have been content to draw general correlations from a statistically large population. They have spent little time observing the concrete nature of voluntarism's contribution to the lives of volunteers and their society. Moreover, examination of some women's activism suggests that studies that rely on counting as a means of assessing voluntary organizations may produce a highly inaccurate picture of women's effectiveness (or lack of effectiveness) in achieving organizational goals. Ethnographic study of Latino organizations in Boston has shown that women have a crucial role that would not be evident if evaluation relied solely on counting.[11] Even more striking is that fact that, while rates of organization in woman suffrage groups in Switzerland and the United States differed little in the early twentieth century, American women achieved universal suffrage seventy years before Swiss women.[12] Counts of participants cannot fully explain the political value of group participation.

The usual conceptual frameworks through which we study the connection between voluntarism and political activity and attitudes only allow us to paint in very broad strokes.[13] Furthermore, "voluntary" is a loosely defined category; most quantitative studies make only a minimum of distinctions among types of associations that qualify as voluntary. This is unfortunate for democratic theorists. For example, the differences between voluntary membership in a labor union or professional association and voluntary membership in a neighborhood recycling organization may be too great to ignore, especially in terms of what they say about or contribute to a person's citizenship.

Because women's volunteer activities differ from men's in important ways, we must have more detailed information about the inside of volunteer organizations if we want to explore the relationship between voluntarism, gender, and citizenship. Much of the research on gender and voluntary memberships, however, is dominated by an adherence to concepts that are indisputably sexist. Scholars have devoted themselves to trying to explain how and why women volunteers are different from men. What women volunteers actually do and the ways in which the voluntary experience molds women's political perspectives are subsumed under assumptions based on male patterns, as is the political participation literature that I discussed in the previous chapter.

Describing a few of these sexist concepts may be a helpful demonstration of why, if we want to understand how voluntarism affects women's political perceptions, we should look at women's voluntary work from the position of participant observer. In the agenda-setting article "Sex and Social Participation" (1972), Alan Booth tagged differences in the types of organizations that men and women belong to by categorizing them according to a dichotomy that is condescending toward women's membership patterns, not to mention unhelpful in defining real distinctions. The organizations in which women were more likely to spend their time included school or youth programs, church-related societies, recreational associations, fraternal service organizations, and health and welfare organizations such as the Red Cross. Organizations to which men belonged in higher numbers included professional, trade, and commercial associations, political parties or protest groups, and veteran's organizations.[14] Booth described men's membership patterns as "instrumental" and women's as "expressive." According to Booth, "Instrumental associations, groups organized to cope with the external environment, entail more aggressive than accommodative behavior on the part of members. . . . Expressive groups are organized to prevent deviant behavior. Their activities, basically accommodative and nurturant in character, include socialization and personality integration."[15]

The different pattern of women's involvement in voluntary activities is confirmed by the 1995 Verba team study, *Voice and Equality*.[16] The authors of this more recent study are less openly dismissive of women's potential for political involvement than Booth, and they are careful to explain that when women do participate in American politics they do not seem any more bound by narrow constraints than are men; however, the authors fail to seek a deeper explanation of the avowedly "non-political" quality of much of women's voluntarism. They write off voluntary activities in which politics are not discussed as not leading to political participation except in the narrow sense of teaching skills that could be used later in political arenas.[17]

Certainly, men's and women's associational patterns are qualitatively different. But the instrumental-expressive dichotomy serves only to obscure the meaning of those differences. Such a dichotomy does not clarify why, for example, a professional association would *not* serve primarily to prevent deviant behavior. It is furthermore impossible to discern how members of the Red Cross or a school-related organization can *avoid* contact with the external environment. Major components of both the instrumental and expressive categories fail to fit the concept definitions.

Booth's use of the dichotomy had a substantial patrimony in the work of Talcott Parsons.[18] Perhaps that is why the instrumental-expressive categories show up unquestioned in more recent studies of gender and voluntarism. The passage I just quoted is also quoted in an article from 1982 that argues that women develop fewer contacts and can access fewer resources through voluntarism than men can.[19] The same section is quoted in an article from 1990 about farm women's activism, where scores on an instrumental-expressive dichotomy are used as a means of determining to what extent women's activism comes to resemble men's when women have off-farm employment.[20]

Women employed off the farm do show higher membership in "instrumental" organizations than women who are not off-farm employed, but considering the fact that a major component of organizations classified as "instrumental" is made up of professional, trade, and commercial associations, the findings seem truly unsurprising.[21] It makes sense that women join more of these "economic" organizations when they hold paid employment—just as we might expect that employed, adult men join more such organizations than men who are unemployed or students. Exactly how such a fact changes a woman's experiences as a member of society or a citizen in politics is, regrettably, a question left for future inquiry. Careful, ethnographic examination of women's experiences in voluntary organizations such as Ōizumi's Sagyōsho is a means of challenging the limits of Booth's dominant categories.

Moreover, seeing the volunteer world through the eyes of volunteer-housewives such as Tanaka-san can be an opportunity for exploring the equally disturbing constraints in much of the women's studies' literature on voluntarism. Viewed through a feminist framework, women's volunteer activity is seen as a substitute for real careers in the paid work force. According to this interpretation, women who are involved in the voluntary sector are understood as conservative or repressed. Consider Doris Gold's characterization of volunteer activity in her article "Women and Voluntarism":

Serving as a dedicated person without payment in a money culture invariably results in the assumption of attitudes of superiority and the halo of goodness.

Women who become volunteers because they want to "do something useful" are most often merely lonely and empty.

[F]or women voluntarism is a hybrid of work and role playing, more closely linked to "occupational therapy" than to work accomplished in the economic sense, [and thus] this psychodrama which has created a virtual subculture among women might seem to offer little else but "therapy" to the volunteer. From a feminist and/or progressive unionist point of view, voluntarism is clearly exploitative.[22]

Gold's presentation of voluntarism as a simultaneously self-serving and exploitative "psychodrama" is, perhaps, among the most extreme views about women and voluntary action. But other students of voluntarism and gender are notable for their defensiveness toward positions such as Gold's. While being more generous in their assessment of the worth of voluntary activity, they nevertheless seem to buy the broad outlines of Gold's thesis. Herta Loeser writes that "the women's movement has become suspicious of volunteering, as yet another means by which our male-dominated society subverts women's liberation. Therefore, I must justify my conviction that my advocacy of volunteering as an important means for many modern women to enrich their lives and those of others is entirely consistent with women's liberation."[23] Loeser argues in defense of voluntarism that volunteer activities can be "professionalized" much like a paid career and that volunteer experience is a valuable resource in preparing to enter or reenter paid employment. She has accepted Gold's main point—voluntary activity is a substitute for real work in the paid workforce.[24]

More recently, scholars have attempted to place women's voluntarism in a better light. In the edited volume *Lady Bountiful Revisited: Women, Philanthropy, and Power,* histories of various volunteer movements in the United States and abroad are used to demonstrate the ways in which volunteer women were able to use voluntarism to "expand the parameters of their influence and reshape public discourse on the content and meaning of their lives."[25] Arlene Kaplan Daniels makes the best available examination of the content of different types of volunteer activities and the perceptions of women participants in *Invisible Careers: Women Civic Leaders from the Volunteer World,* but even Daniels is determined to portray volunteer activity through its structural parallels with careers in paid employment.[26]

Volunteer activity as an aid to democratic life, as a source of values that is *alternative* to the state or marketplace, is given little investigation. But, as I show later in this chapter, Japanese women volunteers perceive their work as alternative to the state, even *against* it in a certain way.

Looking at Japanese voluntarism from the inside challenges us to step back from the task of categorizing voluntary organizations according to how they fit into *our* understanding of what makes politically significant data. We should examine the possibility that, in their understanding of being a volunteer, Japanese women call the relevance of our idea of "politically significant" into question in a basic sense. In voluntarism, there is a hint that politics ought to be treated as insignificant in human affairs.

The Shape of Voluntarism in Japan

As I noted earlier, cross-national research on voluntarism indicates that voluntary activity is much less prevalent in Japan than in many other advanced industrial democracies. Like France, Japan seems to have suffered a constraint in the development of its voluntary sector that may be the result of a strong-state tradition.[27] Difficulties in comparing data across nations may hinder drawing any firm conclusions. While "voluntary association" can be stretched to include even labor unions in some scholars' perspectives, the "voluntary" in Japan is usually considered to be a more proscribed sphere of action.

The volunteer activists whom I studied all participated in associations that fit a category known in Japanese by an English loan-word—*borantia*—for volunteer. In Japanese, *borantia* includes the idea of action taken without compulsion, but it also encompasses a clearly normative understanding of such action. *Borantia* action is freely chosen, unremunerated, social welfare-oriented, and occurs regardless of the profit or loss of the actor.[28] Nearly all of the action known in Japan as *borantia* would, of course, fit under Booth's "expressive" association category, and the membership is overwhelmingly dominated by women.[29] In Japan, however, this "expressive" *borantia* is not contrasted with a more legitimate "instrumental" *borantia,* nor is there any reason to believe that the Japanese would see *borantia* activities as unconcerned with the external world. What is more likely is that memberships in groups like professional and trade associations are viewed as neither voluntary nor unremunerated.

Individual Japanese volunteer organizations are prolific in their production of written material regarding organization goals and accomplishments, but, other than this healthy stream of pamphlets and newsletters, little has been written about Japanese voluntarism. Statistics demonstrate that membership in organizations leads to increased political participation among Japanese citizens, but as is the case in American literature that counts membership in a broad variety of associations, the independent effect of participation in organizations that rank as *borantia* enterprises is indeterminate.

Interestingly enough, male organizational membership rates and political interest peak when men are in their forties: voter turnout among men declines fairly quickly after age sixty. Voter turnout among women maintains its vigor much longer; they report a sense of duty about voting even beyond age seventy.[30] While levels of labor union and trade association membership become almost zero among the population aged sixty to seventy, membership in groups classified as "women's organizations," although declining, still continues at visible levels well past age seventy.[31] Once again, the effect of *borantia* activity cannot be directly measured with this data, but it seems safe to assume that some of the groups contained in "women's organizations" are *borantia* in nature.

Easily discernible or not, the possible effects of *borantia* action in Japan are likely to increase because voluntarism has been increasing steadily throughout the postwar period.[32] Between 1981 and 1987 women's voluntary activity increased by several percentage points in all areas.[33] This may be due to the large numbers of well-educated, post-childbearing-age women with free time on their hands—full-time housewives and women with part-time jobs—for whom volunteering presents an attractive means of participating in their community.[34]

The volunteer has had a not so subtle impact on local-level politics as well. Between 1979 and 1991 women at least doubled their representation in assemblies at entry levels below the national Diet, and notable among these increases were the electoral successes of party-independents who had gotten their start in community service through such voluntary activities as school lunch programs, welfare services, and nuclear power opposition groups.[35] Certainly, school and welfare services, *borantia* types of activity, provide some women with experience and an organizational background that can be footholds for steps into greater political influence.

Social welfare voluntary activity in Japan often occurs with the assistance of, or in close relationship to, agencies of the government. In Nerima, tremendous growth in the number and types of volunteer associations and the number of members also occurred following the beginning of the Nerima Welfare Council's volunteer promotion seminars in 1968, continuing until the present.[36] Welfare councils, originally suggested by the MacArthur administration under the Occupation, are quasi-public institutions designed to promote both the growth of voluntarism and the matching of existing community needs with volunteer resources. In an interview, a Nerima Welfare Council staff member described welfare councils as part of a vision of a more democratic Japan, and explained that the council perceived itself as a force for democratic community development. Nerima's welfare council has a skeleton, ward-supported staff that runs a volunteer center, near the central Nerima ward government office buildings, and two branch operations, or volunteer corners, one in Hikari-ga-oka and one in Ōizumi. The salaried welfare council staffs the volunteer center, but the volunteer corners are operated by uncompensated volunteers.

The volunteer center and corners take responsibility for registering potential volunteers on a roster that includes their available time, volunteer interests, and experiences.[37] These welfare council branches also act as contact points for people or organizations that might seek volunteer services, such as schools or facilities for the handicapped, elderly who find it difficult to get out on their own, or mothers of severely retarded children who need temporary day care. The welfare council exerts energies in volunteer promotion as well. It encourages registered volunteer associations, individuals, and service-receiving organizations to participate in ward bazaars and festivals.

Regular newsletters let volunteers and volunteer service clients know about new programs, new associations, and volunteer training opportunities. They provide "human interest" stories about individual triumphs in volunteer activity as well. The volunteer center sponsors free workshops and seminars where individuals or associations can hear talks from experts and "network" among each other. Finally, the welfare council takes the responsibility for studying the development of volunteer activity in Nerima. It surveys registered volunteers, tracks the growth of new groups and projects the likely areas of expanding needs for volunteer services.

The volunteer associations and services listed through the welfare council do not encompass all of the volunteer alternatives available in the ward. For example, I never properly registered through the Ōizumi volunteer corner, but I participated in a volunteer seminar, was a regular member of two volunteer groups, and attended a variety of special events connected with volunteer associations or activities. Particularly individuals, who might dip in and out of the volunteer sphere through the encouragement of a friend or a chance encounter with a group's activities, could slip through the net of welfare council surveys and general accounting. Volunteer work related to one's employment or sponsored by a labor union or political party might also fail to fall into the welfare council's notice.[38]

The volunteer center and corners were able to see the general *shape* of volunteer activity with relative accuracy. Because of the assistance that they could receive in advertising, coordination, and communication, among other things, volunteer associations and beneficiaries of volunteer service have incentives to develop a relationship with the volunteer center. The picture that the volunteer center was able to draw of Nerima voluntary action was comparable to what I found in my own exposure to the ward.

In 1992, 76 groups of a total of 703 individuals were registered through the volunteer center or corners.[39] More important than the number of registrants are their attributes. In a slightly earlier, more detailed report, 85 percent were women, 74 percent were between forty and sixty years of age, and 70 percent listed themselves in the "housewife/unemployed" category. Most had lived in their neighborhood from ten to twenty years. The greatest number of volunteers were concentrated in the residential areas in Ōizumi and around the adjacent train station, Shakujii-kōen. (This area was the neighborhood in which I lived.) Of the 70 percent who fell into the "housewife/unemployed" category, 90 percent lived in this area.[40]

Sagyōsho: Life Inside a Volunteer Organization

Volunteers grasped the implication of Diet candidate Ono's housewife rhetoric. Yet, as we will see in this chapter and in the chapter on Ono's campaign, in almost all other respects, the volunteer world and the world of Ono's campaign organization contrasted starkly. The contrasts I saw in the two organizations foreshadowed the barriers to political action that I would find in Sagyōsho. For Sagyōsho members, "politics" was associated with many of the aspects of Ono's campaign that differed from the Sagyōsho group. The "pedigreed" participation of Ono's organized political campaign was distasteful to volunteers who recognized how deeply it contrasted with the "grass-roots" ethos of their organizations.

In Ono's office, everyone, even the "volunteers," came with political pedigrees—badges of favor and indebtedness to other politicians or powerful political actors. Everyone was an "insider" in some respect. They had worked for other candidates or powerful, supportive corporate interests, or trade or commercial associations. They had graduated from Ono's school or were related to another Liberal Democratic Party politician. The web of "insider" or "pedigreed" relations was a powerful undercurrent in the organization's daily business. Even my own complicated introduction to the campaign demonstrated as much.

The volunteer world was as perhaps as opposite in its construction as possible. I literally walked in off the street. On the way to the post office on a Friday afternoon, I chanced to notice a used clothing and handmade crafts sale in the lobby of a home security company. The miscellaneous mixture of old and new sale items piled against the large lobby windows startled me. The lobby had caught my attention on other trips to the post office because it was more spacious, brightly painted, and fashionably furnished than the fronts of most of the other businesses on the busy street. I read a sign that described the sale as a bazaar to benefit handicapped people, and I went in to look around. I asked the woman collecting money for purchases to tell me more about the bazaar and the organization it benefited. She told me she was only indirectly related as a volunteer staffer of the Ōizumi volunteer center, but she took my business card.

Saturday morning at nine, the ringing phone jarred me awake. On the other end of the line, a voice I did not know spoke excitedly. "We heard that you saw the bazaar and that you want to study us. I'll be by to pick you up in fifteen minutes. I'm driving a blue van." Somehow I threw together an outfit and transported myself to the curb. I did not know who I was meeting or where I was going, but I took some paper just in case.

The woman who picked me up was Satō-san, one of the chief leaders of a volunteer organization called Sagyōsho no Ie, or Sagyōsho for short. As we wound through the back streets up a hill, into a neighborhood of single-family homes a bit farther from the station than where I lived, she told me that the volunteer corner woman at the bazaar had contacted her, telling her that I was interested in "women's grassroots activities." "Grassroots—that word fits us to a T," she said.

Satō-san took me to what had once been a small, two-story home. The upstairs was used mostly for storage, and downstairs there was only a bathroom, a kitchen, a tiny tatami-mat living room, and a garage. A Western table with chairs nearly filled the kitchen. A low Japanese table took up most of the floor space in the small living room. The garage, open to the street, was filled with old clothes, books, toys, and household items—a regular "garage sale" but an unexpected sight in Tokyo.[41]

In all of the open areas in the house people sat. Some were elderly or handicapped, some, judging from their speech or demeanor, were mentally handicapped or suffered from mental illness. Most everyone was involved in making small handicrafts. At the kitchen sink two women, who, like Satō-san, were dressed in the sweaters, slacks, and aprons that I often saw on housewives, were assisting a woman with cerebral palsy in washing and chopping vegetables. Satō-san sat me at the kitchen table with a cup of tea, and, amid the crowded confusion and the others who joined in from time to time, she told me the story of Sagyōsho.

Satō-san had started Sagyōsho more than thirteen years previously, when she was new to Ōizumi, a young married woman with preschool children. In college she had worked with handicapped people. She wanted to do something for them after she got married, but with her young children, she had found it nearly impossible to get out of the house. Finally, she got together with other mothers she knew and some handicapped people and elderly living alone in the area to form what Satō-san called a "chance for people who find it difficult to get out to make friends." Yanagi-san, the woman with cerebral palsy, was one of the first to join the group.

At first the group met at Satō-san's "small house" once a week or so, and the mothers carried their babies on their backs. With the motto that, handicapped or not, everyone in the community could learn to work and live together, the group members made small crafts like seashell key rings and shared meals. Satō-san and the other mothers raised money to cover their expenses by selling old belongings and their handicrafts at charity bazaars. Eventually the group grew and decided to increase the frequency of its meetings. A local patron assisted the women in leasing, on favorable terms, the small home that I visited that first Saturday.

Sagyōsho met Tuesdays, Thursdays, and Saturdays from 10:00 A.M. until 4:00 P.M., opening a three-day-a-week "recycle" (thrift) shop in order to earn money to cover the expenses of the house. The goods sold in the "recycle" shop were collected from around the neighborhood according to a word-of-mouth system. For example, it turned out coincidentally that Ueda-san had brought old clothes and furnishings to Sagyōsho even though she was not really a member; she had heard of the project when she met Satō-san through the PTA. Ueda-san explained that women in the neighborhood had established a Sagyōsho ethic. Rather than throw unwanted things out they gave usable items to Sagyōsho for free, but purchased, when possible, items they did need from Sagyōsho rather than buying new. The practice guaranteed Sagyōsho a minimum income.

The responsibility for providing meals and overseeing the "recycle" shop was rotated among Sagyōsho's housewife members, two of whom would be present on each day. Often they rotated their Sagyōsho duty at noon, allowing those with younger children to be home in the afternoon, and others a chance to prepare a noon meal for elderly parents or a husband who was home on Saturdays. As Sagyōsho grew, it developed a second sort of volunteer contingent, women who had less frequent but nonetheless continuous relations with the organization. For example, Sasaki-san taught embroidery there once a month. One of the few women in her group of friends who had easy access to a car and felt comfortable driving on the hectic streets, she also ran a recycle store pick-up service, collecting boxes of goods from Sagyōsho patrons who called in donations but did not have transportation. An actress in musicals who sang benefit concerts added Sagyōsho to her list. Although she seldom had time to visit on her own, the profits from blocks of concert tickets, sold by other volunteers, gave Sagyōsho a financial boost.

The Volunteer Ethic

At Sagyōsho, as at other volunteer organizations, volunteers seemed to possess a distinctive ethic for conducting daily business that, in the end, circumscribed the place of politics in the volunteer domain. One could, for example, say something like, "I would have said something when it happened, but I was at Sagyōsho," or "I thought it was odd, too, but, then it was Sagyōsho," or "We could just do it the way we do at Sagyōsho," in the same way that my sponsor's wife had described the ethic of goods trading among patrons of the Sagyōsho recycle shop. Of course, the proper action in any particular situation was often a matter for debate, but, in general, I think it fair to argue that most volunteers had a sense of a Sagyōsho ethic that valued openness, equality, flexibility, and respect for individual difference with a general emphasis on "humanity" in relations (as opposed to rank, custom, or prestige).

Some of this ethic might be assumed, given the sort of work that the organization performed. In other words, people who did not share such values would have little time to spare for Sagyōsho. However, Sagyōsho's "volunteer ethic" also derived substantial support from the fact that the housewife identity and the volunteer ethic were mutually reinforcing; each produced evidence of the value of the other. Moreover, Sagyōsho's members were exposed to powerful messages about the volunteer's place in society through experiences at Sagyōsho and in the other volunteer venues where Sagyōsho members were likely to travel from time to time.

Tanaka-san, the volunteer I described as having "turned away" from politics at the beginning of the chapter, was a clear example of a volunteer whose sense of the volunteer ethic was interlocked with her housewife identity. An unemployed housewife who had moved several times with the transfers her husband received as he moved up the corporate ladder in a large company, Tanaka-san had few links with the Ōizumi community when she moved there in the early 1990s. Because her children were older—one was in high school and one in college—she had few occasions to make many friends by meeting the mothers of her children's friends. Her days of going to the park and to PTA meetings were over. Tanaka-san had one possible social resource, however; she had experience in volunteer activities in her previous city of residence.

Tanaka-san was strongly, if sometimes frustratingly, identified as a housewife. She claimed that she followed a very traditional role orientation in her daily life and attributed this mostly to a "country" upbringing and her husband's own stubborn traditionalism. She often referred disparagingly to her lack of experience in paid employment, and she said that, because she had never worked, she had never developed economic or social independence, although she said she was an independent thinker.

Tanaka-san described society's image of the housewife as "in the home cleaning and the like" and said that she had a "housewife's complex," or a fear of not fitting into society. What bothered her most about being a housewife was the fact that she felt society did not recognize her as valuable. She did not have the means that people in the workforce had of demonstrating their useful skills. "I have no special licenses," she lamented. Tanaka-san had given up any ambitions for even a part-time job because she said her husband opposed her receiving a salary, but she had not given up a desire for a vocation.

"There were lots of housewives in Sapporo who met their friends every day and just talked and drank tea and went shopping and played golf. That's fine, but I don't want to be that kind of housewife," she said. Volunteer work offered Tanaka-san a route to what she perceived as a socially valuable position that did not require a challenge to her housewife identity—a challenge that she clearly seemed to want to avoid, despite her dissatisfaction with her social status. Through volunteer activities, she could make friends in new towns, employ herself without having special licenses, and contribute to society in a way that she thought was important and sensible. Tanaka-san became a volunteer, in part, because it fit her housewife's role. Of course, we might give feminist scholars credit for documenting similar phenomena elsewhere. Nevertheless, I do not believe that the connection between Tanaka-san's volunteer activity and her housewife status was a "psychodrama." Nor was it merely exploitative.

Tanaka-san had been hospitalized for an illness many years previously. Realizing what a strain her care placed on both her family and the already overburdened medical professionals at the hospital, Tanaka-san had become convinced that there was a need for volunteer work. After leaving the hospital, Tanaka-san had tried to volunteer at a local facility for severely handicapped children, without success. The helplessness of the children depressed her, and it seemed as if the other facility volunteers all worked as part of groups like Sōka Gakkai, an evangelical religious group that Tanaka-san felt uncomfortable about joining.[42]

But Tanaka-san tried again, attending a volunteer seminar sponsored by the Sapporo city government. She made friends, and she heard about a volunteer center that prepared meals for shut-in elderly. Tanaka-san joined the group and worked delivering meals to the people whom the group served. She said she soon realized that giving the people she visited her time was often as important as delivering the food. Tanaka-san became a person for the volunteer group's clients to talk to, and she said that gave her a real sense of fulfillment.

When she moved to Ōizumi, she sought opportunities to continue her volunteer service. She attended a ward volunteer seminar run by the Nerima Welfare Council. After the seminar, volunteer center workers suggested that she try placing herself at Sagyōsho because it was close to where she lived. Tanaka-san became one of the regular weekly workers, responsible for making meals and supervising the store along with one or two other women, housewives from the same general neighborhood. She mentioned the satisfaction of making "human connections" with the people she helped. But she seemed to place equal value on her friendships with other volunteers and the variety of activities and the flexibility of her schedule as well.

At Sagyōsho, Tanaka-san met Kawashima-san, who included her on our Karuizawa holiday. She met Sasaki-san also, and they pursued hobbies together. Sasaki-san introduced Tanaka-san to another volunteer group that met at a welfare facility for mentally handicapped adults. Through women she met at this group, Tanaka-san received invitations to Saturday afternoon bazaars and festivals and to charity concerts. She joined a large group that traveled to downtown Tokyo to see a performance by the musical star who so often gave Sagyōsho benefit concerts. When Sagyōsho went on spring and fall outings to the countryside, Tanaka-san went, too. She also became involved in recording for the blind and worked with other members in producing newspaper recordings.

Just as the housewife identity tended to level differences like education or background in a group of women by playing up their equal attachment to their roles as wives and mothers, the "housework" quality of volunteer work created a sense of equality and openness within a volunteer organization. Sometimes a strong claim on a "housewife's" role actually worked to a volunteer's benefit. The fresh-from-college staffer who was hired when the original Sagyōsho recycle shop expanded its activities was chided by the housewife volunteers for her difficulty managing everything from various conflicts with mentally ill activity participants to calculating needs for meal preparation. She needed a housewife's experience, she was told. When the staffer gave a small speech at the annual end-of-year party, she said that she had come to Sagyōsho as "a bride."[43]

While Tanaka-san spoke highly of her volunteer companions, she also seemed to enjoy volunteer work because it called on her to use skills in which she was confident because she used them every day in her role as a housewife—everything from lending a patient ear to cooking an economical meal. Even her tremendous interest in gardening came to her aid. She helped landscape the garden at the second house Sagyōsho rented when it expanded. She helped teach mentally handicapped adults from the facility where she volunteered to grow vegetables; she was even able to offer their teachers advice on the gardening project. When we went hiking with Sagyōsho, Tanaka-san could pick out and identify the interesting plants along the trail.

Especially because the work that volunteers did was often designed to assist those with disabilities to perform daily life tasks as independently as possible, the common ideology held that anyone could do what, in fact, some did much better. Tanaka-san needed no special entree to gain the right to employ herself in gardening or cooking. Like other volunteer women who contributed talents for sewing, cookie baking, or pottery making to the repertoire of a social welfare facility's activities and money-making enterprises for its clients, Tanaka-san found a use for special abilities that otherwise were unremarkable parts of her daily work as a housewife.

The widely held belief that volunteer work was unspecialized, house-wife-like labor meant that Tanaka-san could not take credit for being a great gardener, but it also meant that she needed no credentials, no special pedigree to jump in wherever she had the courage to tread. And since, in actuality, volunteers' contributions were differentiated, informal rewards in the form of praise from friends or repeated requests for assistance on the same task were frequent. Significantly, what the volunteers liked about their world contrasts with what the housewives who are discussed in the previous chapter considered to be characteristic of politics.

Inclusiveness and openness were such hallmarks of volunteer activity that great delicacy was called for at times when information was held confidentially or not well communicated or when someone was excluded from a particular event. As in my own case, the fact that Tanaka-san was a newcomer was officially irrelevant. The status of "volunteer" contained an assumption that one would have other, more pressing obligations. Juggling volunteer duty with housecleaning, cooking for one's family, or personal hobbies was acceptable, even encouraged. *Muri shinaide* (don't try to do the impossible — or, basically, don't overextend yourself) was a common phrase.

Volunteers could move into and out of the organization with few serious penalties, so taking time off for children, elderly parents, a part-time job, or a personal crisis did not threaten a volunteer's ties with other volunteers. Because it was assumed that society's need for volunteers could never be satisfied, there was no logic for excluding a returnee from full participation. Since most volunteers were housewives who suffered unpredictable fluxes in the demands on their time, the flexibility of volunteer work was valued. When volunteers had the opportunity to describe their own reasons for participation, they nearly always mentioned a friendly, inclusive atmosphere in which they could put even limited time or skills to use.

Social Welfare and the Volunteer Ethic

The volunteer ethic was also forged by the manner in which volunteers interpreted their encounters with the social institutions on which they exerted their energies. Social welfare institutions, bureaucracy, and politicians seemed to fail the world in which volunteers exerted themselves. Social welfare perspectives that centered on political remedies did not seem to appreciate the special *humanness* of the volunteer's contribution.

In their activities, volunteers necessarily felt the pressure of public opinion, the power of public policy, and the strength of social networks. Even the most practical information about a volunteer activity could not escape reference to the broader social milieu. Volunteers were schooled in an understanding of volunteer activity that presented their experiences as particular kinds of public undertakings that we could say gave them a volunteer-citizen consciousness, although paradoxically it resulted in constraining their political integration and, thus, constraining real citizenship.

In caring for handicapped people Sagyōsho volunteers came to amass knowledge about social welfare institutions and practices—everything from the amounts of disability insurance available to individuals to the location of ward mental hospitals. Volunteers expanded their wealth of social information when Sagyōsho worked cooperatively with other welfare-oriented organizations. Recovering alcoholics heard about Sagyōsho through an Alcoholics Anonymous program; they volunteered in order to develop a new focus in their lives, but they brought with them information about problems and programs beyond Sagyōsho. People who volunteered at Sagyōsho often volunteered at other organizations, too, and that gave them and those with whom they talked broader perspectives.

Unlike organizations that offered activities such as tea ceremony or painting classes, Sagyōsho provided an easy atmosphere for conversation. Making lunch or tending the store, sharing afternoon tea, baking cookies or running a loom were all activities that left room for talk.

Often discussion was limited to chitchat or neighborhood gossip, but at other times discussion bore more directly on the relationship of the volunteer activity to the outside world. A decision about whether to participate in a ward volunteer bazaar required discussion about the cost of bazaar booths and debate over the purpose of the event. Did Sagyōsho really benefit? What did the ward do with the money from the booths? And wasn't the event just another popularity-boosting showcase for the ward chief's flagging administration?

From time to time, Sagyōsho received complaints from neighborhood residents who felt uncomfortable about having mentally ill or handicapped people congregating in the area or who thought that the organization was too noisy or attracted too much traffic. Every Sagyōsho special event was preceded by a trip around the neighborhood to apologize to all of the residents for any inconvenience. The events were also preceded by lengthy discussions of modern society's coldness or the attitude of "not in my backyard."

Some people took advantage of the open atmosphere to gain a forum for their ideas. An environmental activist who lived in the neighborhood stopped by for tea and talked about his latest projects. He stopped by again and plugged a candidate whom he was supporting in the upper house elections. More common, however, was sharing of less explicitly political information—the mention of a new facility looking for more volunteers, or circulation of a petition for ward support of substance abuse prevention groups.

Volunteer organizations sometimes had more formalized means of distributing information. Sagyōsho had newsletters and executive committee meetings. The mentally handicapped facility where I also volunteered along with Tanaka-san, Sasaki-san, and a group of other women not connected with Sagyōsho set aside a special time after each session for volunteers to chat with a facility staff person.

Staff members explained crucial matters like changes in the facility schedule or the nature of special events in which volunteer assistance would be necessary. Most of the meeting time, however, was devoted to general information about the facility's state of affairs. Questions from volunteers about facility problems prompted wistful remarks from the staffer about funding inadequacies, excessive demand for service, or poor choices by the administrative "higher-ups." She would sometimes even make oblique references to political corruption that led to the misuse of already scarce funding.

The most formal structure for volunteer information sharing was probably the welfare council's "volunteer seminars." I observed a three-day seminar for veteran volunteers attended by members of both Sagyōsho and the mentally handicapped facility groups as well as other groups throughout Nerima. On each of the three days, a volunteer "expert" gave a lecture related to improving volunteer activities. Following the lectures, seminar participants divided into groups to discuss what they had learned and brainstorm about ways of making the lecture's contents practically applicable in specific situations.

Each day of the seminar was quite different from the others, but throughout the three days ran a theme of tension between government's social welfare institutions and policies and volunteer activities—a tension that was equally visible in the less formal conversations I observed in the course of regular volunteer activity. Borrowing words from one of the lecturers, I characterize this tension as a trade-off between *gyōsei* and *yaruki*. *Gyōsei*, a combination of the characters for "to undertake" and "politics," generally means "administration," as in the combination of the ward's policies and actions in a given social welfare situation—care for the elderly, for example. *Yaruki* compounds the words *yaru* (to do) and *ki* (energy or feeling) to describe an attitude of willingness to undertake a difficult project, the spirit of rising cheerfully to any occasion. *Yaruki* was the lecturer's word for the greatest resource of the volunteer world.

Again and again the volunteer spirit, *yaruki*, was contrasted to its absence in the world of *gyōsei*. While all three lecturers made an attempt to argue that *gyōsei* had a proper role in the provision of social services, all three also provided ample information to support the conclusion that *gyōsei* efforts had been half-hearted and unsuccessful. Listening to the volunteers in my discussion groups and in the carpool on the way to and from seminar sessions, I realized that the message they took from the lectures emphasized *gyōsei* failures and *yaruki* successes. Volunteers shared loaves-and-fishes stories with each other about how they had made a project work with few or no resources other than a willingness to work hard and care for their community.

The second of the three lectures got the most interesting reception. The speaker was a man, the director of a private volunteer center in Tokyo's largest ward, Setagaya. His lecture focused on developing a more rational means for matching social "needs" (he used a Japanese transliteration of the English word repeatedly) with social services. His presentation was full of organizational charts. With facts and figures, he supported a claim that volunteer services were inadequate to meet growing social needs, especially in areas such as care for the elderly. Pointing to other nations for successful examples, he argued that the *gyōsei* must insert itself and its finances into areas where, until now, only volunteers worked.

After his lecture, a woman from Sagyōsho spoke up. She asked if government activism would not in the end destroy the special benefits of volunteer activity. Volunteers were moved by a desire to improve their own community life, a *yaruki,* so to speak. As they helped others who were in need, they developed human ties close to home. She argued that the special network of ties made by individuals working together to make their lives more fulfilling would make the community more human. Government programs might deal better with economic needs, she said, but it was important to realize that the fundamental needs were human. When those needs were met on a voluntary basis, other needs could be addressed through community cooperation. She used the Sagyōsho organization as an example.

The speaker disagreed, and he cleverly drew another organizational chart in an attempt to allay her fears that *gyōsei* involvement would destroy *yaruki.* But he had probably missed the point because he failed to see that the element the woman suspected as corrupting was, in fact, *organization.* Discussion was lively in the car on the way home after the lecture. One woman praised the speaker for being forthright in his criticism of *gyōsei* inactivity. But another complained that the speaker had been so detail-driven that she had nearly fallen asleep, and a third simply marveled at his organizational charts. "I guess he understands organization because he is a *shakaijin,*" she said. *Shakaijin* is a term most often used to distinguish a fully employed self-supporting adult from a college student; in this case, however, I think that she meant a careerist as opposed to a volunteer. In a way, she was damning the speaker with faint praise. She offered a generalized appreciation of his skill without indicating that it could be of any assistance in an operation such as Sagyōsho. She might just as well have called him book smart.

The speaker had argued that politics needed an adjustment. Too often *gyōsei* depended on the volunteer world. Volunteers, however, were unwilling to perceive their sort of action as a means for effecting political change. Just as non-active housewives felt that they could not turn generalized political concern into action because they were not and could not be part of a political organization, volunteers saw the nature of their work and the nature of administrative organizations as incompatible.

This view makes sense in terms of two important characteristics of these volunteers' experiences. First, they had no reason to perceive themselves as connected to *gyōsei*. Their position as volunteers vis-à-vis *gyōsei* was parallel to their position as housewives vis-à-vis a work-oriented society. Their status was unclear. The "volunteer" label, just like the "housewife" label, was a catch-all for everything from janitorial labor to food service, sales, and counseling. Volunteers saw themselves as similar to but not of *gyōsei*.

This may have been partially due to the second reason that the voluntary and administrative worlds seemed disparate. The volunteer's *yaruki* ethic and the *gyōsei*'s ethic were so differently ordered that neither could easily maintain its value when combined with the other. The *gyōsei* ethic, at least as volunteers saw it, was task-driven, but the *yaruki* ethic was spirit-driven. In *gyōsei*, human individuals were subordinated to the process of completing tasks. In *yaruki*, tasks were undertaken for the support of human individuals. Personal, flexible, individual efforts at human connectedness were the organizing principles that made the bag of disparate chores under the catch-all "volunteer" label coherent.

A Brush with Politics at Sagyōsho

An odd thing happened to politics in the volunteer world. Despite the volunteers' suspicion of mixing political interests with social problem solving, the women were not unaware of the power of politics to create or alleviate such problems. In fact, the longer a woman participated in the volunteer world, the more likely she was to blame politics for social situations that she found unacceptable. Nevertheless, this blame seldom drove a volunteer to conclude that she must dedicate herself to changing the structure of politics and policy to eliminate those situations. Instead, she often remained committed to avoiding politics when possible. Volunteers spoke of the importance of individuals, of the world close to home, of "human networks."

Sagyōsho had over fifty regular volunteers and more than one hundred people on its list of patrons. Because it participated in ward festivals and because, through its contact with disabled and mentally ill ward residents, it had frequent occasion to deal with the ward social welfare bureaucracy and other organizations like itself, Sagyōsho was even better known in Nerima than its membership and patron lists suggested. Sagyōsho seemed to possess sizable political resources — at least in the area of welfare policy. Yet, with the possible exception of one campaign, Sagyōsho members construed their organization as explicitly apolitical.

When I first began to go to Sagyōsho, Satō-san and other volunteers stressed the small, individual-level nature of the project. Satō-san framed her discussion of Sagyōsho by pointing to the scarcity of legal protections for the handicapped. With the exception of textured route markers for the blind, most mass transportation in Japan has highly inconvenient handicapped access or none at all. Schools seldom make allowances for disabled children. The high cost of living coupled with discrimination in the workplace and low social security allowances make it nearly impossible for most disabled people to live on their own. Families who do not want to risk ridicule or burden their neighbors by asking for assistance hide their handicapped children.

Despite the fact that many of these difficulties, especially workplace discrimination and handicapped access problems, might seem to call for broad legal remedies, Sagyōsho volunteers hoped to make a contribution to solving these problems without turning to a legal, or political, arena. They spoke of using Sagyōsho as a means of heightening awareness of individual responsibility for bettering one's community, but this Sagyōsho brand of community activism excluded *political* activism.

Satō-san admitted that Sagyōsho members had signed petitions for changes in the ward administration's handicapped policies, but she insisted that "changing things from the top doesn't really work." Sagyōsho's real purpose lay in working from "the bottom," helping the housewife volunteers and handicapped members of the organization to develop self-confidence. People must believe that, by changing themselves, they could make individual-level changes in the conditions around them.

Sagyōsho members resisted opportunities to act on a broader plane. A local non-party woman political activist, Motō Ryō, who ran for ward chief had asked for Sagyōsho's support in her 1991 campaign.[44] She promised to increase ward attention to social welfare issues if she were elected. Sagyōsho decided that it would be improper to participate in an election as an organization. The majority of members at that time did help hang posters, but I had been at Sagyōsho a long time before I knew about the campaign participation. In fact, I found out when I interviewed Motō after meeting her at a Sagyōsho party, where she was introduced only as a role model of an active woman and a supporter of Sagyōsho from the community.

When I brought up Motō's campaign, some women said they barely remembered it. Others stressed that Sagyōsho had not been involved—only its members. However, one woman spoke at greater length when we were alone. Everyone had been generally excited about the campaign, she said. They had worked hard and been disappointed when their candidate lost. But, after the campaign was over, Motō had not come around Sagyōsho very often; her involvement in the volunteer world was not hands-on. Motō had just used Sagyōsho to have an attractive image, the woman said, with a rare degree of bitterness in her voice. The woman did not accept the logic that working on the campaign could have been a matter of forming a strategic alliance with a political leader. Furthering an *interest* was not what Sagyōsho was about. In the volunteer woman's eyes, Motō's actions smacked of an absence of a deep personal commitment to Sagyōsho's human network. Motō, it turned out, was just as *political* as the current ward chief.

The volunteers were probably greatly influenced by the nature of the specific political events to which their volunteer activities exposed them. Had Motō won her bid for ward chief and influenced ward policy in a manner that benefited Sagyōsho or the community members that it served, the critical woman's perceptions might well have been different. However, there is no escaping the fact that Sagyōsho's political potential remained untapped.

Gyōsei Meets *Yaruki*: Sagyōsho Expands

In the end, it became ironic that Sagyōsho had been used at the seminar as an example of volunteer success in meeting social needs through a *yaruki* that did not rely on *gyōsei*. Only a few months later Sagyōsho more than doubled its operations with the assistance of ward financing. It became an example of how the power of *gyōsei* could shape a volunteer project, all the way down to Sagyōsho's growing difficulties with organizational charts.

Over the years, attendance at Tuesday, Thursday, and Saturday Sagyōsho meetings had grown until the little house and garage were literally unable to contain a single person more. Saturday lunches often averaged twenty people, and they were practically sitting in each others' laps trying to eat. By placing handicapped Sagyōsho members at part-time jobs in ward facilities, working at the volunteer corner, and helping out at other ward and volunteer welfare undertakings, Satō-san and Sagyōsho developed connections with ward administrators. When Sa-gyōsho was suddenly pressed for a larger operating space, the ward of-fered the organization a deal.

Sagyōsho agreed to operate from 9:00 until 5:00 six days a week and to accept more members, especially people who had been treated at and released from ward facilities. In return, the ward would pay the rent on a larger home and the salary of a full-time staff person, and assist in covering other expenses from food to supplies. Through a Sagyōsho supporter who had moved overseas, the organization obtained another low-cost lease, this time on a larger home. Sagyōsho opened the second home as the Sagyōsho Clubhouse. Meals were all served there, but the small home and recycle shop remained open at its former three-day-a-week schedule. At the new clubhouse members could take classes from volunteer instructors in everything from tea ceremony to weaving to English (the last of which I taught, rather poorly). Members made and sold cookies and items hand-woven from strips of rags as a means of making money and teaching Sagyōsho members new skills and disci-pline.

From the first, the Sagyōsho expansion produced tensions among the volunteers. Before the clubhouse opened up, I asked two of the regular Saturday volunteers about plans for the expanded Sagyōsho. "I don't know anything; it's Satō-san's project," one said. "Won't extra volun-teers be needed?" I queried. The volunteers shook their heads. Yes, more volunteers would be necessary, but they could not imagine where they would come from. "Who will the staffer be?" I asked. Again, they re-ferred me to Satō-san. They were dubious. "Once we deal with money from the *gyōsei*, we will have to follow all sorts of regulations. None of us knows how to do that."

Confusion reigned the day the clubhouse opened and for a while afterward. Most difficulties seemed to stem from communication prob-lems. A few volunteers were reputed to have quit because they felt "out of the loop" when the changes took place. Most did not quit, but, when I met volunteers away from Sagyōsho, I often heard complaints. "I didn't know," or, "There ought to be a better way of letting everyone know," or, "Volunteers won't feel very important if they aren't told what is going on."

Part of the communication problem came from the fact that the organization was in the process of change. Some things, such as the daily schedule, were not clearly decided at first. Activities that had not even existed at the old Sagyōsho were introduced at the clubhouse, and volunteers found it difficult to stay abreast of all of the developments. More volunteers, more members, and more services made the whole process of delivering information cumbersome. There was more information to be shared, and it was easier to forget someone.

A more critical reason for the information gap was a transformation in the nature of Sagyōsho with which many volunteers felt uncomfortable. I went to my first Sagyōsho Christmas party shortly after making my initial connection with the organization. The party honored members, volunteers, and patrons with lunch, short speeches, and a gift exchange. The theme of the speeches focused on individual development, friendship, community development. The speeches at the party in December of the following year were not much different, but in subtle ways the atmosphere had changed. In fact, everyone kept struggling to remember not to call the event a "Christmas" party. Although, there had been almost no Christian significance to the event in the past, once Sagyōsho was receiving ward funds, even the name "Christmas party" could signify a breach of the constitutional separation of church and state.

The "Christmas party" change was just an example of a subtle shift in Sagyōsho's style. I saw open conflict at an executive committee meeting. Members of the committee, Satō-san, the full-time staffer, and four Sagyōsho volunteers of many years were attempting to plan a general volunteer meeting with the objective of "renewing everyone's consciousness about the purpose of Sagyōsho." One member of the committee brought up what she called the "problem of the recycle shop." Volunteers at the recycle shop had been complaining about their relationship with the clubhouse. One volunteer had apparently gotten very upset, but, at any rate, there had been a string of incidents that amounted to something of a turf battle.

Questions had arisen about clubhouse supplies used at the recycle shop and vice versa. Did the shop have to pay the clubhouse for sugar it borrowed from the clubhouse kitchen for morning tea? When a patron donated good furniture or household items to the recycle shop, could the clubhouse make use of the items without officially purchasing them? Some of the problems had developed because volunteers were unclear about the extent to which the disposition of Sagyōsho resources must be made accountable to the ward administration. Even when policies were clarified, however, tension remained.

A woman speaking for the recycle shop volunteers said they had a "vague feeling that the meaning of Sagyōsho was being lost." Shop volunteers felt "lonely," left out of the goings-on at the clubhouse, generally ignored. She and another woman insisted that the recycle shop was no longer appreciated as a contribution to the Sagyōsho effort. Furthermore, the separation of shop and clubhouse activities meant that volunteers working on different projects saw less of each other than in the days of the old Sagyōsho. The human friendliness of Sagyōsho was endangered, some women argued.

Certainly, the atmosphere had changed since the establishment of the clubhouse. The old Sagyōsho had more of the feeling of an informal sewing circle thrown together on an empty afternoon. Everyone was working or talking within a few feet of each other, so it was hard to feel disconnected. People in the neighborhood and patrons with goods for sale wandered in and out of the shop sticking their head in at the sliding glass door to the living room. I can remember being sent on my bicycle to the store to buy snacks with change from the store kitty when an unexpected number of people came for afternoon tea.

With the expansion to the clubhouse, the volunteers and members were separated into two buildings, three blocks apart. The clubhouse was large, and it had an office upstairs where the staffer and Satō-san often worked, apart from the others. Sagyōsho was still informal, but the spur of the moment feeling had been altered. "Drop-ins" did not happen at the clubhouse much. A huge scheduling board hung along the wall in the main room, and what was once just custom — tea at 10: 00, lunch at noon, tea again at 3:00 — was marked up for all to see, each day, a month at a time. People no longer dashed out on bicycles for more snacks; in fact, borrowing sugar between the two Sagyōsho houses was probably a questionable practice in terms of ward finance policies.

Satō-san suggested that the upset shop volunteers were far too concerned with their own satisfaction. Sagyōsho, she said, was a welfare facility to serve handicapped people. Katō-san, another committee member, spoke in support of Satō-san: "It's nice if the volunteers can make friends with each other, that's one thing. But it's another to help out the handicapped, and that's what we want to do." Even Satō-san had to admit that things felt different, though. "We all feel cold because the Sagyōsho organization has gotten so big," she said.

The committee arranged for the general volunteer meeting several days later. There Satō-san passed out chronicles of Sagyōsho's history and gave a short speech about the Sagyōsho vision. Following Satō-san's speech, the volunteers each spoke about how they had come to be involved in Sagyōsho and what they most enjoyed about volunteering.

Satō-san's speech was similar in many ways to her discussion with me on my first visit to Sagyōsho, but it had an important difference in emphasis.

In her speech Satō-san seemed to demonstrate a conflict Sagyōsho experienced as it was moving into cooperation with the *gyōsei*. When we first met, she had described the organization as a chance for people who otherwise did not get out to make friends. She had seemed to place equal importance on the friendships of housewives and handicapped members of Sagyōsho. This new speech had a changed emphasis.[45] She spoke at length about societal discrimination toward the handicapped, and about taking responsibility for community change. This "community change" responsibility replaced what she had said earlier about the importance of developing the confidence to change oneself.

Satō-san emphasized Sagyōsho's achievements of organizational growth, the institutionalization of new activities. The tenor of the change in her speech could be summed up in the two-page Sagyōsho chronicle she had distributed. At the beginning of the first page, Satō-san had noted that Sagyōsho had started with the motto "Working To-gether, Living Together." On the second page, below a list of Sagyōsho's most recent developments, she had written, "We hope that we can help people who are considered mentally ill (spiritually handicapped) return to health while building connections with others to avoid solitude and working together at the clubhouse."

The Sagyōsho volunteers had different narratives, mostly stories of their individual awakening to precisely what Satō-san had mentioned in her original explanation of Sagyōsho to me — greater self-confidence and a feeling of being a larger part of the community that came from making a new group of friends. They claimed a thrill at feeling that they were useful. They extolled the inclusiveness of Sagyōsho. Even without spe-cial licenses or skills, they had found a place there. Of course, the vol-unteers spoke enthusiastically about the relationships they had devel-oped with the various handicapped, ill, or lonely people who had come to Sagyōsho. But they did not seem to see Sagyōsho as a developing social welfare institution.

In some ways, Satō-san did not take that view either. In the end, her shift from viewing the Sagyōsho project as a means of individual-level confidence building to seeing it as a collective force for community-level change still wavered uncertainly on the border of *gyōsei*. The *gyōsei* may distribute money, she said, but community members should never rely on it to take up the burden of caring for others. To make her point, she used the example of a ward proposal to increase voluntarism by offering to contribute pension funds corresponding to the hours someone worked. This sort of political program would destroy the meaning of what the Sagyōsho volunteers were doing, she said. People who volunteer knowing that later they would receive pensions were no volunteers at all. As far as Satō-san was concerned the practice would inject volunteers with interest, and interest, like politics, had no place in the volunteer ethic.

The volunteers seemed to agree generally with Satō-san on that point, and the meeting ended congenially. When I talked to Satō-san the next day, however, she was frustrated. The Sagyōsho staffer who had also attended the meeting had told her that she doubted that the organization was strong enough in itself to stand without Satō-san at the helm. Too many of the volunteers thought of themselves as "mere volunteers," Satō-san reasoned. Sagyōsho needed volunteers with a commitment to change their thinking and lifestyle, but she had no idea how to make that change in the consciousness of the volunteers. First and foremost, Satō-san said, the volunteers were concerned with their own homes and their families. She did not know if she had the right to ask them to change that.

Conclusion

When I left Japan, Sagyōsho was looking for a new staff person. Its first staffer had a new job at an experimental school. Otherwise, Sagyōsho seemed to go on harmoniously enough. The shop workers had made a special effort to eat lunch at the same time as the clubhouse volunteers and members, and no one was complaining very much about the changes. Nevertheless, conflicts remained to be resolved. Certainly volunteers were not prepared to perceive their work as an extension of *gyōsei*. They saw it more as a drama of the human spirit, or *yaruki*, that was conducted, as Satō-san had once suggested, on an individual level. Even while housewives can be community activists, they will not be likely to see their action as politically important. They hold fast to those aspects of community work that resemble housework and to a justification of commitment to one's community that is grounded in concepts that relate easily with their understanding of the nurturing responsibilities of housewives.

In this story of the volunteer world, citizenship stops short at the level of a hand-crafted human network. It is full of compassion and dedication, but it resists taking responsibility for altering policy and institutions because, as their distrust of *gyōsei* shows, housewives tend to think that politics will ruin what they do. As Satō-san's frustration with the growing Sagyōsho seemed to show, voluntarism can bring the housewife to the brink of citizenship but often no farther. Citizenship—involvement in the community on a political level—requires a different ethic, a willingness to see politics, daily life, and community service as rightfully integrated. The volunteers could not believe that they and politics could coexist because they assumed that politics always existed coterminous with a set of values and practices that would corrode the important work that housewives could do in organizations like Sagyōsho.

As Satō-san's comment that the problems of handicapped people in Japanese society cannot be solved with a "top-down" effort illustrates, housewife volunteers thought their work was necessitated by the very fact that those "on top," the political and administrative leaders, were ineffective. Experiences such as the discouraging stories they heard from staffers in ward facilities, the inconstancy of political activists who wanted to use Sagyōsho as a forum but seldom volunteered themselves, and the changes Sagyōsho experienced in its own organization as the result of a need to correspond with ward policies all helped confirm for volunteers that the "political world" was ill-suited to community-building work. After all, in the eyes of many volunteers, "official policy" seemed likely to render Sagyōsho unable to respond quickly to an unexpectedly large number of guests for tea. The openness and flexibility represented in hospitality toward the unplanned guest was exactly the sort of value that volunteers perceived as their long suit, and they jealously guarded it from encroaching politics.

CHAPTER FIVE

Toward a "Housewifely" Movement

The Seikatsu Club Co-op's Daily Life Politics

In the October following the summer elections of 1992, I was again making notes in Hikari-ga-oka, the neighborhood of high-rise apartment buildings where, as I mentioned in earlier chapters, the House of Councilors' candidate Ono had delivered a speech to a remarkably sparse audience. This time, however, I had come to attend the *Iki-iki Matsuri*,[1] a safe-food, safe-soap, information festival and market sponsored by the Seikatsu Club Co-op. The *Iki-iki Matsuri* was a far less explicitly political event than Ono's election campaign stop. Nevertheless, the Seikatsu Club Co-op is a self-consciously political organization. The purpose of the festival, to introduce the co-op and expand its membership, was, politically speaking, very similar to Ono's objective in delivering a speech — to gain recognition in the community and increase supporters. My purpose at the co-op festival was much the same as it had been in Ono's campaign. I wanted to know how women did or did not enter into a consciously political relationship with their community.

Studies of women and politics in Japan usually begin on a note of disappointment. The academic feminists who write them almost inevitably point to what Sandra Buckley calls the "reality gap" between the actual opportunities available to Japanese women in the workforce and in politics and those "guaranteed" to them by law.[2] In spite of the fact that Japan's constitution already contains the sort of equal rights article that the American women's movement dreamed of appending to the United States Constitution, and in spite of equal employment opportunity legislation in 1986, Japanese women have not attained economic or political successes in numbers that demonstrate their social position as anywhere near comparable to that of Japanese men. Even more disheartening, Japanese women's participation in formal political activities and representation in the ranks of elected officials remain yet slimmer than their educational and economic advancements would seem to suggest.[3]

Perhaps echoing the sentiments of many of her colleagues, a frustrated Buckley writes of "the extent to which Japanese women have internalized the popular projection of the 'happy, full-time homemaker' and the ability of the nation s/State we are calling 'postwar Japan' to recuperate or absorb isolated moments of resistance." She calls for a continued examination of the ways in which the "subjected condition of 'being-woman' " has been "in a constant state of production" at the "level of the family (social organ) and the State (body politic)."[4]

Certainly, the intractability of the gendered division of labor in Japan and its concomitant consequences for women's representation in politics are problems worthy of extensive research. However, in devoting a great amount of our efforts surrounding the gender division problem to the role of amorphous entities such as the "s/State" and society in perpetuating the "subjected condition" of Japanese women and their "internalization" of a "happy homemaker" role, we have missed important opportunities to see the gendered division of labor in its fullest complexity. Common academic terms such as "internalized" and "subjected" have led us to look *outside* Japanese women for the determinants of their experiences. We tend to assume that traditional gender roles always subject women, and we imply that women who knew better would toss their gender identities aside immediately. When they do not we are frustrated. Either an insurmountable oppressor must keep women from re-labeling themselves or women must have corrupted psyches—they must have "internalized" the values of vague oppressors such as the "s/State."

In fact, while much of our research focuses on the importance of the removal of legal and social barriers to women's capacity to participate equally in male-dominated spheres such as politics, those Japanese women who have made a place for themselves in politics have often done so more by manipulating existing barriers than by removing them. Moreover, although women's representation in local politics is still low, it has been growing unabatedly since the early 1980s; much of this growth can be attributed to the electoral success of women who make contacts and gain experience by participating in groups such as the PTA, block associations, and social welfare volunteer and environmental protection groups as housewives searching for a way to fill free time or represent their families.[5]

In the previous chapter, I examined how housewives who volunteer in social welfare activities may be seeking a citizenship on terms alternative to those available in political parties, through elected officials, and in governmental bureaucracies. The Sagyōsho housewives could be said to practice "bicycle citizenship" because they seek a public community unencumbered by politics. But some housewife activists—even many who are members of Sagyōsho—come to believe that they must enter the political world in order to effect the community changes they seek. In this chapter, I will discuss the Seikatsu Club Co-op and its political wing, the Nettowāku (Netto). The most active members of the Seikatsu movement consciously seek a voice in political arenas, and they try to do so without losing touch with the personalistic, egalitarian ethic that motivated the Sagyōsho volunteers. In some ways it may be fair to say that they try to transform political routes to conform better to their ethical standards—they try to "bicycle" into a political life where "taxis" predominate.

The political endeavors of the Netto make an especially good model of investigation. The Netto has grown from the election of its first representative to the Nerima Ward Assembly in Tokyo in 1979 to 117 representatives elected at all levels of local assemblies in 1996; in Kanagawa Prefecture, the Netto calls itself a "local party," and even ran three candidates (unsuccessfully) for election to the national House of Representatives in 1993. The growth of this citizens' new party movement makes the group a powerful example of the increasing significance of citizens' movements in Japan's local politics.[6] To the extent that the Netto is able to manipulate its electoral success symbolically, its policy concerns may be heard at higher levels and in organizationally better-endowed camps, much as environmental movements at the local level in the sixties and seventies won the attention first of progressives and then conservatives who hoped to assert or maintain control over the policy agenda.[7]

Perhaps the most significant aspect of the Netto movement, however, is the fact that its elected representatives are entirely women, many of whom were "regular full-time housewives" before running for office on a Netto platform, and the membership of the Seikatsu Club Consumers' Cooperative from which the Netto draws the majority of its support is overwhelmingly female. Netto representatives, the Netto organization, and Netto rhetoric are also undeniably the product of a gendered consciousness made public. The Netto does more than attract supporters at loose ends in a de-aligning political climate; it encourages them to express their frustration with establishment politics in terms of a *housewife identity*.[8] The same gendered separation of political identities that has long been perceived as a barrier to women's political participation in Japan[9] is the origin of the Netto's rhetorical and organizational force.[10]

A Lively Festival: The Seikatsu Movement

The Netto's manipulation of gendered imagery has paradoxical effects, and those paradoxes reveal the constraints of a housewife's bicycle citizenship. Most of these paradoxes were visible at the October festival, the *Iki-iki Matsuri*, I attended. *Iki-iki Matsuri* are held annually in localities where the Seikatsu Club has co-op branches. The one I went to was held in the public park, on the far side of the high-rise development from the station entrance where Ono's campaign band had gathered. The park where the *Iki-iki Matsuri* set up was more crowded on a fall Saturday afternoon than the hot station entrance had been when Ono visited the area. But it would still be fair to say that the festival drew a vigorous attendance in its own right. In fact, the co-op event was as lively as Ono's band of politicians and campaigners had been lonely. Amid the shouts of co-op contracted farmers marketing their produce and the hum of a band playing music from the fifties and sixties, groups of middle-aged women and young mothers, sometimes even fathers, with children in tow, strolled by rows of stalls containing co-op information displays, snacks and drinks sold by co-op volunteers, and bargain-priced, freshly harvested vegetables. At a play area, co-op members helped children build towers out of used aluminum cans and make tunnels out of old cardboard boxes. The ward had set up its earthquake demonstrator, and people, mostly children, waited in line for a turn at the machine-simulated tremors.

The festival ran from 11:00 until 3:00, but at 1:00 the stall selling juice as well as many of the other snack stalls had already sold out of their products. Women passing through the park stopped to fill their bicycle baskets with vegetable purchases, and the tent for resting and sipping tea and coffee supplied a fairly steady crowd of chatters. Women gathered to watch co-op members demonstrate the effectiveness of the co-op's environmentally safe soaps on grease-coated screens. The festival scene was so alive that it would have been hard to judge it as anything other than a success.

Whether the event's success in drawing a crowd would increase the ultimate influence of the co-op's consumer and political movements, however, was unclear. The festival's enthusiastic reception might have been partly credited to the fact that its connection to the co-op's social and political agenda was not necessarily apparent. The festival's Seikatsu Club sponsorship seemed underplayed. Although blue banners at each end of the rows of stalls and the Seikatsu delivery trucks parked behind the stalls identified the co-op as sponsor, one could easily shop the stalls without taking much note of these signs. People seemed to slide by the more detailed information booths. For example, I did not see anyone read a poster display comparing the quality of co-op and other brands of cooking oils through charts and statistics. There was a long line to buy *yakisoba,* a traditional fried noodle snack, but very few of the festival-goers stopped to purchase the co-op soaps and detergents. Only a few of those who had watched the soap effectiveness demonstrations and listened to the co-op members' explanations of how most commercial soaps damage the environment actually bought the product.

Activists in the co-op's Netto political organization roamed among the other festival workers, but they did not make speeches, nor was there much evidence that they attempted to impress a political message on the crowd through other means. One of the activists, a woman who had campaigned unsuccessfully for a second co-op seat in the ward assembly in 1991, walked around wearing a sandwich board advertising the co-op's volunteer counseling service. Beside her walked a representative of one of the co-op's milk contractors dressed in a cow suit. The cow caught children's eyes, but most of the mothers who paused while their children touched the furry costume did not talk about either the co-op or counseling services with the activist.

I stopped at the rest-and-tea tent for a cup of coffee and watched a co-op member as she made a half-hearted attempt to recruit two women sitting there. "Are you a co-op member?" she asked one of the women. "Haaa-," the woman answered, making a sound of hesitation, indicating that she did not belong while simultaneously failing to make a clear denial. She seemed to want to avoid any discussion of the co-op.[11] The co-op member offered the women information pamphlets. One woman took one, but the other declined, saying, "Oh, no, we came together." She spoke with the sort of politely refusing tone of voice that I had grown used to hearing during the Ono campaign when I offered posters or pamphlets to onlookers who were not necessarily supporters.

The co-op member gave up on her recruiting and walked away. I listened while the women remarked on what a fun afternoon it had been. "We ought to go to more ward festivals together," one woman said, and it occurred to me that it was quite possible that she might not have distinguished the co-op's event from similar ward-sponsored events. Perhaps she thought the co-op recruiter was just a bothersome interloper with no real connection to the bargain produce and the cheery music. The energy of the co-op festival in comparison to Ono's campaign event at the same location might have been just as attributable to the fact that the co-op event appeared so *apolitical* as to the vitality of the Seikatsu movement in contrast with Ono's organization.

In a sense, the *Iki-iki Matsuri* embodied the ambiguous relationship between politics and the Seikatsu Club Co-op, and, in turn, that relationship is a good model of the housewife's ultimately ambivalent construction of the political world. Undoubtedly, the largely housewife-controlled Seikatsu Club has achieved some real success at uniting the concerns of the housewives' daily-life world with social and political concerns. The co-op's political movement has made strides, as well, in promoting the political participation of "regular housewives" in its "proxy movement."[12]

As we'll see in the next chapter, compared to Ono's campaign, the co-op's Netto is a true grassroots movement of otherwise truly "unorganized housewives." Perhaps because this is the case, the Seikatsu movement is also an unavoidably faithful reflection of the paradox-driven condition of a housewife's bicycle citizenship. The Seikatsu movement explores the full promise of the housewife's outsider position in the political system. But as it succeeds in realizing this promise, the movement also brings the distressing side of housewife-citizenship into relief. "Housewife" consciousness can be a convenient tool for describing and justifying the Netto movement's political goals and for elaborating shared organizational principles. However, once put into play, the "housewife" consciousness also introduces constraints on the movement in terms of both goal refinement and organizational development that present potential barriers to the continued expansion of Netto gains in a liberal political world. The confrontation of Netto housewifery and establishment politics draws a picture, in bold outlines, of the possibilities and impossibilities of modern Japanese citizenship for women *and* men.

Later in the chapter, we will see that co-op members feel uncomfortable about the demands of political action on both their individual, home-centered lives and the shape of the co-op organization. The fact that they are housewives means that the co-op members are, in many ways, perfectly situated to build the sort of successful grassroots efforts that they envision. Yet, the co-op efforts are also bound by constraints and considerations that, once again, might be largely attributed to the fact that its members are housewives. Thus, the co-op can be viewed as a meeting place for the most complex issues of gender and citizenship in a postmodern liberal democracy.

The Seikatsu Club Co-op as a New Social Movement

The story of the Netto electoral movement is always one full of paradox. In part that may be a result of its origins. The Seikatsu Club Cooperative was begun by a man as a means of accessing women's role in the home in order to benefit a male-dominated social movement. Despite such a "male" origin, for much of its female membership the Seikatsu Club and Netto have come to represent an opportunity to access social movement politics to make a public space for the *housewife's* point of view. The Netto and its electoral movement are actually an outgrowth of the larger movement, the Seikatsu Club Consumers' Cooperative, which has over 240,000 members nationally. Because consumer cooperatives are legally prevented from operating political parties, the Netto is legally a distinct organization.[13] However, Netto activists are simultaneously Seikatsu Club Cooperative members and activists, and the population from which the Netto draws campaign workers, voters, and participants for its political study activities is largely the cooperative membership. Netto concerns are discussed at cooperative meetings. The Netto pursues policy goals that are in line with cooperative objectives, and one duty of all cooperative branch leaders is to further interest in the Netto and its elected representatives among rank and file cooperative members. In fact, it is fair to say that the cooperative was founded for the purpose of creating a support organization for the Netto established later.

Seikatsu founder Iwane Kunio started the cooperative milk buying that eventually led to the forming of the full co-op because he thought it would serve as a vehicle for mobilizing greater suburban support for his progressive policy concerns. Iwane had become active in the protest politics surrounding the 1960 ratification of the renegotiated U.S.-Japan Security Treaty. Opposed to the treaty, he joined the Socialist Party and became a member of the Socialist youth organization in the growing, suburban Setagaya ward of Tokyo where he worked to increase the local strength of the socialist movement. In 1963, Iwane ran for a seat in the ward assembly, but he lost.[14]

Discouraged by his failure in a local election, Iwane concluded that the traditional labor union-based organization of the Socialist Party could not establish a grassroots following in areas such as Setagaya, where of a population of 600,000, only 10,000 belonged to labor unions.[15] During a petition drive to gather signatures in protest of the hydrogen bomb, Iwane realized that the people whom he met as he went from home to home were full-time housewives. Iwane explained his choice of housewives as the object of organization to me: "The fact that housewives became the object of the movement has to do with the particular structure of Japanese society. The workplace and the home are separated. There are almost no workers who can commute in less than an hour. People who work are not in the community. The people who are left there are children and housewives."

Iwane and his fellow activists hit on cooperative milk buying because Shufuren (a national housewives' association) had been successful organizing women on the same basis. The co-op program started in 1965 with two hundred women who ordered a total of 329 bottles of milk.[16] Iwane is frank about the instrumental manner in which he viewed the founding of the Seikatsu Club Co-op. "The Seikatsu Club . . . was borne through a process of steps. I never once thought that I wanted to make a co-op. At the time I started the Seikatsu Club, I don't think I even knew that there were co-ops in the world." But, he adds, "because social movements are forced to develop in a capitalist society, it is inevitable that those movements must live inside of an economic construction." Iwane says that the co-op worked for his movement because it could tie its economic structure to necessities in its members' management of their daily lives.[17]

Iwane claims that the movement is only coincidentally located among housewives. Eventually society will be restructured through a restructuring of consciousness like that which occurs in the co-op. Then, both men and women will work, but under more human conditions than those that men now experience. Both sexes will have free time and both sexes will do housework. In Iwane's view the housewives should disappear naturally with the growth of the movement to its full potential.

During my first exposure to the Seikatsu movement and throughout most of the time I spent studying it, however, I met only women. That is not surprising considering that, excepting some of the founding activists and some paid staffers, nearly all of both the co-op's and the Netto's membership is female. In fact, the internal theoretical pieces written about Seikatsu politics seem odd when considered from the vantage point of daily Seikatsu activities. The pieces are usually written by men, and they tend to interpret the housewife membership as merely a beginning in a movement that will one day include a greater crosssection of both gender and occupation. In Iwane's view, for example, the most unique aspect of the Seikatsu movement is its approach to the socioeconomic contradictions of life in late capitalist society.

I think it is fair to claim that, in the eyes of the huge majority of its membership, the Seikatsu movement is what it is because its membership is female. Moreover, Seikatsu and Netto activists do not want their movement's feminine tint to fade away. One Tokyo Netto leader and former assemblyperson claimed that replacing remaining male leaders with female is currently one of the movement's most important tasks.

The co-op has its own research office, the Social Movement Research Center, and through this office it produces its own journals, *Shakai undō* (Social Movements) and *Dairinin undō* (Representatives Movement). These monthly publications disseminate basic information about the developments of Netto politics across the country as well as theoretical treatments of the Netto movement, placing it in an international and historical perspective. Seikatsu founders and leaders are also prolific producers of other theoretical and practical material relating to the movement. As far down as the branch level, and even sometimes on an individual level, writings, study groups, and discussions relating to the overarching sociopolitical objective of the co-op abound.

Among scholars and co-op founders and top leaders, the overwhelmingly popular view sees the Seikatsu Club and, in extension, the Netto, as some form of New Social Movement.[18] I think it is better to take a very different tack, eschewing these popular theories to examine the Seikatsu movement through its internal struggle over the proper identification of a housewife's politics. New Social Movement theory is designed for placing a movement in the external environment in relative position with other movements, but it is not effective in helping us understand the internal dynamics of a particular social movement.

The exact definition of new social movements (often referred to in the literature as NSMs) is still a matter for debate, but the category loosely refers to postwar, non-party-affiliated networks of organizations seeking broad social change in issue areas such as women's rights, nuclear disarmament, and environmental protection.[19] Iwane suggests that the Seikatsu Club is a new social movement because it seeks a fundamental change in the nature of society. The co-op brings its members face to face with the system of exchange. It encourages their greater participation in society and politics. And Iwane suggests that long-term goals of the co-op movement might be similar to those aimed at by other organizations he also views as new social movements—the German Green Party, for example.[20] Iwane points out that the co-op movement argues the necessity of social change according to a logic that cuts across the traditional conservative-progressive division of established party politics or "old" social movements such as the socialist labor politics. Moreover, Iwane claims the Seikatsu Co-op movement can be described as new on the basis of its organizational principles. The co-op movement strives for a transformation in each member's consciousness—that is part of why it is a "new" social movement rather than a traditional movement that simply asserts an unchanging agenda based on the members' class consciousness.

In other words, the Seikatsu Club is not "someone else's movement,"[21] but a network of fully active individuals who not only carry out movement duties but also, through their participation, develop a *shutai*. Iwane's usage of *shutai* cannot be rendered into a single English word. Often translated as "subjectivity," "independence," or "autonomy," *shutai* is a concept connoting an individual with the capacity to assess a situation independently, form an opinion of it, and take action based on the process of assessment. *Shutaisei* (*shutai*-ness) is akin to Ralph Waldo Emerson's "self-reliance" or to having the courage of one's convictions.

By focusing on the Seikatsu experience as a means for the development of a person's citizen *shutai,* Iwane presents the Seikatsu movement as "new" in its absence of programmatic, ideological content. The Seikatsu Club's use of a transliteration of the English word "network"— *nettowāku* or *netto*—as the name of its political organization is an attempt to make apparent the *shutai,* or individual, emphasis of the movement.[22] "Citizenship" and the "citizen's *shutai*" are key words in internal descriptions of the Seikatsu Netto's political philosophy. Even when they do not adhere as much to NSM theory as Iwane does, leaders stress the newness of the Seikatsu movement's concept of citizenship.

In his discussion of the co-op's history, one co-op leader, Ikeda Tetsu, locates the Seikatsu Club's formal move to a co-op organization in 1968 as synchronous with the birth of a new type of citizenship. Ikeda explains that, following the social protests of the 1960s, the meaning of "citizenship" was transformed; instead of thinking of citizens as subjects of a State, people talked of a citizen-created society. The State-citizen relationship was turned around so that the State became a subject of the citizen's *shutaisei*.[23]

A new understanding of organization and human relationships grew out of movements during the late 1960s such as the Vietnam War protests. Importance was placed on human relations that protected the right of the individual to express differences with organization, and individuals were encouraged to examine the contradictions within their own positions and develop themselves. While Ikeda admits that the new ideals of citizenship are often practiced less than fully in the Seikatsu Co-op and Netto activities, he encourages a dedication to furthering them.

The Seikatsu Co-op and Netto do conform to social science definitions of NSMs in many ways. Scholar Satō Yoshiyuki concludes that the Seikatsu movement is an NSM because, like women's liberation and the ecology and peace movements, the Seikatsu movement wants to reform both human beings and society. He stresses that the Seikatsu movement also fits with many other NSMs because, unlike the male-dominated organizations of "old" movements, the Seikatsu Club is dependent on a constituency made up almost entirely of women.[24] The concerns for peace, a clean environment, and a greater degree of political and economic self-determination that Iwane describes as Seikatsu Club values do seem to conform to the "postmaterialist values" that Ronald Inglehart has shown have made a significant impact on mobilization in new social movements in European nations.[25] However, NSM interpretations of the Seikatsu Co-op do not allow us to see it as a distinctively housewives' movement. As Lee Ann Banaszak's work on the American and Swiss woman suffrage movements demonstrates, contemporary social movement theory fails to pay sufficient attention to the movement "actors' *perceptions* of the 'objective conditions' " in the political environment in which they operate.[26] Banaszak explains that the collective beliefs and values a movement membership possesses, and the manner in which those beliefs and values are transmitted, will make a tremendous difference in the strategies that movement members believe are available. Thus movement members' perceptions of who they are as actors, or their identities, will have an enormous impact on whether they are able to choose strategies for action that are likely to be successful in a given political environment, but even NSM theory pays only cursory attention to the sources of movement members' identities.[27]

This is a crucial lacuna in NSM approaches to the cooperative and Netto because the housewives who currently embody the movement do not see themselves and their identities as coincidental. Like Iwane, they may hope for better working conditions all around, but that sort of broad-scale social restructuring is not explicit in the way most co-op members I met interpret their actions. They tend to connect their co-op activities with their housewives' roles, and, in fact, when their roles as housewives are altered, their activities in the co-op may be greatly reduced. More than once I heard co-op members remark that their fellow members had quit or become inactive because they had started working.

I did not interview Iwane until my study of the Seikatsu movement was nearly completed. When I did, I was startled by what I saw. I had spent months lunching with neighborhood co-op members, attending co-op branch meetings, and interviewing Netto activists, seated around low tables in cramped spaces, eating homemade snacks. I knew the almost conservative, but practical and feminine clothing a co-op woman usually wore. I knew how she laughed and entreated and leaned forward in enthusiasm when she talked. I knew how personal her accounts of Seikatsu experiences were wont to be, and I knew she would pack my bags and bicycle basket full of co-op wares—apples, soaps, canned juice—when I started home. We would bow to each other several times as I slid out the door.

I met Iwane in the co-op's social movement research center office. The long room was impeccably decorated; there was nothing cramped about it. In fact, it was almost bare. He sat on a sofa, and I faced him on a chair. Iwane took up room, throwing an outstretched arm along the top of the sofa's back, crossing his legs, laying back against the cushions instead of bending forward toward me. It was a rare posture in a society where space is always at a premium. His modish hair was long enough to brush the scarf knotted at his neck, whereas nearly every other Japanese man I met wore a tie. His dark shirt and black denim pants stood out in my mind: not a suit. He plopped a book manuscript on the table between us and, without further ceremony, launched into an elaboration of the relationship between co-op political philosophy and change in modern society. I got no personal stories and no apples.

I was certainly compelled by Iwane's explanation of the co-op movement, but after I had met him, I could not shake my sense of the contrast between him and the co-op's housewife members. It was a bit as if the Seikatsu movement had two distinct faces. Actually, however, many other, if not quite such exaggerated, contrasts could be found throughout the Seikatsu Co-op and Netto. Most of the differences, contradictions, and rifts that I saw could only be partially explained with NSM theory because, in concentrating on the organization and goals of movements, NSM theory fails to offer an explanation of how the social identity of a movement's participants can work as effectively on a movement as the movement can work on its followers.

While Iwane went searching among suburban housewives for his political compatriots, he imbued his movement with the symbolic content of the housewife's world. In doing so, Iwane and his activist companions took a gamble on the fate of the movement, whether they realized they had done so or not. The successes, as well as the failures, of the Seikatsu Club movement are more than the successes and failures of a New Social Movement approach to Japanese politics. The particularities of the movement's development are just as much the product of the housewife's experience, and that experience is often lived in a context full of pressures that work against the establishment of a New Social Movement.

The Seikatsu Club Co-op as a Housewife's Movement

Most of my study of the Seikatsu Co-op and Netto took place in Ōizumi, the neighborhood where I resided during the term of my 1991–93 field study, although during the summer of 1995 I both returned to these old haunts and broadened my exposure to the movement in other areas of Japan. In Ōizumi and elsewhere I met with rank and file members of the co-op and women who had been activists in the Netto movement, both those who had participated in the past and those who were active during my stay. I also attended several consecutive monthly Ōizumi branch meetings. These all-day sessions provided a crucial backdrop to my understanding of how Netto politics and co-op practice fit together.

The Ōizumi branch of the co-op was established in 1974; in January of 1993, it had a total membership of 1,192 households. After eliminating single-person households from the calculations, the branch figured its rate of organization in the Ōizumi area as a little less than 5 percent of available households. The rate of organization for the ward, Nerima, within which the Ōizumi branch falls, is slightly over 4 percent. Compared to the 10 percent organization of Hoya City (one train stop from Ōizumi), the Ōizumi and Nerima ward organization seems low. But the overall organization rate of the eighteen branches in the block to which Ōizumi belongs is only 2.4 percent.[28]

Within the Ōizumi branch, the co-op is organized on two different levels. Directly below the branch is the district. The district is made up of a collection of *han* (loosely, "squads") located in the same geographical area. *Han* are groups of individual members, averaging seven members a group, most of whom live very close to each other. *Han* are the most basic and perhaps, in a day-to-day sense, the most important organizations in the co-op. The *han* makes its monthly order of co-op products on a single ordering sheet, and the *han* makes a single payment for the various purchases of all of its members. Besides gathering orders and money, the *han* specifies one location, usually the home of one of its members, for delivery drop-offs. Products that can be ordered only in lots are divided within the *han* after delivery, and, in the case of products like pork, the *han* is charged with the responsibility of arranging the different orders of its members so that as much of the entire animal will be ordered as is possible.

In areas where *han* cannot be organized but sufficient members exist, the co-op also has an individual household *han* system. Individual households may contract directly with the co-op for delivery of goods, but the selection of available products is smaller and the prices are substantially higher. The "individual household *han*" is not available in all areas. It does exist in parts of Ōizumi, however; my neighbor was an "individual household" member of the co-op.

According to co-op logic, authority runs from the bottom up—from the *han* to the co-op block leaders—but the actual distribution of authority has some aspects vaguely reminiscent of democratic centralism in a communist party. Each *han* selects a leader, the *han-chō*, who is responsible for attending district meetings of *han-chō*. The district selects one of its *han-chō* as a branch representative. The branch representatives then choose an executive committee as well as a variety of representatives and committees to cover different aspects of co-op business—everything from recycling to obtaining contracts with producers for new goods.

The branch has the responsibility of operating in coordination with the block to which it belongs; the block is a group of several branches in the same region of Tokyo. Block business is coordinated at the Tokyo co-op headquarters. The Tokyo headquarters is officially under the direction of a delegation made up of representatives elected from all branches. However, day-to-day delegation business is handled by a board of directors that is elected biannually by the delegation. Technically, the board of directors merely executes the directives established by a deliberation process at the lower organization levels, but the board is widely considered to be more powerful than leaders at the *han* and branch levels.[29]

As co-ops are legally prevented in Japan from extending beyond the boundaries of a prefecture,[30] the Seikatsu Co-op in each prefecture in which it has been established possesses formal independence from the others; these "individual" co-ops form an alliance known as the Seikatsu Club Group. The heads of the board of directors represent their co-ops at the alliance level. In practice, information such as product sources and product quality research is shared widely among the "separate" Seikatsu co-ops through the use of the alliance organization. Furthermore, the alliance offers a unified system through which producers can deal with the various co-ops that contract with them to provide goods. The co-op makes yearly contracts with producers for the direct supply at a set price of a set amount of goods meeting certain quality standards.[31]

By making most cooperative product purchasing decisions at the *han* level, Seikatsu Club members learn to work collaboratively on things such as the least wasteful means of ordering meat products or the most efficient means of collecting area garbage for recycling. They come to understand the collective effects of individual decisions and usually develop close relationships with neighbors who join their *han*.

The Seikatsu-sha Nettowāku, or Netto, is the wing of the cooperative movement that handles politics—campaigns for office, accumulation of political funds, research for policy positions, and activities designed to encourage greater political mobilization among the cooperative's rank and file membership. Although I talk about it here as a single entity, the Netto is technically a federation of local organizations, the smallest component of the Netto federation. These are organizations of political activists grouped on the basis of ward or municipality. Therefore, cooperative members involved in Seikatsu politics in the Nerima ward would belong to the Nerima Netto; cooperative activists in Setagaya belong to the Setagaya Netto, and so on. Local Netto are brought together under umbrella organizations at the prefectural level. The Nerima and Setagaya Netto both belong to the Tokyo Prefecture Netto. Local

Netto in Kanagawa Prefecture are joined under the Kanagawa Netto. Because all Netto organizations are distinct from the Seikatsu Club co-operative branches only by means of a legal technicality, all Netto nationally are united by an emphasis on shared goals, organizational strategies, and use of research, networking, and publications centers that serve all Netto. However, the prefectural Netto are centers of key decision-making powers. As I will discuss briefly, later in this chapter, tensions frequently develop between prefectural-level and municipal-level Netto over the matter of defining directions for further development.

Cherishing their reputation as an anti-establishment, citizen's movement, the Netto organizations have eschewed representing themselves as "political parties" or "political organizations." As a Tokyo Netto activist explains, the Netto wants to differentiate itself from "interest group politics." The image of a "network" incorporated in the name Nettowāku is intended to distinguish Netto representatives and supporters from those of established parties, which, in contrast, are perceived as tightly organized, hierarchical, and excessively constraining on individuals in lower ranking positions. However, many Netto activists around the country have considered moving toward a tighter form of organization—a *rocaru pāti,* a Japanese transliteration of the English words "local party." In fact, the Kanagawa prefectural Netto has recently begun to refer to itself as a "local party," or, in a punning reference to its attempt to combine global concerns with community-level activism, *gurocaru*—"glocal"! "Local party" is a term currently popular with citizen's movements seeking to take advantage of the breakdown of the "1955 System" of LDP dominance to grow beyond the level of single issues or a few representatives to capture real policy-making power. By using the "English" words for "party" and "locality," a movement can indicate that it is, simultaneously, different from established parties and more clearly committed to responsible self-government than single-issue interest groups.

By and large, the membership in any local Netto is a tiny percentage of the cooperative membership in a given ward. In Nerima, the Netto membership hovered in the thirties throughout much of the 1980s and early 1990s, growing only with the expansion of representatives to the Nerima assembly in 1995. The Nerima Netto was the first Netto branch to elect an assemblyperson in 1979. In 1985, the Nerima Netto elected two women. Again in 1991, Nerima hoped to elect more than one woman, but the Tokyo prefectural Netto also insisted that Nerima remove Katano Reiko, the woman first elected in 1979, from the candidates' list because the prefectural Netto had voted to establish a three-term limit for all Netto representatives (the Kanagawa Netto has a two-term limit). Katano ran as an independent, taking some of the cooperative support with her. Takada Chieko, the woman first elected in 1985, ran with two other Nerima candidates; the new faces failed to win assembly seats. In 1995, Takada stepped down, and three non-incumbent candidates, including one of the losers from the previous election, successfully competed for seats. Katano was also returned to office, assuredly with a large measure of cooperative support.

The capacity of the Nerima Netto to field three candidates for the assembly successfully (especially when some potential votes are drained by a related, out-group politician) demonstrates the fact that the official membership of the Netto in no way reflects the numbers of supporters the organization is capable of mobilizing. Available support is best counted in terms of cooperative membership, but even there, the totality of organizational resources available to a Netto at any level is not exhausted. As one seasoned Netto activist from the neighboring Hoya *chiiki* (local area) explained, "Women have other networks like the PTA, school. . . . I raised three sons, so I have *tsukiai* [semi-formal to informal social ties] with other children's mothers."

The Hoya activist's comment highlights, again, the importance of cooperative and Netto members' gender identities to their organization. Ueda-san, also a member of the co-op, conducted a survey of branch members during her 1991 tenure as a representative to the branch committee. She found that the majority of branch members tended to be in their thirties and forties, with a sizable number in their fifties. Over 50 percent of her respondents were full-time housewives. Another 25 percent worked only part-time. According to her survey, therefore, somewhat more than three-fourths of co-op members in the Ōizumi branch might be safely assumed to be home-centered in their labor and obligations. Although it is difficult to ascertain the accuracy of her sample, neither Ueda-san nor anyone else I met in the Ōizumi branch or elsewhere in the Seikatsu and Netto organizations found the results surprising, and they seem only slightly different from the calculations of social scientists.[32]

In order to understand fully the nature of co-op politics, an understanding of the members' "home-centering" is indispensable. Even more than the small branch survey could demonstrate, co-op members were "home-centered" in their orientation toward Seikatsu activities. While

Seikatsu founder Iwane came to the co-op movement as a full-time po-litical activist seeking followers, those "followers," the women who joined the co-op, most often came as housewives. They joined as *house-wives*, in contrast to joining as workers or activists or even as simply women. The distinction is important.

When they entered the co-op movement as *housewives*, these women were extending their duties to a prearranged communal structure, their families. No matter how much of a member's co-op experience might be an experience in *individual* terms (for example, an increase in her understanding of economics or a development of her public speaking skills), the bottom line is that she joined as a *representative* of another social unit—the household. That household is intimately connected to the justification of her co-op membership and is the social structure to which she owes her primary allegiance. The household, therefore, per-meates the co-op, and its housewife members see that as an eminently reasonable expectation.

The Housewife as a
Defining Movement Concept

Netto movement interpreters such as Iwane Kunio em-phasize the fact that both the cooperative and the Netto are as commit-ted to the creation of a new, gender-neutral *shutaisei,* or new citizen's subjectivity, as to the achievement of any other programmatic goals. But as both Netto critics and Netto activists point out, the movement's sub-jectivity is anything but gender neutral.[33] The Netto subjectivity is more available to women than men. This means that the potential for the success of the sociopolitical transformation that the cooperative-Netto movement seeks to *engender* rests on the movement's capacity to reno-vate the current architecture of male-female divisions in public life. We can support these suggestions by examining the most prevalent repre-sentation of the movement's ideal subjectivity (*shutaisei*), that of the *seikatsu-sha.*

Seikatsu-sha, or "daily life/ordinary life person," is part of the official title of the Netto— Seikatsu-sha Nettowāku. The name of the coopera-tive, the mother organization of the Netto, is Seikatsu Kurabu (club) Seikyō (cooperative). A popular motto of the movement is *"Ikikata wo kaeyō"* (Let's change the way we live), and the *iki* of *ikikata* is the same character as that used for *sei* in *seikatsu*. The root character of *ikikata* and *seikatsu* means "life" or "to live." It is used in numerous ways to sym- bolize the Seikatsu Club—for example, the *Iki-iki Matsuri*—literally, "lively (or fresh) festival." *Iki-iki* might be written without ideographic characters or it might be written with the root character *sei* twice. For festival signs and publications, however, *iki-iki matsuri* is written using the character *sei* for the first *iki* and the character for the *katsu* in *seikatsu* (which may also be pronounced "*iki*") for the second *iki*. Local Netto organizations each produce political newsletters charting policy con- cerns and activities of representatives; as in Nerima and Setagaya, these newsletters are usually titled something such as *Seikatsu-sha Nyūsu* (news). The electoral movement has even been referred to as *seikatsu- sha no seiji*, or "politics practiced by *seikatsu-sha*." Understanding pre- cisely how the terms *seikatsu* and *seikatsu-sha* are perceived by movement members and activists is key to understanding what sort of subjectivity movement members think they are constructing as the product of their movement.

The term *seikatsu seiji* seems to have come into prewar Japanese po- litical thought as a means of characterizing a form of citizen mobilization that would stand in contrast to fascist understandings of mass political movements, but it became associated with consumer's movements dur- ing the postwar high growth period in the sixties, when it was first adopted by the Seikatsu Club.[34] *Seikatsu* can mean a variety of things. Generally, the word is translated as either "daily life" or "lifestyle." The cooperative's adoption of this word might be interpreted as an attempt to use both meanings. *Seikatsu*, meaning "daily life" or "ordinary life," may stress the practical, non-elite nature of the organization, its acces- sibility.[35] *Seikatsu*, meaning "lifestyle," is a reflection of cooperative rhet- oric emphasizing the necessity of changing even the priorities by which one lives.

As Amano Masako explains in her history of the usage of the word *seikatsu*, cooperative organizers in the 1960s found the word attractive as an alternative to "consumer" because it evoked an image of non-elite participants in economic processes without necessarily reifying com- mitment to a capitalist system in which production and consumption were the definitive or most valued human undertakings.[36] The idea of a *seikatsu-sha* or "daily life" person could be understood as a gender- neutral attempt to restructure the categories by which we conceive of human beings. But as Amano claims and my research demonstrates, *seikatsu-sha* as used in the Seikatsu Club and Netto *is* gender-specific.

Because the movement is a movement peopled by housewives among housewives, the image of the *seikatsu-sha* has been rendered female.[37] In short, as movement members see it, many—even men—might achieve a *seikatsu-sha* subjectivity temporarily or at different periods and in different tasks in their lives, but the premier *seikatsu-sha* is, by definition, the housewife. My work with the Nerima Netto and Ōizumi branch members provides vivid evidence of the "housewife" appropriation of *seikatsu-sha* imagery.

A good model of the primacy of a housewife identity in the movement's employment of *seikatsu* politics is Miura-san. Miura-san's narrative of her transformation from a "regular housewife" with an "allergy to politics" to an activist in the Seikatsu Club's Netto movement rang like the refrain of a familiar song; I heard it in bits and pieces from nearly all of the co-op activists whom I interviewed. In her tale of growing political consciousness, Miura-san unites a concern for the development of a citizen's subjectivity with her belief in the special qualities of a housewife's point of view. Where Iwane may have seen the housewife's world as a convenient starter kit for a movement with gender-neutral implications, Miura-san's account places the housewife in a much more central position. She interprets the movement as uniting the particularized concerns of private households with a challenge to the structure of political priorities. From Iwane's perspective, an inevitable social movement happened to start among housewives, while from Miura-san's perspective, housewives inevitably started a social movement.

Over her fifteen-plus years of co-op membership, Miura-san had served in a variety of positions, including *han-chō* and branch representative. Her longest service had been as an organizer of the branch's recycling efforts, a position she was still filling when I met her. At age sixty-one, Miura-san was quite a bit older than the average branch member, and, as a graduate of a four-year university, she was also better educated than average. Furthermore, Miura-san was certainly very active. Her participation in a broad variety of available programs, including the Netto movement, would probably place her in the most active 10 percent of the co-op.[38] Her high degree of politicization might seem to encourage her to translate *seikatsu* politics into an ungendered phenomenon, but it does not.

When I asked Miura-san what it was that was most important about the co-op's Netto movement, she said, "It is that just regular housewives are doing politics [tada no shufu ga seiji wo yatte iru]—that has meaning." The Seikatsu movement offers housewives an opportunity for study and discussion of society and the political world that is rare, Miura-san explained. In a short piece Miura-san wrote about her co-op experiences for a literary magazine, she referred to "just regular housewives" more than once in categorizing the movement. After a passage where she talked about getting praised for a membership drive by the branch committee chair, Miura-san wrote:

When I say "chairperson" it sounds like I am talking about some important labor union or political party leader, but everyone is just a housewife—working without pay from the ward election to ward assembly observation—from petition drives to administrative matters—from pollution studies to interaction with handicapped people—they are taking on a workload that can never be finished. They are all people who can't quit because they are thinking that somewhere there must be a good way to deal with all of this.[39]

The connection between the co-op and housewives means more to Miura-san than that housewives have a place for social action and leadership experience. Housewives have a particular outlook on the world based on the primacy of the home in their daily lives. The co-op taps special resources more readily available to housewives than others. In a practical sense, housewives, especially full-time housewives, have the large amount of free time necessary for co-op activities. However, beyond the time factor, Miura-san's understanding of the "goods" of the Seikatsu movement are tied to the "housewifeliness" of its membership, even when she does not always make the tie explicit.

The Netto movement, she says, has as its greatest political value the fact that it is completely amateur. Members are not paid, and they do not represent established interests. Miura-san's friend made the point that, tied to their companies and, therefore, the companies' interests, husbands are more likely to operate in accordance with or, at the least, be accepting of establishment interests. Because housewives exist outside many social channels—the regular employment system, for example—they are less accepting of establishment views.

This means of thinking about the housewife's position suggests that Miura-san and her friends' understanding of the relationship of the social movement is undeniably gender specific. In the Miura-san view, the basis of the division of labor according to gender lines does not change. The women's housewife role is simply seen as more important than previously, because, in Miura-san's eyes, it is the source of an antidote to political ailments. If men and women both worked and did housework, few if any would meet the "amateur" criteria that Miura-san and her friends see as so valuable in their movement. If they were not housewives, they would be disqualified.

The manner in which this housewives' amateur position opposes establishment politics is an even greater key to the link between the housewives' position and the co-op as seen through Miura-san's eyes. At first Miura-san could not tell me what the Seikatsu movement's political principles were, and she attributed this inability to the housewife membership. She said the co-op had no ideal image of politics because "it would be too difficult to get the housewives to all agree to it. Everybody has different opinions. In order to get them all together we would have to cut something . . . in deciding what comes first. And we have too many contradictions among us."

Nevertheless, a political image did come out of Miura-san's discussion of the purpose of her activities, and this image could be symbolically connected to a "housewife's" world not only by Miura-san, but by others as well. She recalled that she began to really understand the value of the co-op movement when she participated for her first time in a Netto movement campaign to elect a representative to the ward assembly. Although she had joined the co-op to get good, safe food for her growing children, she gradually came to comprehend the necessity of the broader meaning of the co-op reflected in the Netto movement's slogan, "Let's change the way we live" (*ikikata wo kaeyō*).

Miura-san and her friends agreed that "*seikatsu-sha* politics" could be a way of characterizing the co-op's image of ideal politics. She laughingly commented that she had noticed other politicians employing the word recently, and she wondered if they might be trying to capitalize on the co-op's success. More important, however, Miura-san identified *seikatsu-sha* as a gendered, home-centered concept. She said that the word *seikatsu-sha* evoked the picture of someone concerned with the management of daily life, the home and family, and she argued that the image did not fit men who were away from home, at work most of the day.

In all formal interviews, I asked my informants to describe how they pictured a *seikatsu-sha*. Many, especially the younger ones, were less likely to say that men could not be *seikatsu-sha,* but nearly unanimously they tied the *seikatsu-sha* to presence in the home. A common answer was, "A *seikatsu-sha* is what a person is when he [or *she*—in Japanese, gender would not be specified here] is at home, when she is taking care of daily life." Most of my informants claimed that, as housewives, they took by far the greatest measure of responsibility for the home and the management of the daily lives of all of the household's members.

Therefore, even when the *seikatsu-sha* concept may have seemed to be gender-free, it remained home-centered and, thus, placed squarely within a realm of expertise and responsibility that housewives claimed for themselves. Whether or not *seikatsu-sha* symbolism produced an image of woman-centered politics, it did allude to a set of political values that prioritized a "home-life" arrangement. This meant prioritizing a world where a housewife's role could be, and, in the housewife's eyes, usually was pivotal.

Miura-san's unusual education and activity made her tendency to frame her co-op experiences within a "housewife" identity all the more compelling. Indeed, considering her broad exposure to the Seikatsu movement, Miura-san's adherence to her housewife's position is striking. When a little-educated, inactive member characterizes the movement as a "housewife's activity," one may assume that the member has yet to have experienced the transformation to a broad social and political consciousness of the type that Iwane envisioned, or that she has too deeply internalized more powerful social messages about gender norms. But, in the case of long-time, active members who, like Miura-san, continue to speak of a "housewife's point of view," the inevitable conclusion is that the Seikatsu movement and the housewife's position have been inextricably linked. The movement comes to represent the "housewife's consciousness" for these members as much as, if not more than, the housewife has been influenced by movement consciousness.

Yamamoto-san, an activist branch member in her early forties, similarly linked the co-op with the *seikatsu* politics image, and, in turn, admitted that this image evoked the housewives' world. Yamamoto-san was more self-conscious about her housewife identity than Miura-san. She had worked as a dietitian before marrying, and, although she quit work to bear three children in quick succession, her original intention had been to go back to work by the time her last child was in kindergarten. Somewhere along the way, Yamamoto-san's life as a housewife, including her work as a co-op member, became absorbing. Yamamoto-san did not return to work. Instead, she began to see her housewife status as akin to a profession in its own right. She explained herself as involved in *shufugyō*, the trade or vocation of being a housewife.

Like the majority of co-op members whom I met, Yamamoto-san said that she had joined more as a matter of convenience than anything else. She had three small children, and going to the market, which was far from the new Ōizumi development where she lived, was difficult. Having good food delivered to a home nearby was attractive. She saw other neighborhood women involved in the co-op and asked if she might join. Unlike others, however, Yamamoto-san actively pursued leadership positions within the Seikatsu organization. She became a branch representative after only a few months of membership. Positions as branch committee chair, festival executive committee chair, and, within a few years, executive committee chair for the second Netto-sponsored ward assembly candidate soon followed. Even Yamamoto-san saw her path to activism as extraordinary. "I have been involved in an amazing way," she said. "Wherever I could, I have gotten involved."

Yamamoto-san is a committed political activist who, like Iwane, sees the Seikatsu movement as possessing sweeping significance for the problems of modern society. She resents the image she thinks many people have of co-op members as middle-aged ladies with too much time on their hands and says that she would welcome being paid for the work she did if that were possible. But, finally, she will not separate the housewife and the movement.

Yamamoto-san explained that she saw the difference between the Seikatsu movement and established political parties as a matter of point of view or way of looking at something. "The Seikatsu movement faces real *seikatsu* [daily life] problems. They [movement members] care for people so, for example, when they think of the handicapped, they are thinking of how to really make a town easier to get around," she said. When Yamamoto-san stressed experience with caring as a source of the Seikatsu movement members' distinctive point of view, she was referring to experience with care for children and the aged, duties that, in Japanese society, fall primarily to the housewife. Co-op members acquired the experience behind their point of view because they were women in a society with a gendered division of labor.

"It's not nature but environment," she explained. By "environment" she meant the daily situation of the housewife. "Women are different about organizations and power. Men just give in to them. They say *shō ga nai* [there's nothing to be done]." Yamamoto-san's views echo those of Miura-san's friends. Because they must operate outside the usual power channels, co-op women have remained "amateurs," and this has given them a distinct capacity to resist the interested and corrupt policies of the established power politicians.

Housewife Consciousness as
Political Currency

If an internalized housewife consciousness were simply a barrier to a woman's political participation, those who were most successful in politics could be expected to be least likely to represent themselves as housewives or think of their political undertakings as related to housewifery. However, the Netto case suggests that women are not always mere subjects of their housewife consciousness. The "housewife" as the identity of the *seikatsu-sha* politician was clearly present in the narratives of Netto politicians and their organizers, and at times it seemed to work to their advantage.

A woman who had been a major campaign organizer and volunteer office assistant for Katano Reiko, the Netto-sponsored member of the Nerima ward assembly from 1979 until 1991, explained the predominance of women among Katano's supporters by referring to the special ability of housewives to participate in local politics. The campaigner used herself as an example. Despite the fact that she was dependent on her husband's income for her livelihood, she was freer than he was to use her time as she chose. The campaigner explained that she possessed a sort of independence that her husband did not.

The new Seikatsu Club electoral movement in Mizusawa, Iwate Prefecture, also offers proof of the importance of a peculiar "housewives' independence." In the 1995 local elections, this Netto elected the second woman sent to the Mizusawa City Assembly in the past forty years.[40] But the activists who staffed the campaign were almost entirely full-time housewives. The current members of the proto-Netto organization that acts as the representative's back-up are *all* unemployed housewives, despite the fact that the Mizusawa Seikatsu Club Cooperative has a high number of members who are employed, at least part-time in family farming, small businesses, or the like.[41] Mizusawa movement members complained that working members of the cooperative expected those who were "just housewives" to take responsibility for the movement. They explained that full-time housewives had to bear the brunt of key organizational work in groups such as the PTA or Seikatsu because few others had time do it. The activists also pointed out that, because it was dominated by housewives, their movement was capable of bringing an important new point of view to policymaking. "Women come directly up against social problems that men don't think about," one woman said, and she claimed that male supporters had thanked the group for bringing a female perspective to local issues.

In Nerima, Katano's assistant further pointed out that, as a housewife, the campaigner was in the locality most of the day while her husband and the husbands of many of her friends commuted far away to the center of Tokyo, often not returning to the ward except to sleep before the commute again in the morning. It was she, the housewife, who knew the ward and understood its problems. It was she with a child she hoped to rear in a good environment, she, the housewife, who was really in touch with what was needed in the local administration. Takada-san, a Netto-sponsored assemblywoman in the Nerima ward until 1995, made a similar argument when I asked her if it was difficult to defend a housewife's entry into wider and wider political arenas.

Whether it's kitchen work or raising children, parents deal with a variety of problems and do a lot of questioning in the process of doing it. Many times when you are deciding what would be best to do about some problem, you find that society's usual way of dealing with it won't work. In the midst of thinking "What do I want to do about this?" I think the housewife's relationship to politics becomes, conversely, quite clear. There are some people who understand this right away, but it can take time. It took me time.

None of the politically active Seikatsu women argued that the experience of being a housewife was sufficient to prepare oneself completely for political life. A Netto member of another suburban ward assembly in Tokyo told me that she found the rough and tumble dialogue among the assemblymen hard to deal with at first because it was so different from the interaction she experienced in her previous, female-dominated activities. Katano-san recalled that she had been ridiculed as a nagging old lady during her first years in the Nerima assembly, and Takada-san said that she had struggled to develop her public speaking abilities. The three new women elected as Netto representatives to the Nerima assembly in 1995 underwent a form of teasing that they called *Netto bashingu* — net bashing. In fact, Takada-san said that the mainly housewife membership of the co-op was especially unskilled in dialogue. Learning the courage to express an individual opinion is one of the greatest challenges facing co-op members if they are going to expand the thrust of their movement, Takada-san said.

All of the past and present Netto activists with whom I met spoke emphatically about the need to study in order to develop knowledge and skills that, as housewives, they had not thought of as important. But the acknowledgment of a general lack of preparedness for political rigors did not lead Netto activists to conclude that their "housewife" identities were a handicap. Takada-san and others pointed out that most other, non-housewife assemblypersons were similarly ill-prepared, and, worse, Netto women declared, these other assembly members seldom felt compelled to "study."

These co-op activists used their concern for study to demonstrate sincerity. It seems that by admitting that they were still learning the ways of politics, as Takada-san did in a newsletter to her constituents, the women were calling once again on the political value of an outsider's status in the same way they did when they said that they were housewives. We could say that the Netto activists were attempting to demonstrate an arrogance on the part of "experienced" or "professional" politicians through their own example of the hard-working regular housewife-citizen. The "outsider" component of a housewife's political identity places the content of "housewife" symbolism at odds with established political power holders of all types. In part, this may be a strategy women feel forced to practice. Certainly women are underrepresented among elites of all parties; "experienced insider" is not an image most can easily support. However, the housewife symbolism is more than just an excuse for lack of mainstream political experience. References to "home" experiences are often references to aspects of daily life that are crucial to both men and women but that are *managed* by women, such as child care and meals, and in such references women can claim a more authoritative experience than men.

Feminism, to the extent that it is a cry for redress of injustices perpetrated on the female gender, is not usually a part of "housewife" symbolism. Instead, the symbolism implies a call for the reevaluation of aspects of life that, in the process of being relegated to women, were improperly ignored by the agenda-setting power structures of society. When I asked Netto women if they were concerned with altering the status of their gender through the efforts of the Seikatsu movement, they said that they hoped to do so eventually, but that other social problems were more pressing. When I proposed that the increasing number of women employed outside the home would reduce the number of full-time housewives capable of carrying on Seikatsu activities, I was told that, in the future, the structure of work should be changed so that not only working women, but also men, could participate in

Seikatsu-type volunteerism. Netto women did not seem to see their movement as a way to step out of their housewives' roles.

Within the call to reevaluate the importance of a housewife's *seikatsu-sha* perspective lingers an argument for reevaluating the status of women and their work. The totality of the reevaluation expands beyond gender to the nature of cultural priorities that affect both men and women; yet women are ingeniously presented as more capable than men of conducting this reevaluation. By introducing·the importance of the housewife's point of view to effective policymaking, Netto women are manipulating social understandings of the traditional housewife in an attempt to create a *non-traditional* political space for themselves. "Feminist" or not, this manipulation is gendered. The picture of alternative political priorities embodied in the "home"-centered *seikatsu-sha* cannot be as easily employed by men because they do not certify their *seikatsu-sha* expertise by claiming to be housewives.

Netto symbolism is ripe with implications for the social significance of gender division. Traditional gender roles cannot be viewed merely as a means of constraining women's participation in public life. In some instances, role conceptions may act as cultural reservoirs in which are preserved challenges to the social interpretation of what public life is and how that life ought to be organized. The "housewife citizen" strategy perceptible in these Japanese co-op activists' narratives may be one demonstration of the universal possibilities for power contained in traditional gender symbolism. When anthropologist Joann Martin studied the political activities of women in a rural Mexican community, she found that women employed traditional images of motherhood and domesticity to exert an influence over the political sphere. "When women began organizing formal political groups, the widespread mistrust of politicians had undermined the greater legitimacy of male politicians, leaving women an opportunity to offer alternative conceptions . . . women viewed men as self-interested and easily corrupted because of their lack of connections to the domestic sphere. They argued that the tie of a mother to a child should be the paradigm for a more honest politics."[42] Martin argues that by referring to traditional gender roles women created political opportunities for themselves that allowed an expansion of their role definition both in their own narratives and in the eyes of the community.[43] Kunihiro suggests that, in some ways, Netto housewives redefine the sphere of their housewifery. "Viewing housewife women as '*seikatsu-sha*' is none other than establishing women who were 'family housewives' as 'neighborhood housewives.' "[44]

The "housewife" works as a condensation symbol that provides the Netto movement with some important advantages. By targeting housewives in recruitment drives, the Seikatsu Club and the Netto assure themselves a constituency with a large amount of discretionary time, usually spent in the location where the movement is active. Housewives bring their own networks with them. For example, I found that, once I became acquainted with a member of an Ōizumi volunteer group who also belonged to the cooperative, it would be easy to find several similar trails of overlapping membership between the two groups. A PTA member who joined the Seikatsu Club would be likely to have brought several other PTA friends with her, and vice versa. Once motivated, many of these women were free enough time-wise and economically to pursue electoral activities with vigor. Duties they undertook in their housewife roles—visiting a child's school, representing the family in the block association, establishing friendships with neighbors, even shopping— tended only to expand and strengthen the webs of human relationships they had in the very communities that could provide electoral support.

The association of Netto candidates with housewifery provides a metaphor for a special worldview that justifies Netto political endeavors as a valuable contribution. Just as housewives are seen as outside hierarchical, economically powerful organizations, Netto representatives are seen as outside hierarchical, interest-oriented political establishments. Just as housewives make do in the home, scraping and saving to give their families the best, Netto representatives put citizens first and avoid the self-serving glamour of more traditional politicians. Netto women are caring amateurs. Established-party politicians are entrenched, unfeeling elites. The language of Netto activists is replete with references to their children, or their homes—even when what they seem to be talking about is "hard-core" politics. So, when Takada-san wanted to explain how much the new crew of Netto representatives elected to the Nerima Ward Assembly in 1995 would have to learn, she said: "There were things that—if you hadn't gone out and done them yourself—I couldn't make myself understood [by the new representatives] with just words. Now that they have gotten out there, they are starting to say, 'That's what you were trying to say!' No matter who you are, there are things you could say that about—*if you don't become a mother, you won't understand a mother's point of view*" (emphasis added). Or when another activist wanted to explain the special policy viewpoint of Netto women, she said, "They have a saying that women see old age three times—their parents' old age, their husbands' old age, and their own old age."

By subtly reminding their audience that they are housewives, Netto leaders can access a rapid-fire challenge to the nature of liberal politics as they exist in Japan today. Their association with housewifery is simultaneously a criticism of hierarchy, of large, impersonal organizations, of the pursuit of a politics of interest over a politics of compassion, of the absence of communal values, and of a lack of willingness to work hard for one's achievements. When asked, even housewives say that they think that the *idea* of a housewife-politician is an unworkable one because in a *shikoku shakai* (credentialist society) housewives could never claim to have the proper experiences. Curiously, however, the Netto's housewife manipulation of *seikatsu* politics *is* a means of claiming an advantage of a sort of politically important experience — experience with human beings over experience with organizations.

The Housewife Identification: Latent Political Conflicts

The manipulation of a gendered *seikatsu-sha* image provides the Netto movement with multiple advantages, but it also carries with it some risks. In using a housewife subjectivity as a resource, the Netto also catches itself on the horns of a dilemma: the image that gives this movement a justification for a claim of a special political view is also the image that undercuts the legitimacy of politics as a priority for women. The most obvious risk lies in the fact that, if Netto activists can readily see the primacy of housewifery in the definition of *seikatsu-sha,* others, with less general good feeling, will also be able to see the connection. Certainly, the negative aspects of the housewife's social image can stick to Netto activists. I have never met a Netto activist who served as an elected official who did not complain that she had been heckled by her male colleagues. When I attended the general question session at the opening of the Setagaya Ward Assembly in June 1995, I was surprised by the intensity of animal-like, harassing sounds that assemblymen made when assemblywoman Morita Itsuko gave her presentation as representative of the four Netto seats. Moreover, the housewife identity that may lend weight to a Netto representative's comment about welfare policies for the aged at the local government level where all parties are largely concerned with such social welfare issues might be seen as a barrier to productive policymaking at other levels of government. As events in prewar Japan suggest, a woman's voice in community "house-keeping" issues such as health and sanitation may not translate to a bigger voice in national politics.[45]

Despite the obvious challenges to winning respect from the outside world that the "housewificization" of *seikatsu* politics presents, the greatest potential difficulty in the Netto's gendered consciousness is actually the set of constraints that consciousness may place on the movement's internal organizational development. The gendered quality of the Netto image has acted in some ways as an authenticity seal on the Netto's claims that it is a "citizen's" organization. Precisely because they could not inhabit the halls of corporate or political power, housewives could be trusted to be "just regular folks," and, in an important corollary, the Netto movement could be trusted to be a group of "regular citizens." The newsletter that the Nerima Netto sent out to supporters just after the elections in 1995 reinforces the importance activists place on the "regular citizens" image of the organization. In a section of the newsletter where the three victorious candidates and two of the campaign organizers offer individual reflections on the most rewarding part of the campaign, each woman claims that she most enjoyed "meeting others, making friends, joining with others" or something very similar.[46]

As the Netto movement grows and becomes more ambitious, however, it begins to need an organizational structure than can support it. Women who joined the Seikatsu Cooperative or become involved in Netto activities often see that sort of growth as a challenge to their housewife identities and to the anti-elite, anti-organizational ethic bound up with those identities. Sometimes the challenge is a practical one—responsibilities in the home conflict with responsibilities in the movement. Sometimes the challenge is ideological—big organizations are hierarchical, subversive of the individual, and not to be trusted.

When the Seikatsu's rank and file members expressed dissatisfaction with the co-op, they usually explained their feelings in the form of the co-op's intrusion on time that they needed for their role as housewives. The free time and independence that many activists touted as the housewife's advantage are unreliably supplied. Many housewives are like doctors who are currently free from the hospital but still on call. When their families do not need assistance housewives can devote much of their days to movement activities, but family needs usually supersede all other claims. I heard members complain that *han* business sometimes required calling other co-op members at night when their families were home and husbands or children needed their attention. Order deliveries prompted other problems. Some said that they did not have enough room in their homes to store deliveries for an entire *han*. More often, though, members complained that they could not be home during the day to receive the deliveries. One Ōizumi *han* depended on a single member to receive and hold deliveries for distribution. The woman and her family lived with her aging mother who seldom went out; the elderly mother could collect deliveries when her daughter was out at volunteer activities or busy taking her children someplace.

Aging parents could be more of a hindrance than a help, however. More than one co-op woman in my Ōizumi neighborhood had to care for ailing elderly relatives, and it was not rare for members to declare themselves unable to take branch or *han* leadership posts because their time was already sapped by duties to sick parents. Long drives to medical facilities with long waits for the relative to be seen could absorb entire days. The parent who had so helpfully collected the deliveries might later be the reason a *han* member felt compelled to choose between quitting the co-op or allowing other members to perform an uncomfortably large share of her duties.

The fact that a member's obligations to her home always came before the co-op was clearly visible at branch meetings as well. Like most other housewife-centered activities I had attended, co-op functions were almost always scheduled for midday on weekdays. Branch meetings officially started at 10:00 and lasted until 3:00, but hardly anyone arrived on time. Around 10:30 women would begin to come hurrying in, apologizing for having been busy at home. On clear days when the family wash might be hung to dry before women attended meetings, they tended to be even later. Regardless, it was unlikely for the meeting to run much past schedule no matter how far behind the branch committee was running according to the agenda. At one meeting I attended, that meant not dealing with Netto-related business at all.

Branch members complained bitterly if they had to stay too late; they had young children coming home from school to meet or shopping to do and dinner to fix. The same women who had been late might easily dash out early. One district whose *han* leaders had young children decided to select more than one branch representative so that they could rotate meeting days and switch off morning and afternoon attendance in order to be home as much as possible for their children. From their perspective the arrangement was probably ideal, but at branch meetings it led to gaps in communication and the need for branch officers to repeat explanations and announcements when the information flow among the women representing that district had been inconsistent.

The image of political work as time-consuming put a real damper on the number of Seikatsu members who became involved in the Netto. One woman with kindergarten- and preschool-age children said that she had assisted in the 1991 campaign for two Seikatsu candidates to the Nerima Ward Assembly by hanging posters and making some phone calls. She did not want to do more than that, however, and she said that she would be reluctant to participate in another campaign. While she appreciated the Netto's political efforts, she was too busy with her children and parent activities at their schools to be politically involved, she explained.

Sasaki-san, the woman we met in Chapter 2, made a related comment:

I think that these [Netto] women are trying their very best, and I admire their efforts. But I wonder if they can really be taking good care of their families when they spend all of their time politicking. I want to help my community. That's why I do volunteer activities and joined the co-op, but I don't think it would be right for me to be out everywhere, even at night, doing politics. I am a housewife, and I have responsibilities at home. Katano-san is not married, so it is all right for her to be involved this much in politics.

Cognizant of exactly this sort of attitude, the Netto has established a tradition of preparing meals for the families of its candidates when they are in the midst of a campaign. Feeding the candidate's family is an important part of ensuring her readiness for an election.

Many co-op members seemed to interpret their Seikatsu activities as a means of extending their capabilities as housewives by allowing them to provide their families with nourishing, safe foods at cheap prices. These members appreciated having a community voice through the Seikatsu that encouraged recycling, environmentally safe soaps, and administrative efforts for environmental protection. They explained that all of these were important for raising healthy, happy children. Beyond that level, however, most members eschewed politics.

The Netto active membership roster for 1992 came to less than 1 percent of the Nerima Ward Seikatsu's total membership. Exposure to the Netto among the rank and file co-op members was actually much broader than this figure would indicate because Netto-related policies and problems were discussed at regular cooperative branch meetings and then disseminated to the *han* verbally and in information flyers. Nevertheless the Netto seldom got a high ranking on the crowded agenda at co-op branch meetings. At a meeting I attended, consideration of a

Netto request to recruit able candidates for the upcoming Tokyo prefectural assembly elections got only the most minimal attention. The candidate pool turned out to be too small, and the Nerima Netto could not find anyone to field in the election.

Some of the conflict that comes from the presence of the housewife identity in co-op affairs is evident in problems surrounding the co-op membership drive. Ceaseless, the membership drive usurped the greatest amount of time of any agenda item at all of the meetings I attended. If it did not maintain certain membership levels, the co-op could not maintain its product base and range of services without large price increases. Members left the co-op at a fairly steady rate for various reasons. They moved from the area, or their children grew up and moved out, making the practice of ordering larger quantities far in advance seem impractical. Sometimes a member felt unhappy with the relationship among members of her *han* or quit to avoid being rotated to onerous duties in the position of *han* or branch leader.

To both make up for dropout members and to expand the existing strength of the Seikatsu movement, branch representatives were required to maintain a constant membership drive. As branch representatives reported on the progress of their membership drives at each monthly meeting, it was easy to see that the "housewife" or home-centered aspects of the co-op were much more attractive than the "political." The branch member with the most constant recruiting success during the time of my research was a young mother of preschool-age children. She recruited largely from women she met in parks where her children played or from among the mothers of her child's preschool friends. Older co-op members complained that they did not have these options; without the home-centered bonds of children, they did not meet other women.

A pamphlet explaining the difference between the quality of co-op pork in comparison with grocery store pork was declared the all-around best recruiting tool. Members got testy when at one meeting a young male co-op staffer told them that the pork pamphlet was in short supply and they should make use of others. On the one hand, branch representatives explained that the pork pamphlet was concrete, and it related the importance of co-op thinking to the everyday food with which prospective members were really concerned. On the other hand, members protested that having to explain the co-op's program of rotating leadership and its political involvements made recruitment difficult. Prospective members wanted co-op goods; they did not want to campaign for co-op representatives in the ward assembly.

The cross-pressuring responsibilities of home and cooperative and the reluctance to take politics "too far" bled into specifically Netto activities as well, as is demonstrated by an argument that occurred at a meeting organized by the Netto for the purpose of educating branch representatives in Netto political principles. The explicitly political purpose of the meeting seemed to draw the paradoxes of the Netto's ideal of housewife citizenship into relief. Netto members found themselves heatedly debating a young co-op member who sought to depict Netto politics as the business of a large, hierarchical organization operating on a distant plane from most home-centered co-op members.

The meeting was part of a four-session series that Netto leaders explained they hoped would help prepare co-op members not active in the Netto to take part in campaign efforts in the upcoming Tokyo prefectural assembly elections. Because branch committee seats were regularly rotated, few sitting branch officers and representatives had held branch seats during the previous Netto campaigns for Seikatsu ward seats in 1991. The Tokyo co-op leadership required that branch officers from the branches in the Nerima ward attend the Netto sessions. There the combined branch leaders took turns reading and summarizing Satō Yoshiyuki's book about the Seikatsu movement. Netto leaders said that, through discussions of the book, the branch officers would come to understand the necessity of the Netto political efforts to the entire Seikatsu Club. Once educated to the importance of politics, these branch officers would be better able to organize their branch members for campaign support.

Branch officers seemed less than enthusiastic about the education program. Absences from the monthly meetings were frequent according to a Netto organizer, and it was clear at the meeting I attended that most of the branch officers had done only the most cursory review of the book pages assigned them. Few had made any notes or were prepared to deliver a detailed summary of their sections, and complaints that the work was "putting them to sleep" floated through the room just prior to the start of the meeting.

Ōizumi officers were the first called on to deliver their section summaries. They treated the contents of their section, a review of the history of co-op activism, with marked circumspection. "We were impressed by the efforts that the *senpai* [our seniors, our superiors] had to make," said an Ōizumi branch executive committee member. Another of her fellow officers was more interesting. "We were surprised to hear how it happened, that they were involved in politics from the very beginning, and that they were laughed at, and it was very hard. Those people were really doing it with enthusiasm. We were very jealous to think of how things are now." A third Ōizumi leader flipped nervously through the pages when it was her turn. "It was very interesting. I haven't, uh, really got it in my head yet, but, anyway. . . ."

One of the most senior of the Netto women began to complain that the branch officers had not been conscientious enough in their reading and referred to a summary by another Netto member as an example. She continued along the same vein, insisting that the branch members must have found something in the text that they did not understand, something that could be brought out before the group for further discussion or explanation. That prompted Tsubokawa-san, a thirty-ish officer of the Hikari-ga-oka branch, to offer the comment that the co-op movement's past might, perhaps, be less relevant today when the co-op was a "large organization." A fierce disagreement between the senior activist and the young member ensued.

The senior activist insisted that the co-op was a democratic organization in which any member could have a voice: "Sometimes we felt we were being used by the headquarters [in the early days of co-op politics]. But after I read this [book], I thought, 'Oh, it's not one person's hands — we are not being pushed by other people's hands. It's everyone together.'" Tsubokawa-san disagreed. In the *han* people did not feel involved, she said. *Han* members were being "pushed from above." At the *han* level it was difficult to see the connection between the reality and the ideals of the co-op movement, she said.

The senior activist's voice grew quite a bit louder as she insisted that the connection had already been made; it had been made in the 1960s when the co-op founders had learned from their experience in the 1960 U.S.-Japan Security Treaty demonstrations that political movements must be connected with daily life. She suggested that Tsubokawa-san's dissatisfaction with the co-op was unreasonable. The young woman replied that the Hikari-ga-oka branch might be peculiar, but that it was certainly the case that members felt that the co-op was undemocratic.

Even if members were *technically* free to express all of their grievances, the *atmosphere* of the co-op leadership put a lid on rank and file members, Tsubokawa-san said. She complained that as a branch leader, she was forced to compel other members to participate in activities specified by leaders higher up. Members were afraid to say anything because they did not want to offend her. When she herself had complained to the headquarters about such things as meeting schedules and time-consuming practices that made membership difficult for women with jobs, she was told to develop her consciousness and sent away. While Tsubokawa-san spoke, a member of the Ōizumi delegation nodded her head vigorously in agreement, but, perhaps embarrassed by the increasingly heated atmosphere, neither she nor any of the other Ōizumi leaders said a word.

I had heard Ōizumi members' gripes about co-op higher-ups before, and I thought that their refusal to speak out here could only be an example of the forbidding atmosphere to which the Hikari-ga-oka officer referred. Early in the argument, one Netto member tried to convince the senior activist that the young woman's comments that the co-op needed to change could have some merits. But, as the word exchange intensified, the efforts of others who spoke seemed intended only to quiet the Hikari-ga-oka officer. Another Netto activist agreed that relationships between the *han* and the branch could be difficult. She suggested that, in order to right her problems, the young woman should engage in a process of self-criticism.

"What is 'self-criticism'?" asked an angry Tsubokawa-san. "Is that discovering that I am different from the Seikatsu?" She continued. "I think you are saying to us 'reform yourselves,' " she said, pointing out that when she or her branch members tried to express views critical of the co-op movement, they were shut down. "We are giving advice, not telling you what to do from above," countered the Netto member who had taken the branch officer's side earlier.

A few moments later, the senior activist burst back into the discussion, yelling at Tsubokawa-san, "You are not a follower of this movement if you cannot get rid of this idea [that you are being controlled from above]. You'd better *reform* this part of yourself really soon." The discussion dissolved into an analysis of Tsubokawa-san's character. "Are you always so dark like this when you talk?" yet another Netto member asked her. When Tsubokawa-san admitted that she was not always very cheery, the Netto officer who had at one point taken her part said a bit sarcastically, "Oh, she is so pitiful." Other Netto members made similar comments.

The Netto member who had escorted me to the meeting tried to explain the conflict to me. She told me not to take the episode seriously as some people are just bound to be troublemakers. She repeated an insistence made earlier by a fellow Netto activist that the co-op could not fail to be democratic because any member who wanted to could become a member of the board. I did my own checking, asking other Tokyo activists how the board selection really worked.

As one woman described it to me, self-selection did indeed play a large part in forming the list of board candidates. Drawing up a model of a branch selecting its candidates, she explained that, for example, three names of interested women might be forwarded to the branch committee. But one woman might withdraw her name because her child was in an entrance exam year, and on reconsideration she decided she did not have time. Yet a second woman might withdraw after her husband was transferred to another prefecture. Usually candidate nominations came from among the branch representatives, and often the selection was decided as in the process just described—by asking nominees if they felt that they could really do it or not.

"It is really a housewife's approach, isn't it?" this woman said of the selection process. It is important to point out that the fact that they were *housewives* really did influence the way in which board members self-selected. Certainly, a taste for co-op activities and a desire to lead were important. Co-op members I met who had held many leadership posts were usually noticeably extroverted. With only the presence or absence of leadership ambition as a determinative factor, board selection could be viewed as democratic.

However, beyond personality, the particular circumstances of a member's home situation could greatly influence her decision to self-select. Given the amount of time that co-op activities could occupy, a woman with demanding obligations at home—young children, aging parents, an economically necessary part-time job—might easily feel that she faced substantial barriers to her rise in the Seikatsu Club hierarchy. And consciousness of these barriers might lead her to conclude that she faced a trade-off between her "housewife" role and a larger political role. Why the young Hikari-ga-oka branch officer with a part-time job might perceive the co-op as a closed, elite-dominated organization becomes clearer.

The same Netto activist who had labeled the young woman a troublemaker had her own bad turn with Seikatsu hierarchy a few months later. I happened to meet her and ward assemblyperson Takada-san on the street outside their office when they were returning from a campaign effort for a Seikatsu member who was standing for election in an experimental school board primary. Spring was coming and, with it, the time for Tokyo assembly hopefuls to make their impending candidacy in the June election (1993) known to supporters. I had heard of Netto candidates in other Tokyo wards, but not in Nerima, which surprised me because I had witnessed meetings and branch agenda items attesting to an election build-up and a candidate search.

Over tea in the Netto's narrow office, the two women launched into a bitter-voiced explanation of Nerima's decision not to field a candidate. In the end, Nerima had been unable to find a candidate who met the expectations of both the Nerima and the Tokyo Netto members. In the process of explaining this, the Nerima women strongly criticized the Tokyo Netto's operation regarding the upcoming elections as undemocratic. According to their explanation, more powerful board members had decided to seek endorsements and campaign assistance from the Socialist Party. The Nerima Netto strongly opposed such a move. They felt that a previous Seikatsu Tokyo assemblyperson had been unduly influenced by the Socialist Party endorsement she received and, that, at any rate, the Socialist Party was on its way out as a national political power.

Worse than seeking the endorsement, however, was the manner in which the powerful board chair had forced the idea on other Netto members, Takada-san said. The woman who had escorted me to the reading group described the structure of the Tokyo Netto: "The Tokyo prefectural level Netto came about after a few of the local Nettos [like the ward-level Netto in Nerima] developed. There was a lot of opposition because some said that it would create a pyramidal structure [both women formed a pyramid with their hands], and that is exactly what has happened. Now the Tokyo Netto tries to tell us what to do and everything comes from up above."

Takada-san jumped in again. "The board chair [she pointed out angrily that he was a man] used to be a socialist, and now he wants to go back." She claimed that when the Nerima Netto expressed opposition to Tokyo Netto policies, other wards just stood by silently, even though they probably agreed with the Nerima women. The Tokyo Netto even threatened to stomp Nerima's attempts at independent action contrary to Tokyo-level policy. "That is completely anti-democratic," said Takada-san, "but what is worse is probably what is not said."

The other activist complained that in their desire to expand the political power of the Seikatsu movement, the Tokyo Netto had lost sight of the importance of individual democratic action at the local community level. The woman twisted a necklace around her throat in agitation as she talked: "I look at this thing [the meeting about the assembly elections], and I think I am not a person cut out for large organizations. I keep seeing more and more about what's really going on. When I first joined the co-op, I didn't like the idea of a co-op organization. But what they said about getting your own self straightened out—what they said was good."

She began to talk over ways of changing the Netto structure to allow for more local autonomy. She and Takada-san admitted that they thought of quitting. In the end, she said she blamed the situation on the other local activists who had been unwilling to express their opinions. No one was willing to think on her own, she said. The Nerima Netto members did, but, unfortunately, they were locked into the co-op's undemocratic pyramid, and every time the Nerima women stood up in opposition, everyone looked at them as if to say, "Oh, no, not you again."

"We can never be innocent again," said Takada-san, ruefully.

Evaluating Netto Potential in the Long Run

Two years later, Takada-san stepped down as the Netto representative and was replaced by three women who had never held office before. In a new, much larger Nerima Netto office, she reflected on her choice to step down. Takada-san's own words on her "retirement" bear out many of the paradoxes the Netto movement faces. Overall, Takada-san's decision reflected her desire to support the term-limit system that the Tokyo Netto had adopted in 1991. Although the Tokyo Netto permits its representatives three terms and she had served only two, she still felt she had served long enough to endanger the connection between her as a representative and other movement members. She claimed that, from the start of her second term, supporters had begun to ask her if she would stand again. "That's wrong. They are the ones who put me in politics. Those who put me there should decide if they want to keep me. I shouldn't decide," Takada-san said, explaining that, once citizens leave such decisions up to their elected officials, they have surrendered their position as citizens. Still, she admitted to having regrets about leaving her position.

When I reached my seventh or eighth year of service, I finally realized that I was able to say the things I should, that I wanted to say, but hadn't been able to say at first. That's why I understand that, no matter if you are a Netto representative or some other party, it's, of course, the third term where you finally can get things done.

However, if I had decided to go ahead and just do a third term, the whole idea of this movement as something we all do together would break down. It would be left to me. It would be "you are the person who goes out and does it for us." To be frank, it was already starting to break down.

[The point] is not to become a representative because you want to . . . the role is to go out and spread what citizens are thinking—I thought about [my retirement] from that point. If we do not expand the numbers of people who are participating in putting their representative out there, we won't be able to return the assembly to the citizens.

Takada-san gave into her view of the Netto movement as a "regular person's" movement that practices amateur politics, but she had regrets about losing a job she had come to like and concerns about the ability of the new representatives to succeed. In fact, what worried her most about one of the recently elected women was that the woman would not be able to juggle her responsibilities as a housewife and an assemblyperson—even though Takada-san herself had become a representative as housewife, and when she won her first term, her youngest child had been only a year older than the new woman's kindergarten-aged child.

She [the new person] thought about it for a month and decided, okay, I'll run. She seems to have thought it would be just an election, and then she won. Her husband had thought she would lose so he had patience with the campaign, but he was shocked when she won. . . . When her candidacy was considered, I didn't push for it because I thought it would really be hard for her. I told her it's really hard, especially because she places a lot of importance on raising her children. I'm the sort that can just somehow get [the kids] taken care of and that's good. But I thought it would be hard for her, and I told her maybe it would be good to quit. But she had made up her mind, and once you've made up your mind you've got to go through with it.

Takada-san's comments exhibit concerns echoed currently at all levels of the Netto organization. How can the movement avoid creating "professional" politicians without sacrificing its most experienced activists? How can the movement balance the advantages of its "regular housewife," volunteer image with the need for devoted activists with the freedom and desire to make movement objectives a priority? And although Takada-san doesn't mention it, recently the Netto has been struggling to find a means of employing its growing body of "former" elected officials. Nerima has chosen to pay Takada-san a small salary to continue to work with the Netto as a policy advisor. In another ward, the most senior of the elected representatives in the ward assembly, currently in her third and final term, worries what will happen to her when she retires. In contrast to my first meeting with her in 1990, she is no longer fully supportive of the Netto policy that requires a representative to contribute half of her assemblyperson salary to general Netto coffers. She has divorced since she joined the movement and now uses her representative's salary to support herself; she wants to know what the movement will offer in return for twelve years of her life. In Kanagawa Prefecture, a few women, former representatives to the prefectural assembly, have been working for years on election to the National Diet, but so far their efforts seem bound to failure for a variety of reasons, and I have heard more than one Netto activist complain that such efforts desert the original "grassroots" purpose of the movement.

In many ways, I think it is too early to draw conclusions about the Netto and its gendered political strategy. The instability and confusion among political leaders at the national level ought to leave us uncertain about the future configuration of the Japanese party system. Disaffection in the electorate may prompt a broad, continuous decline in turnout without any altered trend in election results, or it may mean powerful banks of support for a new political group such as a Netto "local party." However we find the Netto activists five or ten years down the road, I am sure that their gendered *seikatsu* politics are provocative now. Netto activists have achieved a *very rare* thing—a political organization dominated overwhelmingly by women who fill traditional gender roles (albeit with many modifications) and still successfully elect themselves to office at a variety of levels. The criticism of establishment politics that these women represent is also rare because it challenges the validity of the ungendered, universal citizen ideal of liberal democracy by arguing that one gender can see some human realities better than the other.

Part way through the question period in the Setagaya Ward Assembly on the day that I listened to the male assemblypeople heckle Morita-san, Ōkawahara-san, the Netto-backed representative of Setagaya in the Tokyo Prefectural Assembly, and her children entered the gallery above the assembly floor. They sat near me, calm and interested while their representative spoke and the suited men of more "mainstream" parties grunted. Those men, of course, retained their "seats of power." But Ōkawahara-san and her children had a stunning dignity—and, besides, in technical terms, she was a higher-level politician than any of the grunters.

The scene brought *home* an important point about the expectations of modern democratic politics. A study of the Netto movement asks us to acknowledge the resourcefulness with which women may greet a gendered identity from which they have little power to exempt themselves. We can see that, even within larger, oppressive "discursive practices" there is room for a type of agency that must command some of our attention. However, the calm "family women" in the sea of grunting men asks yet more of us. We can easily see the disadvantages present in the fact that these women activists are so closely identified with their (often unchosen) roles as homemakers. But what about the disadvantages present in modern politics? The Netto movement forces us to ask: Why is the role of caretaker of other human beings so little regarded? Why does being stamped as the one whose priorities will be the welfare of others *necessarily* impute low status? Why does the "successful" modern citizen turn out to be a grunting, middle-aged man in *nezumi-iro* (rat-colored—a common Japanese term for suit colors) clothes? Why should it be Ōkawahara-san's image as a calm mother with her children that is the oppressive, "internalized" one? Finally, the Netto movement brings even many feminist assumptions into question. If women can parlay the most "privatizing" of all gender roles into a bid for a public voice, into a sort of "sisterhood," how are we to understand, even re-evaluate the goals of feminist analysis of politics? One thing is certain: addressing any of these compelling issues will require that students of Japanese politics go further afield than they have been willing to so far.

CHAPTER SIX

The Ono Campaign

A "Regular" Housewife in Elite Politics

It's 5:30 on July 19, 1992, a Sunday afternoon in the Ginza. Traffic has been blocked from entering the main street in order to create a "walker's heaven." But the "walker's heaven" will end at 6:00, and few have lingered to enjoy the remains of paradise. It is hard to believe that this is Tokyo's most famous shopping district, probably one of the premier collections of clothing designers' shops, swank restaurants, and costly amusement spots in the world. Then again, it is so hot and humid a day that it might be hard to muster the energy to believe in anything. Today, the rainy season has at last come to an end, say weather reports.

This steamy afternoon is the second, and last, "Campaign Sunday" in the eighteen-day official campaign period of the House of Councilors election for 1992. On the coming Sunday, voters will cast their ballots. One of the competitors for those ballots, Ono Kiyoko, a woman member of the Liberal Democratic Party and a current member of the House of Councilors, leads a tired procession down the still shopping street. Ono's words and actions, in the Ginza and other places this day, embody the true dilemma of her campaign. As the picture of her riding a bicycle on the back of one of her pre-campaign leaflets symbolizes, Ono is seeking the same benefits of "housewife in politics" that the members of the Netto movement discussed in the previous chapter sought. However, Ono's position as an elite member of the dominant Liberal Democratic Party means that the use of a housewifery image is inherently fraught with problems.

Ono's 1992 campaign demonstrates how real the difficulties facing the development of the Netto movement are. Netto politicians find that as their movement grows, the requirements of an organization that can be competitive in the political mainstream conflict with important aspects of the very housewife ethic that justifies their followers' entrance into politics. Trying to speak from a "daily life" point of view in the midst of an established political party organization, Ono exemplifies the Netto problem in reverse.

In her campaign rhetoric Ono cultivates an image of a housewife who has reluctantly turned to politics because, as a concerned housewife and mother, she can not overlook the serious issues of her society. Her rhetoric presents housewifery as an antidote to the murky, dirty organizations that voters perceive as dominating politics. Yet, in order to obtain a forum for presenting her housewife rhetoric, Ono has had to immerse herself in the organizational realities of the elite, mainstream politics against which she purports to stand. Her campaign organization is a smoky insider's world of other politicians and back rooms full of men, places where housewives seldom go. Ironically, however, Ono never reaps the full benefits of "taxi" politics. Her housewife-like self-presentation wins her few friends within the male-dominated power circles of her own party, and even when she does manage to present her housewife image to voters, Ono can be undercut by the conflicting messages put out by the surrounding trappings of her elite political world.

To some, Ono may seem to be simply a coldly calculating politician, selling whatever image she thinks voters will buy, but that would be an unfair view of who Ono is. In many ways, though she is seldom in the home, Ono experiences a housewife's distance from political elites with as much if not more acuity than any of the actually unorganized housewives in Chapter 3. Ono experiences, as non-elite women suspect, that she needs a huge organization, money, and men in order to claim her seat in politics, and Ono also experiences, as non-elite women suspect, that those resources are harder for women to come by than for men. When organizational power is divvied up, it seldom goes first to those who speak for the home. When she travels the highways of Japanese politics, Ono finds it difficult to bring her bicycle—and sometimes difficult to hail a cab. When she speaks for the unorganized housewife, Ono knows to whom she refers and, through that referral, with whom she draws a critical comparison.

Ono's Dual Duty:
Rhetoric and Organization Compete

Like the United States Senate, elections in the House of Councilors are staggered so that only a portion of the seats are up for election every three years. A mixed proportional representation and medium district plurality representation system makes the electoral structure a bit more complicated. Of the House of Councilor's 252 seats, 152 are selected by the direct election of individual competitors for seats in a combination of multi-member and single-member districts. These 152 seats are selected on the basis of staggered elections, held every three years. For example, the Tokyo Prefecture has a total of eight seats allotted to it in the House of Councilors. Every three years, four of the eight Tokyo metropolitan area seats come up for election. These four seats are chosen at-large within the Tokyo prefectural unit. Voters select their single most preferred candidate by name, and the four candidates with the most votes win seats. In every House of Councilors election, voters also cast ballots for most preferred party; these are counted for an at-large national proportional representation district. The parties are allocated a percentage of proportional representation seats that accords with the percentage of the total votes for their party. Parties select holders of these seats from a list prepared for this purpose and publicized prior to the election.[1]

In 1992, Ono competed with six major candidates for one of the four Tokyo seats for election. One of those candidates, Ogura Motoi, was from Ono's own party. With exactly a week to go until election day, the readings that campaign staffers were getting from the media were fluctuating wildly, showing her winning in first place or losing altogether. The procession-plus-speech campaign event that took place in the Ginza is known in Japanese as a *yūzei*. As Ono reenacted a *yūzei* like her Ginza procession at location after location throughout the Tokyo metropolitan area, she was performing one of the most classic acts of any democratic political system. She was attempting to persuade the people of her constituency to use the powers of their citizenship in a particular manner — this time to choose her as a member of the ruling class, to elect her to the House of Councilors. When Ono was elected a week later, her efforts at persuasion were labeled a success, but in the months of struggles she faced in achieving that success, we can see a complicated process of delimitation of her political identity, in which the voters were only the most peripheral of participants. In public appearance after public appearance, Ono claimed that, among other things, she hoped to be the "representative of the unorganized housewife." But before the voters could make their choices, the extent to which Ono could really be a housewife in politics was already determined.

The location of Ono's rhetorical presentations varied greatly—from small meetings of fewer than fifty to choreographed shows before an audience of thousands, from the shopping street appearances like the one in the Ginza to *kōenkai* (political support group) newsletters that were sent to the homes of friends and family of her supporters. Her own choice of words and the words of those who presented her were altered somewhat to match the nature of her location. For example, in front of other women LDP activists, she often chose to emphasize the difficult challenge she faced in her opponents, while in an aging shopping district, she usually spoke with concern about the decline of small business. In a downtown business district at lunch she spoke about improving working conditions for female office staff. Although these variations were an important signal of the polymorphous nature of the constituency she hoped to reach, they did not displace a remarkable constancy in her portrayal of herself as a peculiar kind of "ordinary person"—the housewife citizen.

The portrayal of Ono as housewife citizen was probably not entirely her own invention. Theorists like Ueno Chizuko argue that the housewife image is forced on women because it is commodified by Japan's patriarchal capitalist society.[2] Some argue that "motherhood" has become a cult in the wake of the postwar breakdown of traditional communities. Certainly, forced or unforced, a motherhood ideology is present in conservative party politics on a larger scale than Ono's campaign.[3] When I attended a 1992 elections kick-off rally for assembled women's sections of the Tokyo LDP organization, I was struck by the frequent referrals to the audience as the "mothers of Japan" and comments by male politicians such as, "As mothers you can protect the environment . . . think of the peaceful future of Japan and your child . . . you must overlook the embarrassing digression of the Sagawa scandal because the LDP will protect peace and abundance for the future, for your children."

Pragmatic reasons for Ono's cozy relationship with the motherhood image were also readily apparent, however. People I knew often referred to Ono as what is known in Japan as a "talent" legislator. "Talent" is a derogatory label for legislators who earned their fame in a non-political field like acting, newscasting, or, as in Ono's case, sports—she won a bronze meal for her gymnastic performance in the 1964 Tokyo Olympics. "Talent" implies that a legislator has little substance, and Ono could hardly afford to develop a "fluffy" image in comparison with the politically experienced and well-organized opponent from her own party, Ogura. She might have risked the "talent" image for the sheer fact that her better-known name could have earned her some votes, but she was caught in a bind here, too. Another, perhaps more famous, "talent" was in the race, Morita Kensaku. Morita was a clean-looking young television star who was not connected with either the scandal-ridden LDP or the generally unpopular major opposition parties but rather a newer sounding coalition of progressive supporters (endorsed in Tokyo by the Socialists), Rengō-no-kai. Ono could rely neither on the conservative vote nor on the popularity of her name; she needed her own image.

She sought it in a housewife-citizen approach that emphasized her connection to home and family, her hands-on, lifestyle politics, and her general reluctance to be a politician. To an extent, this housewife-citizen image had the effect of reinforcing the political status quo, much in the way Ueno argues that the "loving housewife" role provides the infrastructure for patriarchal capitalism. But it also presented a criticism of the status quo, a recapturing of the elite world in a way that undermined a patriarchalist understanding of proper values. The rhetoric could be read as an attempt to liberate Ono from the thorns of her ambiguous organizational position. She is both of the system—possessor of an LDP organization, representative of "Japan's traditional motherhood"—and not of the system—a relatively inexperienced woman in a man's political world, a representative of the ignored "real" world of home and family.

Ono's slogans stressed her motherhood and her connection with "regular" housewives. They presented her as a nurturer of everything from children to the environment. Her slogans made no explicit reference to politics and her clearly "political" experiences were usually presented in a setting in which they were either balanced with or outweighed by stresses on her "social" or "lifestyle" oriented experiences. The *uguisu-jo* (young, female campaign announcers) in her advertising cars said, among other things: "This is Ono Kiyoko. The Mother Legislator. The Representative of the Unorganized Housewife. The Representative of the Part-Time Worker. The Representative of Working Women and Nurses." Just below the close-up of Ono on the front page of her precampaign period leaflet red letters read: "One step ahead . . . Tokyo living," pointing to her lifestyle orientation. Slightly below this

came another oft-used slogan, "Mrs. Health, Mrs. Freshness, Mother."
These words were highlighted with blue, green, and pink circles. Smaller
black letters above her name, which ran along the bottom of the page
in eleven large, sky-blue letters, identified her as House of Councilors
member and previously Undersecretary for Environmental Policy. On
the flip side of the leaflet a picture of Ono pedaling the sort of bicycle
that Tokyo housewives use to do their shopping ran beside a resume of
her public and professional experiences since attending the Tokyo College of Physical Education.

Diagonally across the inside of the leaflet ran her perhaps most commonly used slogan: "For your health and the health of the globe." Under
this came phrases that appeared again in her official campaign leaflet,
placing the emphasis squarely on her lifestyle politics.

The joy of working; the fun of raising children; the happiness of
relaxation.

An active, full life; a healthy and long-lived society.

A challenge for yourself; the challenge for good health.

Five-day work week; generosity and abundance.

The pictures on these pages had a hands-on flavor. Ono is standing on
the starting line for a roadrace for the Olympic committee. She is standing in the rain in front of trees speaking about the environment. She is
inspecting a drainage creek for pollution from home waste water. She
is distributing bags of tree seedlings to women at an environment week
celebration. She is listening to a discussion on child-care leave at a meeting of the Diet's Committee on Labor and Society. A young woman is
showing her how to recycle a milk carton by using it to make postcards.
The combination is overwhelmingly "green" and caring. Only a single
photo defies the theme, a picture of Ono standing before rows of male
party members, her hands folded demurely and her body ever so slightly
bowed. She is speaking to an unseen audience on behalf of the LDP's
efforts in the local elections of 1990.

Leaflet-sized stickers also distributed during the precampaign period
show Ono in front of a backdrop that looks like a sky with a giant blue
and green globe on it. Across the globe is the "For your health . . ."
slogan in red. The black letters identifying her current political office
and her experience in environmental policy are positively tiny, greatly
overshadowed by a green message along the bottom of the sticker that
uses an exclamation point (extremely rare in Japanese) to proclaim that

Ono shops in her neighborhood shopping street. She is wearing a slate blue jacket without a lapel and a white blouse, the collar of which is a bow tied around her neck. The blouse is patterned with blue hearts. It looks like the sort of outfit affluent Tokyo homemakers wear when they go out with their other women friends.

The inside of her official campaign period leaflet makes no secret of the nurturing theme. It opens to a spread of a small child laying on his stomach in a field of grass. Making a play on the meaning of the character in Ono's name, a slogan in red reads, "One vote for purity; one vote for Kiyoko." Photo insets in the grass at the bottom of the spread are the close-up of her in the heart-printed blouse, the child-care leave bill hearing, the Olympic committee roadrace, a visit to a recycling center and, at the bottom, a picture of young Ono performing her uneven parallel bars routine in the 1960s. Among the promises listed in the written material is one to look at policy, from the problems of the living environment to the problems of the global environment.

Most curious of all, however, is a cartoon figure of a superhero with "Ono" written on the chest of its costume and a small, blue-boxed message by the cartoonist.

Recently Ono Kiyoko has been getting a little fat. Her face looks a little bit like the "*an*" [Japanese sweet] bread man that I draw.

Isn't it just possible that the spirit of honor that fills her heart is fattening her up? Ono Kiyoko is bright, nice, and courageous. She is the ideal Japanese mother.

I'm happy that this kind of person can be among politicians.

On the back of the pamphlet, Ono is seen shaking hands with the long-popular Tokyo mayor. A singer, leaders of sports associations, and a leader of a small and medium businesses association are pictured with their endorsements of her.

The leaflets are perhaps exaggerated portrayals of an image that Ono and her organization sought to construct throughout the campaign in live arenas as well. From one point of view, this "full-hearted mother" image was supremely uncontroversial, suggesting that in the Ono political world all is pink and blue and pure. The current social order need not be questioned because all that is needed for a happy life can be found in the traditional mother and child relationship. At large rallies, time that might have been used for "political" discussion was absorbed with glamorous performances by "healthy" aerobic dancers. Like a cheerleader parading at a football game with the school mascot, Ono appeared at some functions with people dressed in caricatured animal costumes. It was as if to say that Ono represented the bright, good things in life and to make as evident as possible her distance from the dark world of politics.

Aisatsu (greetings and introductory speeches) that many politicians made on Ono's behalf stressed a nurturing image of a reluctant politician. Consider some of the comments made on her behalf by both men and women politicians at a large rally for women supporters.

To Ono's virtue, the first time that Nakasone asked her to run she refused because her children were too small.

I am here as a representative of my wife [laughter] . . . Ono is lively. She was in the Olympics. She has had five children she has raised well, and she has supported her husband. . . . She has been called a "talent," and that's how she won her first election, but she's been working hard and has not had time to get noticed by the media.

I am a behind-the-scenes worker; it's my job to build the office. It's not easy to do this for her. I worry. Ono is praised for being such a good person. That's why I worry.

Ono understands the position of housewives.

You should support Ono . . . don't worry what your husband does. . . . She's beautiful; she has five, well-raised children.

I've been friends with her for a long time. I've talked with her about raising her children . . . the foundation of politics is not just anything. . . . Real life is the basis of politics. . . . She understands this.

The rally was opened with the aerobics act in front of the blue-and-green globe backdrop from her leaflets. Ono's appearance on stage was hailed with a tape replay of the crowd at the Tokyo Olympics where she won her medal. Supporters at the rally received free box lunches and T-shirts with the "Keep to Smile" motto.[4]

This kitschy event would seem to prove that Ono is being sold by the party as a sort of idealized woman in a world where gender roles determine one's fate. Her introducers present her legitimacy as strongly connected to her identity as mother. The apolitical presentation of dancers and sports music would seem to suggest that, while glamorous and successful, she was not dangerous in any sense of the current social order. One might argue that it demonstrated her complicity with the very political order that maintained the domination of a closed, male elite, and the argument would certainly be correct. Ono's own comments stressed both her dependency on this elite world and the incompleteness of her integration into the political arena. Neverthe-less, her words and the words of other women house a latent criticism of the system whose kitschy image they sold.

Ono began by offering her thanks to the organizational world and deprecating her own experience and knowledge. "When I won the first time, I didn't know anything," she said. She then read a list of politicians who had assisted her. "All I can do now," she added, "is ask favors of other people and politicians, ask them to gather their women for me. . . . I must credit Iida-sensei with the name of the Pure Bell Association."

Ono continued to deprecate her own skills, saying that she thought study was important to politics but had not had sufficient time to study properly and hoped, through reelection, to increase her chances to study. But, just like Takada-san, the Netto politician described in the previous chapter, Ono also took care to present her unstudied wom-anhood as an advantage. She pointed to the scarcity of women in pow-erful positions in the party, and she criticized the LDP for failing to provide a sufficient explanation of the new law allowing the Self-Defense Forces to participate in United Nations peace-keeping operations. The party did not realize that it must speak to women with sons, she said.

The ability to explain politics in terms that "regular people" can un-derstand came up again and again in Ono's campaign. The explanation issue seemed to play on the image of the political world as elite and closed, thereby skillfully presenting Ono's "ordinary womanhood" as a key to politics' back-room doors. One woman speaker at the Pure Bell Association rally made an explicit connection between increasing women's political power and Ono's explanatory ability.

I finally understand Ono's character and how serious she is about politics. The power of women in politics has not exploded yet. I want Ono to work in politics (because of her character). But it also has the plus that we (as women) will be able to realize real power. . . .
I have made a lot of friends with women working in this organization. . . . Ono can explain politics in easily understood words. . . . Let's use this association as a foundation; let's get our hands on politics.

A core speech in Ono's repertoire, a speech about the dire state of the global environment, provided a fine opportunity for her to project her-self as an "ordinary woman" with the special ability to see and explain politics. She used pieces of the speech in nearly every appearance I saw her make, but I have reconstructed it here from my most detailed notes of two different, but very similar speeches, delivered to women's groups from other prefectures who had traveled to tour the party headquarters.[5] In the speech Ono does her best to muster the image of a concerned housewife turned politician. She tries to put political issues in "easy to understand" terms and refers often to the authoritative experiences of a mother and housewife.

I want to explain to you today that politics is daily life.

I have been a member of the House of Councilors for six years. I am too busy to spend much time in the home, and so I am ashamed to say that I cannot be a good housewife. But from both my experience in the home and the world, I know that you cannot say that women are not related to politics. They have the number one important relationship. . . .

The small problems of a small house are politics. The global environment is related to our health, and everyone here today must participate individually to protect that environment.

The globe is limited; resources are limited. The Japanese disposal society is unacceptable. Consider the problem of oil pollution in the water, for example. . . .

How can a woman in the home help the environment? (1) proper disposal of cooking grease, (2) use of non-polluting detergents, (3) proper disposal of water for washing dishes. . . .

In various ways these environmental issues are related to your lifestyle. Soon it will become hot. Your daughter will get sick at work because the air-conditioning is too cold. We don't need to make it that cold. If we each cool our homes less by about one degree. . . .

I have been learning about the problem of global warming. If it continues, Shitamachi [section of Tokyo] will be covered with water, and Singapore and. . . .

The problem of dirty water creates problems for farmers. What are these? These are political problems.

The construction ministry and the finance ministry, the social welfare ministry and the Ministry of International Trade and Industry are all looking at these problems—to make strict laws.

Sometimes Ono added a bit about her own daughter's propensity for long morning showers that wasted water and filled the water with polluting shampoo. Sometimes she broke the speech down and spent equal time talking about the problem of the aged, the low birth rate. "The birth rate is falling to almost one child per couple. What if this is your daughter? She wants to work so she marries late; she has children late. And the cost of bearing children is high." Sometimes Ono told a little story about arguing with the men in committee over the writing of a new day-care bill, pointing to things she knew as a mother that they did not understand.

In her housewife rhetoric, Ono was a candidate who promised the rare value of an uncorrupted, daily life perspective and a "regular person's" hard work and sincerity. The words that she said and that others offered about her supported an image of her as speaking plain truths straight from her everyday, daughters-and-showers home to politics. But the connection between her perspective and politics was not quite as direct as it sounded. To make her House of Councilors bid, Ono depended on an organization whose lack of relationship with "unorganized housewife" rhetoric seemed an ironic demonstration of the truth of her words that politicians do not have a housewives' perspective.

The Organization Pressure of Politics

The foundation of Ono's campaign was not "unorganized housewives" but an LDP organization of other politicians and their veteran assistants. In Japanese Diet politics, it is organization that either makes or breaks a candidate.[6] Ono's campaign confirmed as much. Daily life on the campaign was a constant reminder that the moving forces in the LDP political world were links of favor and obligation. Ono moved among other political elites whose support of her was contingent on complex arrangements of political power and had little to do with a desire to bring her "homemade" perspective to politics. Aside from her public self-presentations, much of Ono's life as a politician was dominated by a concern for building and maintaining these power arrangements, and a housewife's point of view was irrelevant to the task.

At a staff meeting during Ono's precampaign period, "organization" was the key subject of discussion. The media had made much of a new conservative party, the New Japan Party, that was established prior to the summer 1992 elections. A successful alternative conservative party could certainly pose a threat to the Liberal Democratic Party in the proportional representation seats, given the large number of unaligned conservative voters in Japan.[7]

Leading politicians in Ono's campaign office argued that although the New Japan Party might receive media attention, the likelihood that, with its skeleton organization and lack of ties to other, non-party organizations, it could really muster the votes to match its image was not great. One of Ono's advisors continued on to discuss Ono's organizational situation. Unlike the New Japan Party, Ono could tap into some of the ready-made organizational resources of the LDP. But, in Ono's case, her organizational relationship to the party was difficult because she was forced to compete for a district seat with another member of her own party, Ogura Motoi. At this particular staff meeting, leaders argued that without strengthened management, especially of the ties to non-party interests, Ono could expect to lose votes to the better organized Ogura.

As Gerald Curtis explains in his now classic work on Japanese elections, the complexity of LDP campaign organizations is, in large part, a result of the intra-party competition that exists in multi-member districts. This is the sort of competition that Ono faced in Ogura Motoi. Because several Diet members are elected from the same district, it is possible that one party may have more than one successful candidate in a district. Thus, sometimes, it can benefit the party to have more than one candidate run. They can split a large conservative vote and take two or more seats. Other times, however, the vote may not be sufficient, once split, to elect two candidates. In fact, it is possible that splitting the vote could make both candidates losers in a situation where a single candidate surely would have won.[8]

The party is led to take a laissez-faire attitude in many elections. Often competing candidates in local elections will run as "non-aligned, conservative," meaning that the party has not chosen to endorse the candidate. If elected, however, it is generally assumed that the candidate will join the LDP and, having proved his electability, may receive a party endorsement in the future.[9] Intra-party competition is credited with increasing the competition for funding.[10]

Historically, the LDP has been divided vertically into factions that recruit candidates and collect and distribute funds.[11] Candidates who could gather funds could join large factions because their fundraising skills were valuable. Powerful factions were able to recruit strong candidates because they offered the best organizational and funding packages. Factions competed with each other for the power to assign prime spots in the cabinet. Factional organization of the party led to further intra-party competition.[12]

Ono is an example of a candidate recruited to politics by a powerful faction leader who was willing to help with organization and funding. As a woman with little or no previous political experience prior to her first election, Ono could not be expected to have an organization of her own. Instead of having to prove her electability and fundraising panache in local elections, she was invited to step directly into the upper house election by the popular prime minister Nakasone Yasuhiro, who had his own factional resources that could fill out her campaign resources.

During his term as prime minister, Nakasone enjoyed the benefit of favorable public opinion, but in intra-party factional competition, he was not as strong. Feeling his position threatened, he called a rare double election of both the upper and lower houses in 1986. In order to demonstrate his power as a popular politician, he needed to field a large number of successful candidates. Ono, already well known—through her Olympic success in the 1960s and her continuing public activities, including appearing on television in a fitness program—may have provided exactly the "easy win" he wanted.

Ono explains that Nakasone twice asked her to run. The first time she was asked in 1980, Ono refused. She says that her five children were still young and required her attention. When she was asked in 1986, however, she accepted. She says her first election was much easier than the 1992 election. She used a book she wrote about child rearing as a way to get her name out, and, although the LDP ran two candidates in her district, LDP support was generally high. Both candidates won; Ono received over 800,000 votes. She had only a small organization and worried little about fundraising.

But in 1992, the party again endorsed two candidates, despite the fact that a less popular prime minister, a controversial United Nations peacekeeping operations bill before the Diet, and a rash of scandal disclosures seemed likely to reduce LDP popularity. Making matters more difficult, the other Tokyo district LDP candidate, Ogura, had built a political career for himself in the Tokyo assembly. He was a member of what, at the time, was overwhelmingly the most powerful faction, the Takeshita faction. He received the endorsement of a large majority of LDP city and ward assembly members. In some wards, he was reputed by Ono and others to have received the support of virtually all conservative politicians.

The argument at general party functions was that running two candidates in Tokyo would likely increase the LDP vote on the proportional representation ticket. Since the Tokyo population is enormous, this could be a true benefit in terms of proportional representation seats. Ono's side paid lip service to the goal, but the closer the election came, the more palpable grew the frustration with the Ogura organization's strength. In conversations and meetings, non-LDP competitors were referred to by name, but Ogura's campaign was known merely as "the other (or opposite) side," symbolizing the importance of intra-party competition to the flavor of the campaign.

Of course, not all of Ono's intra-party relationships were competitive. Because Ono was recruited to politics by Nakasone, she became a member of his faction. When in the late 1980s connections to a political scandal led Nakasone to withdraw as faction leader, Watanabe Michio became faction leader, and Ono thus became a member of the Watanabe faction. When Ono was running for her second term, Watanabe was foreign minister and another Watanabe faction member, Kakizawa Kōji, was vice foreign minister. Kakizawa, a member of the House of Representatives, had formed a connection with Ono when they campaigned together during the 1986 double election, and in the 1992 election he and his staff members took a large role in Ono's organization. It was through an introduction from one of Kakizawa's secretaries that I found my way into Ono's office.

Candidates are dependent on the support of other politicians and wealthy interests and their organizations to raise the funds they need to run a campaign. Furthermore, rather than depending on direct mail, advertising campaigns, or coverage in the mass media, Japanese politicians rely on networks of support organizations to get out the vote. A politician without such a network cannot turn to advertising because, with the exception of the regulated use of posters in the precampaign period, it is virtually forbidden.[13] The crucial role of local organization helps to explain how politicians such as Ono end up in campaign organizations that are really the interlocking networks of other politicians' organizations. These necessary networks of organizations form a corresponding web of obligations that, in turn, accounts for an insider's bias in campaign organization structure, visible in what I call a "political pedigree."

Any politician may have a myriad of small groups of supporters who enjoy benefits that range from meeting with their representative to attending concerts on reduced-price tickets and traveling or gathering with their friends for "political lectures" that may include box lunches and the appearance of a favorite singer. These groups are called *kōenkai*, and their members are given the task of recruiting new supporters from among their friends and colleagues and providing lists of names of acquaintances or potential supporters that the politician might contact during the election period. Often a politician may use a *kōenkai* to gather political funds, but it might also be a means of using money—when funds are distributed to pay for the rental of an auditorium for a *kōenkai* entertainment event, for example.[14]

These organizations provided Ono with an important link to her most supportive, or core, constituency.[15] They helped her do everything from getting posters hung to turning out a crowd for an afternoon appearance at a public hall. However, they may also have assured a certain distance between her and the average voter. One of Kakizawa's aides described how he puts together women's *kōenkai* to gather supporters for his boss. He seeks out "well-known" or "powerful" women in a community. Building a connection with these women, he urges them to gather their friends for chances to "meet" with their politician. Often the proper "powerful" women will be the wives of prosperous small businessmen or local politicians, or already active in another politicians' *kōenkai*, through a family or friend connection. While a large *kōenkai* membership is preferable, group formation practices tend to lead to a rather exclusive membership of well-to-do wives with free time on their hands. And such *kōenkai* may be the closest most politicians come to the "ordinary person."

Certainly, the non-elite women I interviewed often mentioned that they felt politics was overly dominated by organization and, therefore, inaccessible to the average citizen. In Ono's case, her rhetoric strove to portray her as a representative of unorganized women, but, inevitably, her organization more often than not offered proof that male supremacy still rules in Japanese national-level politics. Ono's organization did contain one notable exception to male-dominant politics, a women's support group called the Pure Bell Association, which was chaired by the only woman speaker of a Tokyo ward assembly. Yet even this group was hardly "ordinary." The politically "unorganized" housewife would probably not have felt comfortable at its meetings.

Ono's election operation was complex because, as a single-term member of a geographically and demographically large upper house district, she lacked her own intricate web of support groups. She was dependent on the support organizations of other politicians from smaller lower house districts or local assemblies to provide her forums in which to present herself and lists of potential supporters to contact. As politicians or their secretaries came to work on her campaign, they brought with them their own organizational structures, and perhaps their own assistants. These organizational links reflected not only Ono's campaign needs but also the complexity of relationships within the LDP.

The opening ceremony for the *kōenkai* office that would later become Ono's campaign headquarters was an important demonstration of the forces that would go on to shape Ono's campaign. Men and women whom I met there continued to appear again and again at other functions throughout the period prior to the election, and with the exception of the first day of the official campaign period, I do not think that I saw the key players so completely assembled anywhere else. Ono's office placed great importance on the occasion, hiring extra students to make the event run smoothly and devoting an entire page of Ono's *kōenkai* newsletter to photos and a write-up of the ceremony. The character of the crowd, especially of those welcomed for refreshments in the campaign offices prior to the ceremonies on a vacant lot outside the building, was hardly "grassroots," demonstrating the tug on Ono from an "insider's" or "organization" world and making explicit how much her political character existed within the web of party, or more clearly, faction, lines.[16]

In expectation of a swelling office through the precampaign and official campaign periods, the Ono *kōenkai* moved from its previous headquarters in an apartment near the Diet building to the bottom three stories of an old office building a short taxi ride away. The office opening ceremony was a confusion of men in dark suits, ashtrays overflowing with cigarette butts, and women running hither and thither with coffee, tea, milk, and sugar. Ono's office claims that approximately three thousand attended the opening ceremonies. This figure may have been an overstatement, but probably well over a thousand attended. The first floor rooms were devoted to greeting the event's attendees. The walls of the main reception rooms, the hallway, and the staircase to the second floor were covered with signed endorsements from other politicians and various interest groups, such as small business associations. Nakasone's endorsement was large and hung in a very visible spot. Most of the endorsements were from men.

At a reception table, visitors registered their names and addresses (providing a way to send thank you notes and other information) and offered congratulatory money contributions in ceremonial envelopes. I helped sort through the envelopes later in the day. I do not know what the contributions totaled, but I did notice that many of the envelopes bore company logos. Many guests were "dispatched" from firms that had agreed to support Ono, which partially accounts for the large number of men attending a ceremony on a weekday morning.

Groups of men, many referred to as merely *sensei* (teacher), out of respect for their political experience, were led to smaller reception rooms where they were served tea and talked behind closed doors, smoking furiously all the while. Men who would later appear atop the advertising car at the outdoor ceremony to offer Ono best wishes were ushered to the second floor to meet in a back office with Ono and others key to the campaign. Wherever Ono could be seen, she was bowing and thanking those who had come or signaling frantically to have her workers reduce the commotion. In many ways the event displayed evidence of the elite network that supported and bound Ono's political career, and in the same ways, the event was thus suggestive that Ono's claim to be the representative of the unorganized housewife could be viewed as a relatively weak one.

The *aisatsu* by various public figures lasted over an hour. It included members of the Tokyo LDP, the Tokyo mayor, a popular woman newscaster, the previous speaker of the Tokyo assembly, and the female ward politician and chair of the Pure Bell Association, a group that I will explain later in this chapter. Many of the men who endorsed Ono at this event were politicians whom she had met the previous year while working on the campaign of long-time Tokyo mayor Suzuki, but none of the speakers were, by any stretch of the imagination, ordinary housewives.

Following *aisatsu,* a toast was offered and guests ate celebratory red beans and rice balls and drank tea. Long after most of the guests had returned to their offices or homes and Ono had slipped out on her way to another event, congregations of other politicians' aides lingered to discuss strategy for the coming months. By afternoon, young male aides at the *kōenkai* office had been sent to the Diet office building to make the rounds to offices of any Diet members who had been guests and thank them for their attendance.

"Thank you" rounds were evidence of the political network within which Ono's organization existed. The people whom Ono took the most care to thank were those to whom her campaign was most obligated for various kinds of support in her bid for a Diet seat. I accompanied a secretary who offered another form of *aisatsu* speeches to staff in a Diet member's office — a thank you for assistance up until that point. *Aisatsu* is a general word for a wide variety of formal greetings or communications. "These courtesies are the heart of politics," he told me. "One of the most important political words you can know is *kikubari*." *Kikubari* is a difficult word to define correctly in English, but basically it means demonstrating proper consideration for others, including humbling oneself before others, paying attention to the form of etiquette, the requirements of rank. At the Diet member's office, the aide was scolded by a staff member. Ono's staff had not paid enough attention to *aisatsu,* she said. It wouldn't do.

On another occasion, I rode in Ono's car on an afternoon when she made *aisatsu* stops at a company president's office and a temple. I was not invited into her two meetings, but I witnessed her being particularly upset after her stop at the temple to have found out that her staff had not been out recently to make *aisatsu* on her behalf. She called her main office and demanded an explanation. Without a demonstration of her sense of obligation, she could not hope to bring key supporters together.[17]

Of course, the organizational network did not exist merely as an exercise in etiquette. One of the most well-known Japanese political facts is that elections are costly.[18] The importance placed on *aisatsu* to people or groups may reflect a sense of financial indebtedness as much as anything. Connections with various interests — religious groups, businesses, professional associations, for example — are important because they provide fundraising opportunities.

My study focused on political participation, so I did not make many pointed inquiries into the sensitive area of fundraising, but the circumstances of my own introduction to Ono provide a good example of how such relationships among other politicians and interest groups operate. In February, prior to Ono's July election, I met a young graduate of the university where I was a guest researcher. His mother was a leader of a *kōenkai* for a former member of the Tokyo metropolitan assembly. The graduate I met introduced me to his mother and to the wife of the ex-assembly member. At their invitation I attended a *kōenkai* event for the ex-assembly member who hoped to increase his supporters and recapture the assembly seat in the coming 1993 metropolitan assembly elections. This particular politician operated in a ward congruent with Kakizawa's House of Representatives district, and Kakizawa sent his best wishes to the assembly-hopeful's *kōenkai* in the form of an *aisatsu* by his younger sister. The *aisatsu* had the advantage of conveying the prestige of connections with a National Diet politician on the lower level politician's *kōenkai*. It also offered Kakizawa a chance to demonstrate his willingness to do favors for the little guy and get some free publicity.

At that *kōenkai* I became the beneficiary of one of Kakizawa's "favors." A few weeks earlier, the *kōenkai* chairwoman and I had dropped by the office of Kakizawa's *kōenkai* so that she could introduce me and offer *aisatsu*. I had been sent on to another of Kakizawa's offices where I met a French exchange student working for him. Later, a secretary from Kakizawa's office invited me to participate as a commentator on American affairs at a large Kakizawa *kōenkai* event, ostensibly at the invitation of the French exchange student. I had thus become the provider of a small favor. But, for all of my *aisatsu* and running from office to office, it seemed unlikely that I would ever have the opportunity to meet the female candidate.

At this lower level politician's *kōenkai,* things turned around for me. The *kōenkai* chairwoman introduced me to Kakizawa's secretary and said that I had expressed interest in Japan's female politicians. The secretary introduced me to Kakizawa's younger sister, and, about two weeks later I was shuttled into both Kakizawa's office at the foreign ministry and, at last, Ono's office. In Kakizawa's office, I made a formal request for assistance on my research in Japan. A few minutes later, in Ono's office, Kakizawa's secretary explained to Ono that Kakizawa would like to make a formal request that I be allowed to participate in her election. It was clear that Ono had already assented.

I joined Ono's office as "a helper from Kakizawa-sensei's office." Because I was known this way, I was asked to attend nearly all of the events that Ono attended in Kakizawa's district. I was obliged to serve tea when Kakizawa's supporters attended functions at the office. I was always made aware of the attendance of his wife or sister so that I could take the time to offer them proper *aisatsu,* and his secretaries, particularly the one who first introduced me to Ono, often asked after me.

At first I found it difficult to understand why my identity must be tied to Kakizawa-sensei. Later, as the number of campaign workers expanded, I came to understand that my connection to Kakizawa-sensei was symbolic of a central feature of Japanese electoral organizations. Reference to Kakizawa-sensei served as my political pedigree, an identity tag that explained to others where I stood in the organizational network and how I was to be accepted, and like all participants in LDP organizations, I needed a political pedigree in order to get my foot in the door. On the one hand, political pedigrees tell a campaign observer who came from where and a little bit about what they might be expected to do for the organization. They help make clear with whom the candidate has had relations in the past and who will be influential in the candidate's future. On the other hand, those pedigrees show who does not come to the office, who is not represented in the organization, who will probably not have a voice in future plans.

Other campaign workers had similar pedigrees. A group of women volunteers had been students at Ono's high school. Young women receptionists or organizers were the granddaughters or relations of conservative politicians. Men were secretaries from other offices or politicians in their own right. Even many of the students who carried out office tasks as part-time jobs had been sent to Ono by sports or politics circles to which they belonged at school.

While the differences in political pedigree were not divisive, people commonly introduced themselves to other campaign workers by referring to the person or organization on whose behalf they had undertaken to work in Ono's office. The pedigrees probably reflect both a cultural tendency to efface one's actions for oneself and a desire to be perceived as acting on behalf of others. But they were also quite clearly the glue that kept the campaign edifice together — evidence of a network of obligations and favors that showed a worker to be dependable or loyal. Other scholars have talked about the importance of such networks in the Japanese culture.[19] However, in an enterprise where expanding networks of human relations are key to delivering the product, a favorable vote, such pedigrees served a purely practical purpose as well.

One retired man said he came to the campaign as a representative of "education." He had been a principal of a Tokyo middle school and very active in the national PTA. He even took me to visit the school where he had worked. His major campaign job was calling people who could be of some use to the office and asking favors of them. His pedigree as the "education" worker may have served as a short-cut assessment of whom he could reach and what he could achieve through already established positions and connections. A worker whose background was educational associations would not be expected to deliver the votes of small businessmen, just as a worker from Kakizawa's downtown Sumida Ward could hardly be expected to increase support among leaders of a suburban PTA.

The overwhelming existence of a pedigree, a prior connection to politics, a group with interests in the candidate's actions once elected or the candidate herself, points to something not at first apparent. People do not walk in off the street and offer their services as volunteers. People seldom, if ever, choose to join the campaign because they are ideologically close to the candidate or because they have a desire to further the candidate's particular policy initiatives. Such congruencies may happily occur, but the major motivator of campaign workers is their indebtedness to certain interests or their desire to curry favor.

Those with an interest in Ono's politics but without previous connection to either her or any of her supporters might seek to volunteer. Probably they would not be refused; but they would not be welcomed either. No pedigree would explain their origin or offer guarantees of their skills. The manner in which their volunteer efforts were to be remunerated—with favor or otherwise—would remain at issue. It is hard to see how their labors could be made of use without much ill ease.

I had problems with this issue myself. As a foreign scholar receiving money from the American government, I felt I should refrain from public endorsements of the candidate and from being in the candidate's employ. But no matter how many times I explained my position, it remained frustratingly unclear to some. People would ask why I was not more familiar with the staff of Kakizawa's *kōenkai* office, as if testing the genuineness of my pedigree. Some of the public appearance organizers were frustrated that I refused to be hired to speak in the advertising cars along with the *uguisu-jo*. When I stuffed or stamped envelopes for the opportunity it gave me to talk to campaign workers, staff members apologized for all the help I had offered for nothing. "It is so unfair of us to keep you working all the time," a staff member told me once. "It is a nice day, why not go home." I came to almost regret my refusal to work in the advertising cars because I felt it placed emphasis on my outsider's position, and, after much protest, I finally did accept a transportation allowance and take many of my noon meals in the campaign headquarters lunchroom. I needed to demonstrate my connection to the interpersonal favor network.

Some outsiders to the campaign might be hired to do clerical tasks, but their involvement would be limited, and they would be paid a proper wage. Because the campaign workers are usually gathered through previous channels of favor or obligation, those who have no connection with those channels are not likely to become connected to the campaign. Therefore, as large as the organization might grow, there is little possibility that its actions could be swayed by a swelling of heretofore unorganized sentiment. The heretofore unorganized do not get in.

Ono's connection to the LDP meant that a campaign workforce (of properly "pedigreed" workers) was more easily assembled than it would have been for a Seikatsu Netto candidate. The same connection, however, meant that the campaign was, despite its rhetoric, no place for non-elite housewives with public interests. Although Ono was a female candidate, almost all of the women workers were in a position of "volunteer," and, for the most part, their work was clerical or service oriented. Nearly all of the part-time student workers were men. Among the full-time staffers, nearly all with non-clerical positions were men. One woman dispatched from the women's office of the party headquarters held a non-clerical position organizing events for *kōenkai* and

Pure Bell Association functions. Another woman acted as office administrator, directing the clerical, part-time, and "volunteer" staffs and maintaining the office generally—making decisions on daily issues from lunch arrangements to office equipment. Other women were receptionists or word processors.

The use of the word "volunteer" to characterize some workers should not be misunderstood. The "volunteer" of Ono's campaign sounded like the same "volunteer" of the Sagyōsho in Chapter 4, but the meaning of the word in practice was very different. Nor were Ono's "volunteers" akin to the volunteers we imagine when we think of rank and file workers in American electoral campaigns. Those in Ono's office who were labeled "volunteer" lacked the character of ideologically motivated volunteer activists that is often identified with the image of American campaigns. Even those who referred to themselves as "volunteers," most notably the women graduates and classmates of Ono's high school, received a travel allowance to cover the cost of their transportation to the office. Most others received a part-time wage, including college students who hung posters or set up chairs in auditoriums for Ono's appearances. Some "staffers" characterized themselves as "volunteers" at first, but they were usually on dispatch from a company, party, or political office and remained on salary throughout the campaign.

The use of *meibō*—rosters of members of supportive trade, religious or recreation associations—is also evidence of Ono's dependence on networks of interlocking organizations. During the official campaign period, members of groups endorsing Ono, usually women, made telephone calls to private homes, soliciting support for the candidate. Members of *kōenkai* were encouraged to provide the office with *meibō* or to make calls from their own. But those without *meibō* were given them by the manager of the telephone bank. As they called each number, they listed the responses on the *meibō*. When I asked the leader of the Pure Bell Association for a list of the names of its members, she gave it to me with the caveat that I was not to release it to the public. Much in the way some aides claimed that organization lay at the root of politics, she argued that *meibō* were a campaign's lifeblood. "A good *meibō* will help you win a campaign, and a smart politician will not give his *meibō* away," she said. In the Seikatsu Club Netto, the decision of whether or not to cooperate with established parties may involve a decision over whether or not to release a *meibō* to a group that may be less friendly later. Especially in Tokyo, where many of the residents come originally from elsewhere and are without ties to the community possessed by families who have lived generations in the same spot, *meibō* may produce one of the few practical ways of reaching a potential constituency, and a politician's reliance on *meibō* only further indicates the highly organized quality of public relationships.

Without a doubt, Ono's campaign organization was an "insider's" effort. The closer the election date drew, the more apparent grew the political network that supported her. At public appearances the rooftops of the advertising cars were crowded with powerful politicians — former-Prime Minister Nakasone, Prime Minister Miyazawa Kiichi, and, risking poor health to demonstrate his endorsement, Foreign Minister (and Ono's faction's leader) Watanabe.

But these were only the most outward signs of her connection to political power. As the advertising cars traveled from ward to ward, often without the accompaniment of Ono, who had more pressing scheduling matters, local politicians who were behind Ono climbed aboard and rode through their ward with the *uguisu-jo*. They waved white-gloved hands and took the microphone to introduce themselves and say a few words on Ono's behalf. As part of the endless weave of favor that formed the weft of the campaign structure, ride-along politicians would often slip some "lunch money" to the *uguisu-jo*, urging them to keep up the good work. The first time I rode along, a politician gave them a 10,000-yen bill, approximately 90 dollars. I saw the women get even more from some, and a staff member assured me that such a tipping practice was "expected."

In many ways, Ono's office was probably typical of any LDP Diet candidate's office. However, her operation had one feature that was probably atypical. This was the solely female group of strategists that I mentioned earlier, the Pure Bell Association. These women had taken their name by combining the first character of Ono's first name, Kiyoko, which means pure, or innocent, with the character for "bell." The association leader, Taito Ward Assembly Speaker Iida Tsuneko, explained that the name "rang with the freshness" of Ono—both as a person and as a rare female face in the troubled world of male politics.

Nearly every time Ono made an appearance at a large *kōenkai* event, Iida also offered an *aisatsu* in which she introduced the Pure Bell Association. In general, Iida stuck to a simple theme. The Pure Bell Association brought women into the heart of Ono's campaign, and the Pure Bell Association was striving for a truly "grassroots" (Iida used the direct Japanese translation, *kusa no ne*) campaign. According to Iida, it was people like Ono and organizations like the Pure Bell Association that would bring new life to politics, which had gotten old and dirty.

The Pure Bell Association was more than a rhetorical device. It was a serious parallel to the male-dominated factional organization with forty-six branch divisions representing the twenty-three wards of central Tokyo plus the surrounding areas that made up the election district of metropolitan Tokyo. The association leadership included a number of female ward assembly members; all of the office-holders were long-time veterans of LDP campaign organizing, much like their male counterparts in other parts of the Ono operation. The Pure Bell Association leaders and the leaders of the LDP's all-Tokyo women's bureau overlapped noticeably. The association had its own strategy meetings, and during the official campaign, it operated its own telephone banks. It sent members to participate in Ono's regular street events, and one entire day was devoted to street events organized by the Pure Bell Association. The Pure Bell Association had its own *kōenkai* events, including the All-Tokyo Pure Bell Association Support Rally, held at the LDP national headquarters slightly over a week prior to the beginning of the official campaign period.

Over seventy years old and outspoken, Iida was prominent at her desk in the second floor staff room at the campaign headquarters. Iida seemed dedicated to developing a "fresh new politics" image for Ono. She often said that such "freshness" started in Ono's "grassroots" campaign to prove that Ono could raise money without becoming beholden to "back room politics." At the entrance to the auditoriums and public halls where *kōenkai* events were held, the Pure Bell Association opened a small stall where, with the assistance of *kōenkai* women's section and part-time workers, they sold "Ono Goods"—"Keep to Smile" T-shirts, bells with attached streamers marked with Ono's campaign symbol, and other small accessories like wallets. Because the "goods" were provided by a supporter at a great discount, they could be sold for only a nominal price, Iida's staff assistant explained. Those who wanted to "donate" to the campaign were thanked for paying more than the asked price for their purchase.

Ono's campaign could not have survived on the proceeds from its "goods" sales. In fact, the associated staff assistant told me that most of the profits were distributed to the *kōenkai* women's sections who helped in the sales so that they could use them to provide refreshments for women's section get-togethers. Profits were certainly not sufficient to eliminate the need for other funding sources, and Iida was not surprised by this. More than anything, Iida was a seasoned politician. She wanted increased numbers of *women* elected, but it is doubtful that she expected housewives or "do-it-yourself" tactics to be more than a symbolic boost for women's representation.

The Political Pressures of Disorganization

As the preceding discussion emphasizes, Ono had substantial organizational resources, despite her public characterization of herself as a candidate without an organization. Downtown in a business district, near a busy train station, and full of businessmen, Ono's campaign headquarters was no world for housewives. But her sense of an insufficiency of organization was not entirely without truth, either. I was party to many conversations in which the weaknesses of her organization were at issue. The apparently stark contrast between Ono's rhetoric and her campaign's realities was dampened by the fact that, as a woman with little previous political experience, Ono was not completely at home in the LDP world. She was just enough of a housewife to find that some elite routes to politics were hard going.

In the early part of the precampaign period, the tardiness of Ono's poster hanging came up often as a problem of organization. In April, posters were an important issue to the Ono campaign. She had hung hers later and they were far fewer in number than the posters of the other LDP candidate and another female candidate from the Kōmeitō Party. At meetings at party headquarters, both with the party's women's section and with groups of ward politicians, Ono apologized profusely for the "tardiness of her preparation." But staffers told me that the real issue was less preparation than money. The Japanese economy was generally tight, meaning that funds flowed less freely into party coffers.

Uncertainty surrounded the LDP because of scandal and tough policy issues, and some staffers claimed that the party was tighter than usual with the money it gave candidates. Worse yet, Ono was a woman, and everyone, including Ono herself, seemed to think funds were always harder to gather for a woman candidate.[20] In early precampaign meetings with the party's women's section, representatives of different branches complained that posters had not been delivered or hung in their wards. Often these branch representatives would characterize Ono as "unorganized" in comparison with Ogura, the other LDP candidate in her district. They had a variety of ways of providing such measures:

The people in this ward are divided half and half between Ono and Ogura. Ogura has a lot of posters, and he was also doing baked potato events. Ono has not come out to visit. [Party] people are turning over to Ogura. The women are for Ono, but the young people are for Ogura.

All the ward assembly members are for Ogura. And there are party tickets out for Ogura that were distributed by the branch chief.

The ward assembly members are behind Ogura, but the ward people have no interest. Ogura is unknown so it does not matter if the assembly members support him. There is no party feeling in the ward.

The branch has decided to support both candidates, but, of course, Ogura has been very serious and dedicated. The women are behind Ono, but I, myself, am in the Ogura camp.

Almost all of the assembly members are for Ono, but when you compare posters . . . Takeshita is putting money behind Ogura's posters.

Everything is about the same as last week. The posters are still late, and Ono has not made a personal appearance. Please show your face—and get the posters out. Now it's 14–9 in the ward, Ogura versus Ono.

At an expensive luncheon held for about fifty Kakizawa *kōenkai* women and Ono, the women seated to my left bent my ear with concerns about the posters and the readiness of the Ono operation. This woman had organized her first *kōenkai* when she gathered friends in support of her husband's bid for a seat in a local assembly and spoke with the confidence of her own experience.

The posters still aren't out. Ono must ask people individually to pass them out. If she doesn't they'll take them home, but they won't hang them. But, then they might not hang them even if they do get asked personally. I have seen so many posters for Ogura that, in some places, I have pulled them down. Of course, you're not supposed to do that.

Closer to the office, the "poster problem" was perceived as a lack of organizational mastery, and the causes for such a weakness were interpreted as a scarcity of funds and political experience in the office and the candidate. On one of my early days in her office, I had lunch with one of her staff members and another politician's secretary. The younger Ono staff member was grilled by the more experienced secretary who then gave his own interpretation of events.

The office isn't really organized. There's no flow of information, especially to higher up. Not enough money has been raised. Probably the candidate has limited the fundraising somewhat. [The younger staffer later interpreted this to mean that a woman candidate has difficulty raising money from companies. "They let women give speeches, but they don't trust them as leaders."]

The candidate does not realize how dangerous the situation is. That's why I suggested an opinion poll and am still suggesting it. The posters were not hung early enough—the "other side" already has its posters up.

It will be important to get a lot of people to show up for the office opening on Monday, hopefully over 1,000. But the media hasn't been contacted yet—and if the media is contacted everybody better make sure a lot of people show up.

The same sort of concerns were voiced by others and could be heard until nearly the end of the campaign. The younger staffer who was lectured by his more experienced counterpart had his own complaints about the scarcity of party financial support for Ono and of the inexperience and disorganization of her campaign in comparison with the Ogura office.

Ono also expressed frustration with the problems of organization when I asked her about politics: "Getting money. And elections are nonstop. But worse, your organizations break down [between elections]. You don't remember who was involved and how they were involved. You forget and make too many mistakes, and there are too many appointments. Your time goes away." On other occasions, including after the election, Ono explained that women in the LDP are handicapped financially and organizationally because they do not possess the connections that men usually do. To counteract this in her reelection bid coming up in 1998, she has begun to develop her own women-oriented organization by asking the mothers she met through PTA activities at the schools that her five children attended to gather their friends for "political talks" at Ono's house.

The perception of insufficient organization was prominent among the members of the Pure Bell Association as well. Iida spoke often about the need for strengthened organization. She stressed the idea that if party women did not stick together and organize behind women candidates, they could not expect to improve their overall situation. The perception that Pure Bell Association members had of being outsiders within the party because they were women may be one reason that they chose to bill their organization as a "grassroots effort." Regardless of the fact that the leaders and much of the membership had been long-seasoned in politics and hardly represented the "average" voter, the women may have perceived themselves as non-elites in comparison to other, male-dominated LDP organizations. One member of the Pure Bell Association, the sole female member of the LDP contingent in one of Tokyo's ward assemblies, spoke without prompting and with conviction about the organization-related difficulties that women faced within the party.

The other parties have ready-made organizations to support you in a campaign, but there is nothing from the LDP. You have to build your own organization and then prove to the party that you can be elected. . . .

Look at the female representatives from other parties. Of course, the LDP has the highest number of representatives from a party—but I'm the only LDP woman. . . .

I had to build my own organization. I used the group of friends I had made over twenty years and raising children together. I had been making noises in the community for years but it took about twelve years before anybody understood me.

This woman's remarks were typical of what other LDP women told me about their position within the party. I attended a nationwide gathering at party headquarters for all of the LDP-elected women representatives at every level. In a hot, crowded room, the women addressed male leaders in their party who sat above them at a head table. As, one by one, each woman took the floor to introduce herself and make a short statement of her most pressing party-related concerns, the feeling that the party ignored its women politicians was echoed again and again. And to the astonishment of the party leaders, the room was bristling with real anger by the end of the presentations. If Ono felt like a representative of the "unorganized," the representative of a new and valuable perspective, she likely had company among her fellow female politicians.

A Rhetoric for Whom?

While Ono's self-presentation emphasized private action and a view of the home and family that are undeniably conservative, her use of housewife imagery was not without criticism for the state of society. In fact, it often added up to a picture of a political world that had yet to satisfactorily address fundamental human issues—the living environment, education, the family. Because her party had unfettered dominance of the political system during nearly the entire postwar period, her criticisms were implicitly criticisms of the party. By portraying herself, as her advertising car claimed, as the "representative of the unorganized housewife" she could distance herself from the party, a move that probably had benefits for her constituency relationship but also may have reflected the uncertainty of her own standing in the world of the LDP elite.

The criticism latent in such a portrayal must not be overstated. At first, my interest piqued by her constant phrasing of politics in terms of daily life issues, I perceived Ono as vastly different from the male politicians who surrounded her. She seemed more approachable—really more like "regular people." But when I told stories of her speeches to the non-elite homemakers in my neighborhood, I noticed they were skeptical about the reality behind Ono's housewife image.

In many cases her approachable words must have been drowned by the contrasting messages delivered by the nature of the forum within which she spoke. Of course, as I said earlier, the *yūzei* had to compete with far too much other street media for the attention of the voters. But I think that even at *kōenkai* events, for example, where Ono could have the floor without interruption, the structure of the event must have framed her "daily life" message with contradictory images of the rarefied world of a Diet politician. Usually, at gatherings of fewer than fifty, the room was arranged with a head table where Ono and perhaps other leaders sat. At larger gatherings Ono was on a stage surrounded by local dignitaries, mostly men, although famous women sometimes gave entertaining speeches on her behalf. She wore huge corsages, as did the other dignitaries, and, at the end of her *aisatsu* she was presented with flowers, much as if she were a prima ballerina. Often professionally made banners marked the stage; toward the later states of the precampaign period, the more elaborate globe backdrop added a heightened sense of drama. To much of the audience, the *kōenkai* event must have been like an outing to the theater. (The politician who connected me to Ono actually does have a Kabuki theater outing for his women's *kōenkai*. Local politicians offer short *aisatsu* prior to the show.) In fact, many of the women who attended dressed in kimono or very formal suits. They came with groups of their women friends or with their husbands, and the halls outside the auditorium would resound with the greetings of neighbors who had not been in touch recently and talk about the box lunch contents and the attractiveness of the auditorium. The same groups would leave together later, talking excitedly about everything but politics, often refusing even to carry an Ono poster home. The events were not "regular," and the closer the official campaign period drew, the more choreographed they became.

I usually stood at the reception desk at the beginning and end of these events, and because I was frequently the only foreigner, women who had seen me previously at another function often commented on the fact. In this way I came to notice that many of the same people would attend a variety of functions; the actual pool of supporters who turned out for Ono's precampaign rallies or official campaign period *yūzei* was not as large as it might appear. I also noticed that it was difficult to find young people in the audience. Most of the women were at least middle-aged or older. The older women predominated. The majority of the men who were not politicians or their secretaries were of retirement age. Such an audience meant that Ono's rhetoric reached a limited number of ears. Those ears were probably more attuned to the organizational ins and outs of local *kōenkai* than the specifics of Ono's image. In the final analysis, Ono's rhetoric could not escape being colored by its organizational trappings. As we saw with the campaign photograph of the Hikari-ga-oka event discussed in the beginning of Chapter 3, where Ono was unorganized, her speech as "concerned housewife and mother" turned politician fell on deaf ears. From the standpoint of male politicians in her party, Ono was, perhaps, in the worst way, a housewife politician, but from the perspective of the housewives in my neighborhood, she was still a taxi citizen.

Conclusion

I finished the bulk of my fieldwork and returned to the United States in 1993, just before a wet May turned into one of the longest rainy seasons that Japan has seen in years. Beneath that summer's record-breaking, unceasing downpour, Japan experienced perhaps the most momentous political changes that have occurred since World War II. The Liberal Democratic Party (Ono's party) split, lost a vote of no-confidence, and eventually surrendered its government to a coalition of new conservative parties, recycled Liberal Democrats, and a hodgepodge of old opposition forces. Under the short-lived leadership of coalition Prime Minister Hosokawa Morihiro, Japan flirted with a new, more populist policy agenda and, at long last, reformed the Diet's lower house electoral system.

In June of 1995, I returned to the places where I had begun the field research for this book in order to do some follow-up work. The growth and success of groups such as Sagyōsho and the Seikatsu Club Cooperative's Netto movement over the two years of my absence presented striking contrasts to the chaotic disintegration of established political parties that continues unabated even as I write this. The Netto, especially, had done remarkably well in the local elections of April 1995. Where I had once been a student of a relatively obscure electoral effort, I was now following a group that commanded the attention of journalists and scholars trying to grasp some sense of the shape of Japanese democratic politics in the future.

That same June, an *Asahi shinbun* article about the rise of non-party candidates prior to the House of Councilors election in 1995 ran a sidebar and a large graphic that examined the expansion of the numbers of Netto-sponsored politicians in local assemblies.[1] The sidebar's short text was unremarkable, but the graphic was startlingly revealing of the issues that permeate this book. It was a map of Japan, divided by prefecture. The prefectures where the Netto had succeed in electing representatives to assemblies at some level were blacked in. Around the edges of the national map were symbols of people, grouped and labeled to represent the strength of the Netto presence in each of the blacked-in prefectures. Arrows connected the people-symbol groups to the appropriate locations on the map. For example, several tall people grouped together depicted Tokyo, where forty-nine Netto representatives hold office, while one short person stood for rural Iwate Prefecture, where only one Netto representative holds office. The newspaper graphic was neat and effective, except for one key mistake: each symbolic politician was, most unfortunately, wearing a tie.

I wondered, was it a backhanded compliment to the Netto's political successes that its female elected representatives were rendered as male? In the newspaper graphic the Netto political identity had escaped the narrow boundaries of a gender role. Represented as men in suits advancing to black out a national map, the Netto movement looked impressive. Yet the graphic representation of the Netto success managed to erase one of the most significant aspects of that movement. I considered the effect of making the symbols clearly feminine. The important truth that the Netto had succeeded in propelling women into office in the way many mainstream political organizations had not would not be understood without changing the gender of the graphic's symbols, but then I doubted that an image of the movement's growing power would be as easily conveyed with female politicians. Moreover, the simple flipping of the symbolic politicians' genders would not be adequate to telling the story of the movement in the way that the Netto members understood it. After all, as Ono's campaign organization demonstrated, if Netto representatives were only women in men's parties, the significance of their gender would be relatively slight.

The problem with the graphic was not simply its gendering of the politicians. As Netto activists understand themselves, their difference from other politicians is determined not solely by their gender but by who they are in totality. Netto members are distinguished by the special *seikatsu* (daily life) point of view they acquire by their participation in a particular way of life and ethic of human relationships to which their gender is, in part, responsible for relegating them. In other words, because they are housewives before they become politicians, Netto representatives understand aspects of human existence that are ignored by established party politicians for whom organizational development and interest brokering are central concerns. Netto representatives become housewives and acquire their housewives' expertise because they are women and in their society women are charged with care of the domestic sphere. Changing the gender on the graphic would not be sufficient, although it might be a move in the right direction. In order to be a fair accounting of what the Netto movement representatives seek to be, the graphic must depict the concerns and ethics in which Netto activists are enmeshed, in contrast to those in which mainstream politicians operate. Netto members understand implicitly that a crucial variable in determining political outcomes is the social vehicle one rides into politics, the "bicycle" or the "taxi."

We might be tempted to shake our heads for a moment and then forget the graphic altogether. While an interesting example of the varied political life in Japanese localities, the Netto is probably not the wave of the future. After all, at its new height of power in Tokyo, the Netto could claim only three seats on the 128-member Tokyo Prefectural Assembly. Housewife politicians do not have the numbers to force important policy shifts. Then there is the fact that, as they acquire higher political positions, housewife politicians look less like housewives and more like male politicians. The tension between Ono's housewife rhetoric and her campaign organization suggests as much; the conflicts within the Netto and Seikatsu Cooperative memberships about the growth of big organizations also add to the impression that any marriage between housewifery and politics is likely to be a fleeting one.

However, a housewife's bicycle citizenship is interesting precisely because it does not survive long in arenas of political power—because housewives know as much and thus distrust the political life, politicians, and political organizations. Bicycle citizenship does not function effectively in the thick of politics because it is shaped by an ethic that is impractical for making gains in a world of highly organized, interested competition. Housewives who will be active in the political world must be willing to trade in their bicycle views for the necessary advantages of taxis—literally and figuratively, as I have said before. Ono could not take time off in the middle of her campaign to care for sick parents or arrive late at meetings in order to save time for hanging the laundry, nor could her campaign strategists. Connections at the PTA might win a woman a seat in a ward assembly, but they will not stretch far enough to guarantee a seat in the Diet. Even the most publicly oriented housewife can take her housewife ethic only so far in political life.

Despite all sorts of differences in areas such as political party structure, the relative power of bureaucracy and legislature, and some behaviors of elite political actors, Japan is widely regarded to have achieved a liberal democracy. Yet in Japan at its highest levels, liberal politics — and, thus, an important form of citizenship — is not open to women who take the obligations of a housewife role very seriously. The complaint that citizenship in any liberal democratic polity, while seemingly abstract and universal, actually privileges some members of society in comparison with others is not a new one. Certainly the evidence against the inclusiveness of the liberal citizen model is as great in the case of the United States as we might argue it is in Japan.[2] Nor is there a scarcity of possible schemes for increasing the participation of less advantaged groups of society in politics, particularly with regard to the representation of women.[3] But critiques of liberal democratic citizenship and remedies for its faults all tend to have one thing in common. They assume that citizens will be better off when they are more fully integrated into the political system.

Japanese housewives who, like Kameda-san in Chapter 3, turn their backs on the political world they see as murky, money-hungry, male, and over organized do not believe that their lives would be improved by participation in politics. Even many much more publicly active housewives, such as the members of the Sagyōsho volunteer group or the Seikatsu Club Cooperative, doubt that either their own lives or the social causes they hold dear will benefit from a greater politicization. Most housewives are unwilling to make the trade between the obligations embedded in their gender role and the obligations of a political life. One might try to argue that women who are housewives are afraid to relinquish a gender role — housewife — that receives society's approbation for one that might earn its disapproval — female politician. Perhaps that anxiety is part of the story. The generally low opinion that Japanese women hold of politicians might support such an interpretation.

The ambivalence with which women accept a housewife identity, however, suggests that they do not feel bound to housewifery over politics simply as a matter of acting in accordance with popular opinion. As either a housewife or a politician, a woman would encounter a negative social image. The difference is that, even taking its most negative images into account, women are convinced that their house-wifery has value in the human spheres close to them. Politics, on the contrary, seems like an ineffective tool for operating in the housewife's world of person-to-person ties. Worse, because it attempts to reduce interpersonal obligation to "interest" and measures an individual's success in terms of money, organization, and credentials as opposed to spirit, politics sometimes seems to endanger the world close to home. The anti-political feeling among the Sagyōsho activists discussed in Chapter 4 is a good example of housewives' perception of the danger of politics.

On a day-to-day basis Sagyōsho volunteers encountered social problems — such as the need for more types of care for the aged and better disabled persons' access to public facilities — that might receive more adequate attention if the volunteers were represented in politics. Despite this fact, the Sagyōsho volunteers did not make political participation a priority. To some degree, it is even fair to say they eschewed it. Sagyōsho members declined to make their public actions clearly political because they perceived that an alliance with politicians would mean making their ethics and participation subservient to selfish political interest. Sagyōsho members emphasized their personalistic, flexible, and egalitarian ethic of relationships. They insisted that the localized, person-to-person, *ya-ruki* spirit of their activism was more valuable than the "satisfaction of needs" perspective that government and other social welfare "experts" advocate. Sagyōsho volunteers turned to public activism in search of a particular quality of human relationship rather than as a means of solving a specific policy problem.

Most Sagyōsho volunteers would admit that they knew little about the social policy dimensions of the problems they volunteered to work with when they first joined the group. Even after they become educated about policy problems through their activism, Sagyōsho housewives continue to resist the characterization of their own activity as policy oriented. Sagyōsho is in the business of building human connections. In that sense, Sagyōsho volunteers perceive themselves as dealing with the need for community with others that, disabled or not, all human beings share — a need that by its nature defies generic solution. Undoubtedly, Sagyōsho volunteers would be thrilled if the government prioritized, for example, increased handicapped access to public facilities such as train stations. The presence of enough Sagyōsho-friendly representatives in political assemblies might assure such policy changes. Yet as we saw in Chapter 4, when the human connection aspect of

Sagyōsho's work seemed to be subverted to the expansion of the organization for the purpose of serving social policy concerns, conflict developed; members could not understand the meaning of their voluntarism without the emphasis on their ethic of personal relationship.

Sagyōsho volunteers did perceive their work as publicly important, but they did not perceive it as the representation of interest in a competitive arena. At Sagyōsho—as with other housewives—politics and public life were not necessarily the same thing. When they were told that the Nerima ward government sought policy changes that encouraged voluntarism by making it more "profitable," Sagyōsho members were disturbed. They did not think that community members should be led to view their ties to one another as the product of self-interested trading. As Satō-san explained it to me again in the summer of 1995, Sagyōsho members trusted that their work would foster a mutually beneficial climate of *taskeai* (helping each other—literally, "help and join"), but members did not seek specific benefit trades as a result of their efforts. Sagyōsho members thought people should volunteer because they thought themselves obliged, as members of the community, to lend a hand, and their presentation of their experiences demonstrated that they treasured the knowledge that they were meeting their obligations.

Obligation is at the heart of a housewife's bicycle citizenship, although it would not appear on the Netto newspaper graphic even if all of the symbolic people were rendered female and finds little "representation" in the most radical revisions of liberal doctrines of citizenship.[4] The difference between housewives who are very active in the community and those who are not is probably largely determined by factors such as life stage and personality. But the weight of perceived obligation to family and the nurturing role of housewife is a real barrier to an activist bicycle citizen becoming a taxi politician. If we want to bring more women into the "taxi" arenas of political life, we could focus on ways of alleviating a housewife's load of obligations. The scholarly emphasis on Japanese women's opportunities in the workforce as opposed to their duties in the home is such a focus.[5] More and more flexible child-care facilities and well-established, affordable elder care could reduce the weight of a housewife's responsibility for those around her. If workdays could be shortened so that men worked less, women could probably expect to share a greater percentage of household duties with their husbands. At any rate, the high cost of living, the declining birth rate, and a possible labor shortage combined with the high standard of education among young Japanese women today will probably mean fewer and fewer women are primarily housewives in their role orientations. If the nexus of obligations that keeps women at home and centers them on a housewife role were undone, more women might feel that they are required to trade off less in becoming a taxi citizen. And so, perhaps, more women would become taxi citizens.

We can imagine a dissolution of the social conditions that relegate women to bicycle views and thus hinder their entry into politics on the same terms as men. Given the real frustrations that many women feel toward their position in society as housewives, that may be good news. Of course, the entry of more women into politics does not mean that all barriers to political participation by "regular people" will be eliminated. If fewer women are housewives, more women will probably be available for political life—even if the ratio is far from one to one. But greater differences among the types of women who enter politics may increase. Nonetheless, we should work to understand what kinds of social changes will increase the freedom of women who feel bound to a gender role not of their choosing.

In examining how women might be relieved of the constraints of their housewifely obligations, however, we should not forget the basic tension between citizenship in a liberal regime and the weight of human relationships. We can imagine a system that would put more Japanese women into politics, but unless we reimagine the nature of Japanese politics as a whole, putting women into politics will mean getting them off of their bicycles and into taxis. Even supposing women are no longer held accountable for the maintenance of the ties in the world of *mijika,* the world close to home, those ties will not need less upkeep. Reducing barriers to women's participation in politics will undoubtedly help women in many ways, but it will not cure liberal politics of its allergy to the caring, personalistic, egalitarian ethic of the housewife's world. Interest will still be a more powerful political language than obligation.

Expressing concern about the challenges faced by women trying to escape housewifery is fashionable. Expressing concern about who will do the housewives' work or represent the housewives' ethic when housewives are no more is not so fashionable, but I think it is truly important. When we lament the moral emptiness of the liberal picture of democratic politics, we are often not specific about who is to be held responsible for maintaining the moral content of our lives. We imagine better citizens who, in a shadowy tribute to ancient city-states, are both householders and political animals, skilled equally in the management of their private families and the public consideration of what is most just. We want citizens who put a vision of human cooperative endeavor before the advancement of their interests.

Ironically, considering the fact that the ancients had *men* in mind, the publicly oriented housewives we have met in this book are, in significant respects, the sorts of citizens whom we democratic theorists, in our fuzzy imaginations, desire. The Sagyōsho and Netto housewives, in particular, combine an important degree of leisure time with a broad awareness of their community. They are brought into public life through their association with friends and neighbors, and many of them perceive their most important public task as the development of a network of relationships where all can speak and a spirit of obligation to the community is the most valuable commodity. These women believe that some things are more just than others and that only cooperative action of community members will bring justice to the fore in social life.

While the world of the taxi politician requires money, time, experience, and other resources not readily available to most members of society, the world of the housewife activist requires little of its participants but a willing attitude, and the housewife ethic fosters inclusivity and flexibility, which make it easier for ordinary people to join in. When it comes to providing a rewarding, enlarging experience of public life, the housewife's world—as we see with organizations such as the Netto and Sagyōsho—has more to offer in many ways than the political world of Ono's campaign.

Of course, we must not lose sight of the fact that the housewife does not choose her world or ethic without regrets. The housewife identity is, at best, only a reductive, none-of-the-above label for the constellation of duties that fill a housewife's life. Those aspects of her daily life, such as cooking and cleaning, that most "represent" the housewife are usually the ones she finds least rewarding. When we look carefully at both the housewife and her practices in public life we are confronted by an odd fact. The gender role that disturbs us because it seems to typify women's inequality with men is also the repository of values that we claim we long for in public life. Bicycle citizenship has many admirable, democratic qualities, but women do not become bicycle citizens as a result of an admirable, democratic process.

The housewife activist challenges us to find a way to preserve her ethic without preserving the repressive aspects of gender relationships that make it *her* ethic. After all, we can argue that bicycle citizens are necessary to high quality democratic life because they represent the importance of forming and fulfilling obligations to other human beings.

Political commitment without a sense of such obligations is only interest competition, and in the world of interest competition, the richest, best organized, and most powerful tend to win. The existence of bicycle citizens cannot change the outcome of most interested struggles, but it can provide us a model from which to critique them. Without such a model, where do those who cannot or will not ride in the metaphorical taxis of public life find a means of persuasive expression?

Because the housewife is consigned to be viewed by society as a born caretaker, she can draw convincingly on the authority of her identity to criticize the ways in which society falls short of its role of caring for its own. We should not forget that, despite the difficulties faced by women such as House of Councilors member Ono or the Netto representatives who try, in various ways, to take housewifery to politics, sometimes these women are successfully elected. On some level, their rhetoric and their housewife symbolism are appealing—and, no doubt, are so to a constituency that reaches beyond housewives to members of society who fill other roles but are attracted by what the housewife politician's *seikatsu-sha* point of view represents regarding the capacity of society to answer human needs, both material and spiritual.

Notes

Foreword

1. See, for instance, Linda Basch, Nina Glick Schiller, and Cristina Szanton-Blanc, *Nations Unbound: Transnationalized Projects and the Deterritorialized Nation-State* (New York: Gordon and Breach, 1994); Sherri Grasmuch and Patricia Pessar, *Between the Two Islands: Dominican International Migration* (Berkeley: University of California Press, 1991); and Yasmin Soysal, *Limits of Citizenship* (Chicago: University of Chicago Press, 1994).

2. See, for instance, Anthony King, ed., *Representing the City, Ethnicity, Capital and Culture in the 21st Century* (London: Macmillan, 1996).

3. Pierrette Hondagneu-Sotelo, *Gendered Transitions* (Berkeley: University of California Press, 1994).

4. See also, generally, Zillah Eisenstein, "Stop Stomping on the Rest of Us: Retrieving Publicness from the Privatization of the Globe," *Indiana Journal of Global Legal Studies* 4, no. 1 (1997).

Chapter One. "Supposing Truth Is a Woman"

The chapter title is from Friedrich Nietzsche, *Beyond Good and Evil: Prelude to a Philosophy of the Future*, trans. Walter Kaufmann (New York: Vintage, 1966), 1.

1. The difficulty of literally mapping women's perception of the spaces in which they live (as well as those from which they are excluded) leads Gillian Rose to argue that the discipline of geography has a "masculinist aesthetic" which makes it difficult to see actual relationships between women and space (*Feminism and Geography: The Limits of Geographical Knowledge* [Minneapolis: University of Minnesota Press, 1993]).

2. Jonathan Rauch, *The Outnation: A Search for the Soul of Japan* (Boston: Harvard Business School Press, 1992), 53.

3. The term "Madonna Boom" plays on the propensity of female candidates to portray themselves as clean politicians—political virgins, as it were. It is not a reference to the singer Madonna, who, in a different twist on the image of immaculate conception, claims to be "like a virgin."

4. Lucian Pye and Mary W. Pye, *Asian Power and Politics: The Cultural Dimensions of Authority* (Cambridge, Mass.: Belknap Press of Harvard University Press, 1985); Robert E. Ward, "Japan: The Continuity of Modernization," *Political Culture and Political Development*, ed. Lucian W. Pye and Sidney Verba (Princeton, N.J.: Princeton University Press, 1965), 27–82.

5. Scott Flanagan, "The Genesis of Variant Political Cultures: Contemporary Citizen Orientations in Japan, America, Britain and Italy," in *The Citizen and Politics: A Comparative Perspective*, ed. Sidney Verba and Lucian W. Pye (Stamford, Conn.: Greylock Publishers, 1978), 127–165; Curtis H. Martin, *Politics East and West: A Comparison of Japanese and British Political Culture* (Armonk, N.Y.: M. E. Sharpe, 1992).

6. According to a 1995 *Asahi shinbun* survey of voters in Shizuoka Prefecture, 38 percent of the voters who had claimed to support a particular political party in 1993 had decided that they did not support any party by 1995. See "Watakushi ga shiji wo yametta riyū" [The Reason I Gave Up Supporting (a Party)], *Asahi shinbun* 9 June 1995, 12th ed., 6.

7. Scholarly examinations of the political changes of the early 1990s have seldom focused explicitly on voters. For example, although he notes the growing numbers of disaffected voters and points particularly to women, Takabatake Michitoshi centers on the LDP split and surrounding elites in his coverage of political change (*Nihon seiji no kōzō tenkan* [Structural Shifts in Japanese Politics] [Tokyo: Sanichi Shobō, 1994]). Whether or not the new House of Representatives electoral system will result in greater "democracy" in Japan is examined primarily in terms of how it will affect elite politicians, in Raymond Christensen, "The New Japanese Electoral System," *Pacific Affairs* 69.1 (1996): 49–70. Other examinations of the politics of political reform that concentrate solely on elite concerns are Ōtake Hideo, "Forces for Political Reform: The Liberal Democratic Party's Young Reformers and Ōzawa Ichirō," *Journal of Japanese Studies* 22 (1996): 269–294; Chalmers Johnson, "Puppets and Puppeteers: Japanese Political Reform," *Japan: Who Governs, The Rise of the Developmental State* (New York: W. W. Norton, 1995), 212–231. All of these works devote substantial attention to the political interests of Ōzawa Ichirō. Despite the fact that voter support for such non-party candidates as Aoshima in the Tokyo 1995 mayoral race and continually dropping voter turnout demonstrate that voters are changing as well, scholars persist in focusing primarily on a single set of elite actors. The predominance of the elite-oriented frame in studies of Japanese political participation is evident in a relatively recent article pointing out that political scientists have ignored growing numbers of independents in the electorate, assuming party support as a *normal* state for voters. Tanaka Aiji, " 'Seitō shiji nashi' sō no ishiki kōzō: seitō shiji gainen saikentō no shiron" [Attitudinal Structure of Independent Voters: Rethinking Measurement and Conceptualization of Partisanship], *Revaiasan* 20 (1997): 101–129.

8. Two male readers (political scientists) of my manuscript suggested re-

moving this section of what one considered "male bashing." I, myself, am ambivalent about revealing the "real me" to my readers. However, ambivalence and uncertainty in approaching the political is what this book is all about. Recording a conventioneer's disconcerting reaction to my presence in the political science milieu is not intended as "male bashing" but, rather, a hard-nosed, empirical observation. After all, I was perhaps more embarrassed than my tipsy colleague.

9. Scott C. Flanagan, Bradley M. Richardson, Joji Watanuki, Ichiro Miyake, and Shinsaku Kohei, *The Japanese Voter* (New Haven, Conn.: Yale University Press, 1991). For an indictment of behavioralism by a behavioralist, see David Easton, "The New Revolution in Political Science," *American Political Science Review* 63 (December 1969): 1051–1061.

10. Susan J. Pharr, *Political Women in Japan: The Search for a Place in Political Life* (Berkeley: University of California Press, 1981).

11. For example, a recent English-language work focuses on Japanese women legislators but, again, does not examine citizenship among "regular" women. Sally Ann Hastings, "Women Legislators in the Postwar Diet," in *Re-imaging Japanese Women*, ed. Anne Imamura (Berkeley: University of California Press, 1996), 271–300. Some similar investigation of women's entry into postwar politics has been done by Ōgai Tokuko in "Sanjū kyū nin no dai ikki fujin daigishi: minshū kaikaku no hoshitachi" [Stars of Democracy: The First Thirty-Nine Female Members of the Japanese Diet], *U.S.-Japan Women's Journal* 20 (1996): 31–55. Translations of some of the growing body of Japanese-language work on local-level women is available in Kumiko Fujimura-Fanselow and Atsuko Kameda, eds., *Japanese Women: New Feminist Perspectives on the Past, Present, and Future* (New York: City University of New York Press, 1995). In later chapters I make more thorough examinations of Japanese-language literature on Japanese women and politics.

12. Anne E. Imamura, "The Japanese Urban Housewife: Tradition and Modern Social Participation," *Social Science Journal* 24 (1984): 139–156, and *Urban Japanese Housewives: At Home and in the Community* (Honolulu: University of Hawaii Press, 1987).

13. A good example is Jane Condon, *Half Step Behind: Japanese Women of the '80s* (New York: Dodd, Mead, 1985). Sumiko Iwao complains about this lopsided view of Japanese women in *The Japanese Woman: Traditional Image and Changing Reality* (New York: Free Press, 1993). She does include a chapter on politics and the Seikatsu Co-op movement, although she does not devote attention to non-activists as I do. Her general picture of women and politics examines women's depressingly low representation in elite spheres.

14. See especially Tocqueville's introduction to Alexis de Tocqueville, *Democracy in America*, ed. J. P. Mayer, trans. George Lawrence (New York: Harper and Row, 1969), 9–20.

15. The "official" herald of the liberal democratic triumph in history, Francis Fukuyama, quotes Nietzsche's *Thus Spoke Zarathustra* in his book *The End of History and the Last Man* (London: Penguin Books, 1992), 312. The perhaps more prudent political theorist Thomas Pangle quotes from exactly the same passage of *Zarathustra* in *The Ennobling of Democracy: The Challenge of the Postmodern Era* (Baltimore: Johns Hopkins University Press, 1992), 82.

16. Pangle, *Ennobling of Democracy*. See also Robert N. Bellah, Richard Madsen, William M. Sullivan, Ann Swidler, and Steven M. Tipton, *Habits of the Heart: Individualism and Commitment in American Life* (New York: Harper and Row, 1985).

17. Allen D. Hertzke, *Echoes of Discontent: Jesse Jackson, Pat Robertson, and the Resurgence of Populism* (Washington, D.C.: C. Q. Press, 1993), 245.

18. Bellah, *Habits of the Heart*, vi.

19. John Locke, *The Second Treatise of Government* (Indianapolis: Bobbs-Merrill, 1952), 36.

20. Ibid., 44, 45.

21. Carole Pateman, *The Sexual Contract* (Stanford, Calif.: Stanford University Press, 1988), 91.

22. Kathleen B. Jones, *Compassionate Authority: Democracy and the Representation of Women* (New York: Routledge, 1993), 68–69.

23. Ibid., 70.

24. Iris Marion Young, "Polity and Group Difference: A Critique of the Ideal of Universal Citizenship," in *Feminism and Political Theory*, ed. Cass R. Sunstein (Chicago: University of Chicago Press, 1990), 117–141.

25. Ibid., 136–137.

26. Jean Bethke Elshtain, *Public Man, Private Woman: Women in Social and Political Thought* (Princeton, N.J.: Princeton University Press, 1981); Sara Ruddick, "Maternal Thinking," in *Mothering: Essays in Feminist Theory*, ed. Joyce Trebilcot (Totowa, N.J.: Rowan and Allanheld, 1983), 213–262.

27. Mary G. Dietz, "Citizenship with a Feminist Face: The Problem with Maternal Thinking," *Political Theory* 13 (Feb. 1985): 19–37.

28. For a good explanation of the difficulties of "essentializing" for feminists, see Val Plumwood, "Women, Humanity and Nature," in *Socialism, Feminism, and Philosophy: A Radical Philosophy Reader*, ed. Sean Sayers and Peter Osborne (New York: Routledge, 1990), 211–234.

29. Patricia Boling, "The Democratic Potential of Mothering," *Political Theory* 19 (Nov. 1991): 606–625.

30. Struggling to resolve this essential woman–universal citizen dilemma, Chantal Mouffe defends an idea of citizenship in which citizens are perceived to have a multitude of subjectivities that guide their understanding of public matters. Citizens rearrange the order in which they consider their subjectivities as the matters they consider change. Unfortunately, Mouffe does not make clear how a multiplicity of subjectivities is different in any sense other than name from the variety of interests a typical citizen in a liberal democracy may be expected to possess and, therefore, does not explain the difference of her citizenship from that which occurs in the interest group democracy we have now. See Chantal Mouffe, "Feminism, Citizenship and Radical Democratic Politics," in *Feminists Theorize the Political*, ed. Judith Butler and Joan W. Scott (New York: Routledge, 1992), 369–384.

31. Critical theorists have complained that ethnographers do not acknowledge the transformative power that they exert over subjects when they turn a field into field notes and, in turn, make of field notes a scholarly text. According to critics, ethnographers are actually only presenting a view of the subject that

has been constructed by both the larger social power structure that acts on the informant and the power of the ethnographer's personality, but they disguise this fact, even from themselves, by appearing to allow the anthropological subject to speak in her own words. See Gayatri Chakravorty Spivak, "Can the Subaltern Speak?" in *Marxism and the Interpretation of Culture* (Urbana: University of Illinois Press, 1988); James Clifford, *The Predicament of Culture: Twentieth Century Ethnography, Literature and Art* (Cambridge, Mass.: Harvard University Press, 1988).

According to Joan Scott, scholars cannot escape the influence of power relations on their work, even when they seek a nonjudgmental account of the subjects' experiences, because the unanalyzed "experiences" of a subject have "inner workings or logics" that reflect "not individuals who have experiences but subjects who are constituted through experience," and "experience" originates in a power-dominated world (Joan Wallach Scott, "Experience," in Butler and Scott, *Feminists Theorize the Political*, 25–26).

32. For a good review of much of this literature, see Mary E. Hawkesworth, "Feminist Epistemology: A Survey of the Field," *Women and Politics* 7 (1987): 115–127. An explanation of the difficulty of merely "accommodating" the study of women and politics to the discipline as it exists now is found in Joan C. Tronto, "Politics and Revision: The Feminist Project to Change the Boundaries of American Political Science," *Revolutions in Knowledge: Feminism in the Social Sciences*, ed. Sue Rosenberg Zalk and Janice Gordon-Kelter (Boulder, Colo.: Westview Press, 1992), 91–110. Traditional social science oppositions between subjective and objective knowledge are criticized as inherently "male," in Rita Mae Kelly, Bernard Ronan, and Margaret E. Cawley, "Liberal Positivistic Epistemology and Research on Women and Politics," *Women and Politics* 7 (1987): 11–28; Susan Hekman, "The Feminization of Epistemology: Gender and the Social Sciences," *Women and Politics* 7 (1987): 65–83.

33. Diana Owen and Linda M. G. Zerilli, "Gender and Citizenship," *Society* 28 (July–Aug. 1991): 27–34.

34. Ibid., 31.

35. Ehara Yumiko, "Feminizumu seijigaku no kanōsei" [The Possibility of a Feminist Political Science], *Revaiasan* 8 (spring 1991): 8–9. Carol Hardy-Fanta finds that ethnographic methods are necessary for uncovering the full dimension of Latina women's political participation in Boston because women's tendency to emphasize formal/institutional political structures and positions less than the building of interpersonal connections meant that politically alive Latinas often failed to appear in data collected according to more traditional political science methods (see Hardy-Fanta, *Latina Politics/Latino Politics: Gender, Culture and Political Participation in Boston* [Philadelphia: Temple University Press, 1993]).

36. Ehara, "Feminizumu," 10.

37. Ibid.

38. Ibid., 22.

39. I have borrowed this phrase from Rousseau, who wrote in the opening section of his "Discourse on the Origin and Foundations of Inequality Among Men": "Let us therefore begin by setting all the facts aside, for they do not affect the question. The researches which can be undertaken concerning this subject

must not be taken for historical truths, but only for hypothetical and conditional reasonings better suited to clarify the nature of things than to show their true origin" (Jean-Jacques Rousseau, *The First and Second Discourses*, ed. Roger Masters, trans. Roger Masters and Judith Masters [New York: St. Martin's Press, 1964], 103). Although not all of his "conditional reasonings" please or convince me, I quote Rousseau here because I aspire to the thoughtful and revolutionary spirit that seems captured in this enigmatic passage, and I hope that my readers will find his words as valuable in my prefatory remarks as they were to me.

40. Koji Taira, "Dialectics of Economic Growth, National Power, and Distributive Struggles," in *Postwar Japan as History*, ed. Andrew Gordon (Berkeley: University of California Press, 1993), 181–183.

41. Yazawa Sumiko, "Toshi ni ikiru josei" [Women in Urban Areas], in *Toshi to josei no shakaigaku: seiyakuwari no yuragi wo koete* [The Sociology of Women in the City: Moving beyond the Breakdown in Sex Roles] (Tokyo: Saeinsu-sha, 1993), 35–37.

Chapter Two. Identity of "Regular Housewife"

1. Imai Yasuko, "The Emergence of the Japanese *Shufu*: Why a *Shufu* Is More Than a 'Housewife,' " *U.S.-Japan Women's Journal English Supplement* 6 (March 1994): 44–65.

2. It is customary to indicate one's name and occupation in a letter to the editor, but some women not employed outside the home choose to declare their occupation as "not working" rather than housewife. For the example letters mentioned earlier, in which the author did declare herself as a housewife, see "Genron no jiyū ga nainoka shushō" [Prime Minister, Don't You Have Freedom of Expression?], *Asahi shinbun* (Tokyo) 21 Oct. 1992, 15; "Hitori-hitori ga yūki wo dashite" [One by One, Show Some Courage], *Asahi shinbun* (Tokyo) 8 Oct. 1992, 15.

3. Yoshinaga Michiko, "Seikatsu-sha gawa ni tatteinai: dakkara yominikui" [You Don't Stand on the Side of the Ordinary Person, That's Why You're Hard to Read], *Asahi shinbun* (Tokyo) 26 Sept. 1992.

4. "Ikinokori kakeru fujin sōgō zasshi" [General Women's Magazine Gambles on Survival], *Asahi shinbun* (Tokyo) 18 Jan. 1993, 13.

5. Kunihiro Yōko, "Toshi no seikatsu sekai to josei no shufu ishiki" [The Lifeworld of the City and Women's Housewife Consciousness], in *Toshi to josei no shakaigaku* [The Sociology of Women and the City], ed. Yazawa Sumiko (Tokyo: Saiensu-sha, 1993), 78.

6. For further reflections on this phenomenon see Glenda S. Roberts, *Staying on the Line: Blue-Collar Women in Contemporary Japan* (Honolulu: University of Hawaii Press, 1994); Kathleen S. Uno, "The Death of the 'Good Wife, Wise Mother'?" in *Postwar Japan as History*, ed. Andrew Gordon (Berkeley: University of California Press, 1993), 293–322. Joy Hendry points out that as many as 30 percent of married women remain uninterruptedly in the home, in "The Role of the Professional Housewife," in *Japanese Women Working*, ed. Janet Hunter (New York: Routledge, 1993), 224–241.

7. *Nerima Kusei Gaiyō* [Outline of Nerima Ward Administration] (Tokyo: Wada Insatsu, 1992), 17.

8. Ibid.

9. This sort of urbanization is an undisputed nationwide trend in Japan, and many have suggested that it has led to a fragmented community structure where a large proportion of the daytime population consists of housewives and students who do not fit usual social analysis categories. See Inuzuka Susumu, "Toshika to danchi seikatsu: 'danchi toshi' no sangyō shakai kōsei" [Urbanization and *Danchi* Lifestyle: The Structure of Industrial Society in a *Danchi* City], in *Chiiki shakai to seiji bunka: shimin jichi wo meguru jichitai to jūmin*, ed. Moriya Takahiko and Furuki Toshiaki (Tokyo: Yūshindō, 1984), 26–37; see also Fukutake Tadashi, *The Japanese Social Structure: Its Evolution in the Modern Century*, 2d ed., trans. Ronald P. Dore (Tokyo: University of Tokyo Press, 1989), 99–137.

10. Theodore Bestor's study of tradition in a modern Tokyo neighborhood suggests that the sort of "real" tradition to which my informants refer does not exist even in "old" Tokyo neighborhoods. Bestor says, "Social change itself created many of the features now labeled as 'traditional' and now thought to represent the survival of the past." In congruence with the argument I make about Nerima, Bestor writes, "Contemporary patterns of neighborhood life, therefore, were and are created through the general processes of urban growth, combined with the particular historical circumstances of the community and of Japanese society during the twentieth century" (Theodore Bestor, *Neighborhood Tokyo* [Stanford, Calif.: Stanford University Press, 1989], 258, 259).

11. I put "unimportant" in quotation marks because, over time, I realized that individual women were awake to the distinctions among members of a given group and may even have paid them a great deal of attention. Nevertheless, courtesy required that the distinctions go "unnoticed" when my informants socialized with other housewives.

12. According to the Prime Minister's Office report *Josei no genjō to shisaku* [The Present Condition of Women's Lives and Women's Policy] (Tokyo: Gyōsei, 1992, 100–101), over 50 percent of all Japanese women over fifteen years old have had some form of paid employment since the early 1970s. In 1992, 75.6 percent of those between twenty and twenty-four years old and 72.1 percent of those between forty-five and forty-nine were employed, and this number reflects a steady increase over the years since the 1970s. Over half of women in their chief childbearing years in their late twenties and early thirties are employed.

13. Nearly 70 percent of women in a 1992 prime minister's office survey said that they would like to participate in some form of continuing education; in 1990, 43 percent of all Japanese women over twenty were engaged in a continuing education program (Prime Minister's Office report, 97).

14. Particularly useful are Jane M. Bachnik, "Introduction: *Uchi/Soto:* Challenging Our Conceptualizations of Self, Social Order, and Language," in *Situated Meaning: Inside and Outside in Japanese Self, Society, and Language,* ed. Jane M. Bachnik and Charles J. Quinn, Jr. (Princeton, N.J.: Princeton University Press, 1994), 3–37; Joy Hendry, "Humidity, Hygiene, or Ritual Care: Some Thoughts on Wrapping as a Social Phenomenon," in *Unwrapping Japan: Society*

and Culture in Anthropological Perspective, ed. Eyal Ben-Ari, Brian Moeran, and James Valentine (Honolulu: University of Hawaii Press, 1990), 18–35.

15. Nancy R. Rosenberger, "Introduction," in *Japanese Sense of Self*, ed. Nancy R. Rosenberger (New York: Cambridge University Press, 1992), 1–20; Robert Smith, *Japanese Society: Tradition, Self and the Social Order* (New York: Cambridge University Press, 1983). Although her analysis is now considered overly simplistic, Ruth Benedict pioneered the relational self idea in English in *The Chrysanthemum and the Sword: Patterns of Japanese Culture* (Boston: Houghton Mifflin, 1946). See also Takeo Doi, *The Anatomy of Self: The Individual Versus Society*, trans. Mark A. Harbison (Tokyo: Kodansha, 1986); Takami Kuwayama, "The Reference Other Orientation," in *Japanese Sense of Self*, ed. Nancy R. Rosenberger (New York: Cambridge University Press, 1992); Herbert Hyman, "Introduction," in *Readings in Reference Group Theory and Research*, ed. H. Hyman and E. Singer (New York: Free Press, 1968); Raymond Schmitt, *The Reference Other Orientation: An Extension of the Reference Group Concept* (Carbondale: Southern Illinois University Press, 1972).

16. Americans might say much the same thing about the social quality of their identity definition. However, we might draw an exaggerated but still useful contrast between American and Japanese rhetorics of identity. In the United States, we may concede that we cannot write our identities on a blank slate, but we still place at least a superficial importance on the effort of scraping out a portion of the identity slate that is marked as ours, original, distinguishable from the identity of all others. American rhetoric of identity values the rejection of socially predetermined lines of self-definition; it is a rhetoric of self-ownership. Japanese rhetoric of identity does not concern itself with conceding the power of larger social definitions in an individual's identity because it is not particularly concerned with self-ownership. An American has a "successful" identity when she can claim to have crafted much of it herself, while a Japanese can claim to have a "successful" identity when she can fully fit herself into a ritual space considered aesthetically pleasing. The successful American celebrates her capacity to distinguish herself from ritual; the "successful Japanese" celebrates her capacity to embody ritual.

17. See Takie Sugiyama Lebra, "Self in Japanese Culture," in Nancy R. Rosenberger, *Japanese Sense of Self*, 105–120. See also Anne Allison, "Producing Mothers," in *Re-imaging Japanese Women*, ed. Anne Imamura (Berkeley: University of California Press, 1996), 135–155.

18. Lebra, "Self in Japanese Culture," 106–107.

19. Ibid., 107.

20. Ibid., 110.

21. Ibid. See also Dorinne Kondo's explanation of the "relationally constructed" self, in *Crafting Selves: Power, Gender and Discourses of Identity in a Japanese Workplace* (Chicago: University of Chicago Press, 1989), especially 112–113.

22. It may seem strange to generalize about the character of all modern democracies while operating from a specifically Japanese understanding of the self. However, I would argue that, with further research, a similar self-*seken* relationship might be defined in Western democratic politics as well. For some preliminary evidence of this see Kevin McKillop, Michael Berzonsky, and Barry

Schlenker, "The Impact of Self-Presentations on Self-Beliefs: Effects of Social Identity and Self-Presentational Context," *Journal of Personality* 60.4 (1992): 789–808; Fiona Devine, "Social Identities, Class Identity and Political Perspectives," *Sociological Review* 40.2 (1992): 229–252; Pamela Johnston Conover, "The Role of Social Groups in Political Thinking," *British Journal of Political Science* 18.1 (1988): 51–76.

23. Kunihiro Yōko, "Shufu to iu kategorī: Kōgakureki josei no shufu ishiki to shutai keisei" [The Category of "Housewife": The Housewife Consciousness and Subject Development of Women with Higher Education], master's thesis, Keio University, 1991. One particularly useful question that I borrowed from Kunihiro was "Shufu rashī shufu desu ka?" (Are you a housewife-like housewife, or are you a typical housewife?). Most of both mine and Kunihiro's respondents declined.

24. This is a question suggested to me by Kunihiro and used in her own thesis.

25. One freelance writer who became a housewife has written an entire book to correct what she came to believe was the Japanese media's erroneous presentation of housewives and "the woman problem" (Ueda Miho, *Tōkyō shufu monogatari* [The Tale of a Tokyo Housewife] [Tokyo: Geibunsha, 1992]).

26. She worked as a part-time assistant at her husband's company. She also studied politics for her own benefit.

27. Sasaki-san is probably not at all unusual in her tendency to wrestle with her work identity and housewife identity. Research on Japanese women's working patterns indicates that, partly because of cultural expectation, partly because of discrimination in the workforce, women often expect to place their home and family duties first when they take on a job. In other words, they take jobs with their primary identity of housewife in mind. See Ann Cordilla and Kazuko Ohta, "Central in the Family and Marginal in the Work Force: Women's Place in Japanese Society," in *Women's Work and Women's Lives: The Continuing Struggle Worldwide*, ed. Hilda Kahne and Janet Z. Giele (Boulder, Colo.: Westview Press, 1992).

28. Underreporting of work of this type that Japanese women do in the home is common according to Mary Saso, *Women in the Japanese Workplace* (London: Hilary Shipman, 1990), 27.

29. It should be understood that, although she and others considered the teaching a "favor," Sasaki-san would be paid a regular sum in the form of *O-rei* (thank-you money) by the parents of her pupils.

Chapter Three. Housewives and Citizenship

1. The collection was published as a postelection magazine: Ono Kiyoko, *Kokkai dayori: Anata no Kenkō, chikyū no kenkō* [National Assembly Report: Your Health and the Health of the Globe] 3 (1993).

2. *Uguisu-jo* literally means "nightingale-girl"; it is the nickname for the women who have trained their voices to do the stylized, professional announcing of candidates' names and other information from campaign sound-trucks.

3. For a good English review of the native Japanese literature that has

attempted to broaden the scope of political science but still failed to examine politics from the perspective of non-elite citizens, see Gary D. Allinson, "Politics in Contemporary Japan: Pluralist Scholarship in the Conservative Era—A Review Article," *Journal of Asian Studies* 48 (1989): 324–333.

4. This definition would seem to be appropriate in terms of a theoretical understanding of democratic life. A person who possesses no perception of *political* membership in society is, in essence, a subject of that society's political structures. In discussions of democratic politics, subjects and citizens should not be equated. Subjects cannot be said to have experienced the key component of democracy—a possibility of equal participation on some level in determining the society's nature through politics.

5. See Kabashima Ikuo, *Seiji Sanka* [Political Participation] (Tokyo: Tokyo Daigaku Shuppankai, 1988); Kobayashi Yoshiaki, *Gendai nihon no senkyo* [Modern Japanese Elections] (Tokyo: Tokyo Daigaku Shuppankai, 1991); Satō Susumu, *Nihon no jichi bunka* [The Culture of Japanese Self-Government] (Tokyo: Gyōsei, 1991); Watanuki Jōji, "Yūken-sha to shite no josei" [Women as Voters], *Revaiasan* 8 (1991): 23–40; Aoki Taiko, *Yoron minshushugi—Josei to seiji* [Public Opinion Democracy—Women and Politics] (Tokyo: Waseda Daigaku Shuppanbu, 1991); Theodore McNelly, " 'Woman Power' in Japan's 1989 Upper House Election," In *Electoral Systems in Comparative Perspective: Their Impact on Women and Minorities*, ed. Wilma Rule and Joseph F. Zimmerman (Westport, Conn.: Greenwood Press, 1994), 149–159.

6. Watanuki, "Yūken-sha to shite no josei," 28, 34.

7. Ibid., 35–37.

8. Sugawara Kazuko, "Chihō josei giin ōryō shinshutsu no igi to kadai" [The Significance and Problems of the Large Increases in Local Female Legislators], *Jichi no naka no onnatachi, Jichitai gaku nenpō* 5 (1992): 27–41.

9. Tanaka Yasumasa, "Tokai no shufu to chihō no shufu" [Changing Japanese Housewives in Urban and Rural Areas], *Gakushūin Daigaku Hōgakubu Kenkyū Nenpō* 25 (1990): 1–90; Aoki Taiko, "Shufu pawā no rekishiteki tōjō: 'midori' to gendā gyappu" [The History-making Appearance of Housewife Power: "Green" and the Gender Gap], *Gendai no riron* 210 (1985): 69–77.

10. A good example of this sort of explanation is Susan J. Pharr, *Political Women in Japan: The Search for a Place in Political Life* (Berkeley: University of California Press, 1981). The centrality of the home to women's lives is considered a main cause for Japanese male/female participation differences in Aoki, "Shufu pawā no rekishiteki tōjō," 68–77.

11. Anne Phillips, *Engendering Democracy* (University Park, Pa.: Pennsylvania University Press, 1991), 118–140; Virginia Sapiro, *The Political Integration of Women: Roles, Socialization, and Politics* (Chicago: University of Illinois Press, 1983). Full-time housewives are awarded a 100 percent privatization score in the categorization of woman as privatized and egalitarian, and, not surprisingly, privatized woman are less likely to be politically active (Sue Tolleson Rinehart, *Gender Consciousness and Politics* [University Park, Pa.: Pennsylvania State University Press, 1992], 92–119). For more on the public-private distinction see Carole Pateman, *The Disorder of Women* (New York: Routledge, 1989).

12. Iris Marion Young, "Polity and Group Difference: A Critique of the Ideal

of Universal Citizenship," in *Feminism and Political Theory*, ed. Cass R. Sunstein (Chicago: University of Chicago Press, 1990), 117–141; Jean Bethke Elshtain, *Public Man, Private Woman: Women in Social and Political Thought* (Princeton, N.J.: Princeton University Press, 1981); Carole Pateman, *The Sexual Contract* (Stanford, Calif.: Stanford University Press, 1988). For a Japanese radical feminist interpretation of the categorical exclusion of women from modern society that greatly resembles Pateman's argument about the submission of woman to men prior to the erection of liberal democracy, see Ueno Chizuko, *Kapuchō sei to shihonsei* [Capitalism and Patriarchy] (Tokyo: Iwanami Shoten, 1990).

13. Kathleen S. Uno, "Women and Changes in the Household Division of Labor," in *Recreating Japanese Women*, ed. Gail Lee Bernstein (Berkeley: University of California Press, 1991), 17–41; Sharon H. Nolte and Sally Ann Hastings, "The Meiji State's Policy toward Women, 1890–1910," in Bernstein, *Recreating Japanese Women*, 151–174.

14. Sheldon Garon, "Women's Groups and the Japanese State: Contending Approaches to Political Integration, 1890–1945," *Journal of Japanese Studies* 19.1 (1993): 5–41.

15. Kathleen S. Uno, "The Death of the 'Good Wife, Wise Mother'?" in *Postwar Japan as History*, ed. Andrew Gordon (Berkeley: University of California Press, 1993), 293–322.

16. Sumiko Iwao, *The Japanese Woman: Traditional Image and Changing Reality* (New York: Free Press, 1993), 10.

17. I interviewed a female politician in the rural prefecture of Niigata who said that, for women, the opposite was actually true. Women in the Tokyo area were far more likely to be politically active.

18. This is a rather extraordinary accomplishment, considering that—despite the fact that women make up nearly all the rank and file members and lower officers—PTA president is a job that has been traditionally reserved for men. In 1984, 83 percent of PTA presidents were men (Inoue Teruko and Ehara Yumiko, eds., *Josei no dēta bukku* [Women's Data Book] [Tokyo: Yuhikaku, 1991], 141).

19. According to *Asahi shinbun* research, as many as 26 percent of Diet seat winners in an election were running for a seat previously held by a father, father-in-law, uncle, or grandfather. See "Nisei giin: sannin ni hitori, shidai mo suzukunoka" [Second-generation Legislators: One Out of Three Are from the Next Generation], *Asahi shinbun* (Tokyo), international satellite ed., 15 March 1994, 9.

20. Taxis are an extremely expensive mode of transportation in Tokyo, and I heard this sort of linking of politicians, taxis, and elitism often. Another woman put it this way: "If Diet members didn't ride in cars, but had to walk from place to place, they'd see a lot. They need to see things from the position of weak people."

21. My translation of "that far" is not direct. Her words might also have been rendered as "to that extent" or "to that degree." I, nevertheless, interpreted her words as an inference of distance between her lifestyle and the world of politics, paralleling her understanding of politics with that of other women who do not use distance words such as *mijika ni nai* (not close by).

Chapter Four. Volunteering against Politics

1. Alexander Hamilton or James Madison, "Federalist No. 51," in John Jay, Alexander Hamilton, and James Madison, *The Federalist: A Commentary on the Constitution of the United States* (New York: Random House, 1937), 337.

2. See Tocqueville's passage on Americans and associations in Alexis de Tocqueville, *Democracy in America*, ed. J. P. Mayer, trans. George Lawrence (New York: Harper and Row, 1969), 513–517.

3. Ibid., 510.

4. A recent example of this argument in the American case is found in Robert Bellah, *The Good Society* (New York: Alfred A. Knopf, 1991), 112–113. *The Good Society* is the sequel to *Habits of the Heart*, the Bellah project to reexamine contemporary American public life through the Tocqueville framework.

5. Wuthnow is talking about voluntary sectors in a cross-national perspective; see Wuthnow, "The Voluntary Sector: Legacy of the Past, Hope for the Future?" in *Between States and Markets: The Voluntary Sector in Comparative Perspective*, ed. Robert Wuthnow (Princeton, N.J.: Princeton University Press, 1991), 3–29.

6. Sidney Verba, Kay Lehman Schlozman, and Henry E. Brady, *Voice and Equality: Civic Voluntarism in American Politics* (Cambridge: Harvard University Press, 1995). Benjamin Barber argues that real democratic citizenship is not possible unless individuals are forced to more communal thinking through their participation in civic affairs.

While agreeing with Tocqueville that "local institutions and voluntary associations" are "a key to national democracy in America," Barber does express reservations that organizations that are excessively parochial in their concerns cannot provide participants with a full civic education. He says that voluntary activity in private groups cannot substitute for the contribution that "direct political participation" makes to citizenship.

7. J. Miller McPherson, "A Dynamic Model of Voluntary Affiliation," *Social Forces* 59 (1981): 705–727; Frank Baumgartner and Jack Walker, "Survey Research and Membership in Voluntary Associations," *American Journal of Political Science* 32 (1988): 908–927; Tom W. Smith, "Trends in Group Membership: Comments on Baumgartner and Walker," *America Journal of Political Science* 34 (1990): 646–661. Nicholas Babchuk and Alan Booth, "Voluntary Association Membership: A Longitudinal Analysis," *American Sociological Review* 34 (1969): 31–45.

8. David Horton Smith, "Research and Communication Needs in Voluntary Action," *Volunteerism: An Emerging Profession*, ed. John Cull and Richard Hardy (Springfield, Ill.: Charles C. Thomas, 1974), 111–186. Although this book is over twenty years old, its criticism of voluntarism literature is still accurate. Almond and Verba counted the number of citizens' voluntary association memberships as a key variable in their cross-national study of political attitudes, claiming "members of such organizations receive training for participation within the organization, and this training is then transferable to the political sphere." Gabriel Almond and Sidney Verba, *The Civic Culture: Political Attitudes and Democracy in Five Nations* (Newbury Park, Ca.: Sage Publications, 1989), 256. The

recent Verba, Schlozman, Brady team study takes much the same approach and reaches similar conclusions. Verba et al., *Voice and Equality*, 80.

9. Almond and Verba, *Civic Culture*. See also James E. Curtis, "Voluntary Association Joining: A Cross-National Comparative Note," *American Sociological Review* 36 (1971): 872–880. A high degree of voluntarism among Americans in comparison with other nations may be due to the large number of church-related volunteer activities and the tendency of Americans to join organizations in which they are not active simply because many opportunities to join exist. But some nations, Japan among them, have low levels of voluntary association membership even when researchers' control for church-related, labor union, and non-active memberships. James E. Curtis, Edward G. Grabb, and Douglas E. Baer, "Voluntary Association Membership in Fifteen Countries: A Comparative Analysis," *American Sociological Review* 57.2 (1992): 139–152.

10. Curtis et al., Voluntary Association Membership in Fifteen Countries."

11. Carol Hardy-Fanta, *Latina Politics/Latino Politics: Gender, Culture, and Political Participation in Boston* (Philadelphia: Temple University Press, 1993).

12. Lee Ann Banaszak, *Why Movements Succeed or Fail: Opportunity, Culture, and the Struggle for Woman Suffrage* (Princeton: Princeton University Press, 1996), especially 84–90.

13. We are not even sure what the real causal path between voluntary participation and political participation in the United States is because we have not fully taken account of a third variable, socioeconomic status. Stephen Cutler, "Voluntary Association Membership and the Theory of Mass Society," *Bonds of Pluralism: The Form and Substance of Urban Social Networks*, ed. Edward O. Laumann (New York: John Wiley and Sons, 1973), 133–159.

14. Alan Booth, "Sex and Social Participation," *American Sociological Review* 37 (1972): 188.

15. Ibid., 188.

16. Verba et al., *Voice and Equality*, 256.

17. Ibid., 257.

18. Booth admits this himself ("Sex and Social Participation" 188). He also uses the terms in Babchuk and Booth, "Voluntary Association Membership" 39.

19. J. Miller McPherson and Lynn Smith-Lovin, "Women and Weak Ties: Differences by Sex in the Size of Voluntary Organizations," *American Journal of Sociology* 87 (1982): 883–904, especially 884.

20. John Wilson, " 'Public' Work and Social Participation: The Case of Farm Women," *Sociological Quarterly* 31 (1990): 107–121, especially 112.

21. Ibid.

22. Doris Gold, "Women and Voluntarism," in *Women in a Sexist Society*, ed. Vivian Gornick and Barbara Moran (New York: Basic Books, 1971), 384–400, quotations are from 389, 390, 393.

23. Herta Loeser, *Women, Work, and Volunteering* (Boston: Beacon Press, 1974), 26.

24. Ten years later, Wendy Kaminer was still defending volunteer activity to feminists as an important step toward paid employment, in Kaminer, *Women Volunteering: The Pleasure, Pain, and Politics of Unpaid Work from 1830 to the Present* (Garden City, N.Y.: Doubleday, 1984). She writes: "This [feminism] has

left women somewhat confused about their motives for volunteering. If they have been encouraged, even pressured by the feminist movement to demand something for themselves from their work, many still have a residual impulse to apologize for doing so. Their tendency is to distinguish between the desire for a professional career and the impulse to serve a community as 'selfish' and 'unselfish' reasons for volunteering. It is a distinction that makes no sense at all to me" (53–55).

25. Kathleen D. McCarthy, "Parallel Power Structures: Women and the Voluntary Sphere," in *Lady Bountiful Revisited: Women, Philanthropy, and Power*, ed. Kathleen McCarthy (New Brunswick, N.J.: Rutgers University Press, 1990), 1–31, especially 11.

26. Arlene Kaplan Daniels, *Invisible Careers: Women Civic Leaders from the Volunteer World* (Chicago: University of Chicago Press, 1988). Daniels provides a particularly damning example of social science's volunteer world myopia in her preface. She invited two colleagues, their wives, and an especially accomplished woman volunteer–civic leader to her home for dinner. Having described the volunteer woman's achievements to her colleagues, Kaplan expected them to see the woman as an interesting person to meet and study. She says, however, that "my colleagues had not 'seen it.' They only saw a conventional upper middle-class dowager and were more intrigued with her husband, who represented class interests and values they might wish to study. Interestingly enough the wives of these social scientists did see what I tried to show them" (xv–xvi).

Recently I had the dubious pleasure of a very similar experience when I presented some of this research at a professional conference on communitarianism. The man giving the paper preceding mine spoke about the American voluntarism recognized through former president George Bush's Points of Light Award program. In characterizing the awarded volunteers, the presenter said, "These people do real stuff. This isn't tea and rummage sales." Of course, tea and rummage sales are exactly the sort of work that Sagyōsho, the group I discuss here, does. As the speaker failed to explain why "tea and rummage" sales were "unreal" volunteerism, I was left to wonder if their association with traditionally feminine voluntary sectors was what had tainted them in his mind. After all, the other possible meanings of "tea and rummage sales" are only available to us if we ask, "Tea with whom?" "Rummage sold for what purpose?"

27. Curtis et al., "Voluntary Association Membership in Fifteen Countries," 139–152. The idea of a strong-state tradition in Japan is not universally accepted. Margaret McKean, a student of environmental activism in Japan, argues against strong-state interpretations, in "State Strength and the Public Interest," in *Political Dynamics in Contemporary Japan*, ed. Gary Allinson and Yasunori Sone (Ithaca, N.Y.: Cornell University Press, 1993), 72–104.

28. The definition of *borantia* is explained in English in Koya Azumi, "Voluntary Organizations in Japan," in *Voluntary Action Research, 1974: The Nature of Voluntary Action around the World*, ed. David Horton Smith (Lexington, Mass.: D. C. Heath, 1974), 15–26. "The clearest cases of volunteerism are those involving welfare-oriented, unpaid services by private persons. *Borantia* in Japan refers to persons who engage in altruistic acts" (ibid., 21). Nearly an exactly matching definition is also found in a Japanese publication produced for the

Nerima ward government by the Nerima Ward Welfare Council, a quasi-public body instituted for the promotion of voluntarism under the guidelines of the Occupation's Supreme Command of Allied Power (*Borantia no machizukuri wo mezashite: Nerima-ku ni okeru borantia katsudō suishin no teigen* [Aiming for a Volunteer City: Suggestions for the Promotion of Volunteer Activity in Nerima] [Tokyo: Nerima-ku Shakai Fukushi Kyōgikai, 1989], 1).

29. Some survey data show that men and woman participate in activities that are known as *borantia* at about the same rate, about 6 percent (Prime Minister's Office, *Josei no genjō to shisaku* [The Present Condition of Women and Women's Policy] [Tokyo: Gyōsei, 1992], 51). Why the figures look this way is a mystery. Among the 715 people registered as volunteers at the Nerima Volunteer Center in 1992, only 129 were men, and the center staff indicated that increasing the number of male volunteers was a perennial challenge. In my own field research among volunteers groups, I seldom came across male volunteers. Those I did see tended to spend far less time on group activities than did women. Exceptions were male Christian church staff and progressive political activists who sometimes included volunteer work in their community network repertoire.

30. Kabashima Ikuo, *Seiji sanka* [Political Participation] (Tokyo: Tokyo Daigaku Shuppankai, 1988), 131.

31. Ibid., 123.

32. Azumi, "Voluntary Organizations in Japan."

33. Inoue Teruko and Ehara Yumiko, eds., *Josei no dēta bukku* [Woman's Date Book] (Tokyo: Yuhikaku, 1991), 142–143.

34. Matsumura Naoko, "Seikatsu no gendaiteki tokuchō to shufu yakuwari" [The Characteristics of Modern Lifestyles and the Housewife's Role], in *Josei seikatsu shi dai go kan: gendai,* ed. Itō Yasuko (Tokyo: Tokyo Daigaku Shuppankai, 1990), 235–268.

35. Sasakura Naoko, "Ikiyoi wa toroenakatta josei no shinshitsu" [The Unrelenting Vigor of the Women's Political Advancement], *Ekonomisto* 21 May 1991, 86–89.

36. *Borantia no machizukuri wo mezashite,* 8–16.

37. Registered volunteers receive special coverage under the ward insurance program for injuries they might sustain while involved in volunteer activity.

38. Some labor unions were listed on the Nerima volunteer group roster, however.

39. Some degree of overlap should be expected in this figure, as those registered as individuals may have also belonged to one or more groups, but the number of people who belonged to the registered groups would have numbered well over 1,500 according to copies of volunteer center records.

40. *Tōroku borantia no jittai to ishiki ni kansuru chōsa hōkokusho* [A Report on the Survey of the Nature and Consciousness of Registered Volunteers] (Tokyo: Nerima-ku Shakai Fukushi Kyōgikai, March 1990), 64–68.

41. Tokyo's garbage collection sites are famous for the treasures they contain. One Japanese-American friend of mine acquired a working refrigerator, several televisions, and some serviceable furniture—all of which had been set out for trash collection. Other friends had found perfectly operable washing machines that would have made their way to the dump. Periodicals for English-speaking

foreign residents of Tokyo suggest combing the trash for household items rather than buying new.

42. Sōka Gakkai is the key supporter of the Kōmeitō, or Clean Government Party, a party that many housewives upheld as an example of the distasteful nature of "organization" in politics.

43. This is especially humorous for more than one reason. While she was obviously poking fun at her own inadequacies, her remark could also be interpreted as a jab at the housewife volunteers who played the nagging mother-in-law role to her bride. Such mother-in-law–young-bride jokes are a staple of Japanese humor.

44. She lost by a very slim margin, probably in part because she did not receive the organizational support of the Nerima Seikatsu Club Co-op, which was unable to commit to such a level of political involvement. The co-op is the subject of the next chapter.

45. She also said that it was important for the volunteers to work with the handicapped without developing a "volunteer" consciousness where they saw themselves as lady bountifuls. Of course, only "volunteers" had been invited to the meeting, demonstrating that Satō-san also made distinctions.

Chapter Five. Toward a "Housewifely" Movement

1. Where the Japanese name has important symbolic meanings for the Seikatsu movement, I have chosen to use the original Japanese rather than a translated alternative. Interpretations of the symbolism in words such as *seikatsu* and *iki-iki* are undertaken in this chapter in the subsection "The Housewife as a Defining Movement Concept."

2. Sandra Buckley, "Altered States: The Body Politics of 'Being-Woman,' " in *Postwar Japan as History*, ed. Andrew Gordon (Berkeley: University of California Press, 1993), 347–372.

3. Kunihiro Yōko points out that in 1994 the average representation of women in the two houses of Japan's National Assembly (Diet) was only 6.7 percent, and women make up only 3.4 percent of elected representatives in prefectural and lower level assemblies combined. Women are best represented in urban ward assemblies, at 12.1 percent. While these numbers seem shockingly low, Kunihiro also reminds us that in 1994, American women made up 11 percent and 7 percent, respectively, of House of Representatives and the Senate of the United States Congress. See Kunihiro Yōko, "Chiiki ni okeru 'shufu' no seiji teki shutaika: dairinin undō sanka-sha no aidentitī bunseki kara" [The Development of a Political Subjectivity in the Local "Housewife": From an Analysis of the Identity of Participants in the *Dairinin Undō*], in *Chiiki shakai gakkai nenpō dai nana shū: chiiki shakaigaku no shin sōten* 7 (1995): 121, 123–124.

4. Buckley, "Altered States," 372.

5. Hasegawa Kōichi, "Han genshiryoku undō ni okeru josei no ichi: posuto-cherunobuiri no 'atarashī shakai undō' " [Women of the Anti-Nuclear Energy Movement: A Post-Chernobyl New Social Movement in Japan], *Revaiasan* 8 (1991): 41–58. For statistics representing the growth of women's representation

see: Nihon Fujin Dantai Rengō Kai, *Fujin hakusho 1992: Konnichi no kazoku mondai* [Women's White Paper 1992: Today's Family Problems] (Tokyo: Horupu shuppan, 1992), 285; Nihon Fujin Kaigi, *Onna tachi wa seiji wo kaeru* [Women Change Politics] (Tokyo: Emu kikaku insatsu, 1994); Dairinin Undō Kōryū Sentā, "Senkyo kekka" [Election Results], *Dairinin undō* 9.6 (1995): 21.

6. Gary D. Allinson, "Citizenship, Fragmentation and the Negotiated Polity," in *Political Dynamics in Contemporary Japan*, ed. Gary Allinson and Yasunori Sone (Ithaca, N.Y.: Cornell University Press, 1993), 17–49; Kurt Steiner, Ellis S. Krauss, and Scott C. Flanagan, *Political Opposition and Local Politics in Japan* (Princeton, N.J.: Princeton University Press, 1980).

7. Kurt Steiner, "Toward a Framework for the Study of Local Opposition," in Steiner et al., *Political Opposition and Local Politics in Japan*, 3–32.

8. In their words, *futsū no sengyō shufu*.

9. Iwai Tomoaki, " 'The Madonna Boom': Women in the Japanese Diet," *Journal of Japanese Studies* 19.1 (1993): 103–120; Sumiko Iwao, *The Japanese Woman: Traditional Image and Changing Reality* (New York: Free Press, 1993); Susan Pharr, *Political Women in Japan: The Search for a Place in Political Life* (Berkeley: University of California Press, 1981); Ueno Chizuko, "Shufu ronsō wo kaidoku suru" [Interpreting the Housewife Debates], in *Shufu ronsō wo yomu* [Reading the Housewife Debates], ed. Ueno Chizuko, vol. 2 (Tokyo: Keisō Shobō, 1990), 246–274, and Ueno, *Kapuchōsei to shihonsei* [Capitalism and Patriarchy] (Tokyo: Iwanami Shoten, 1990); Watanuki Jōji, "Yūken-sha to shite no josei" [Women as Voters], *Revaiasan* 8 (1991): 23–40.

10. To be fair, a few scholars have begun to note the connection between women's successful entrance into politics and *shufu pawā* (power). See Aoki Taiko, "Shufu pawā no rekishiteki tōjō: 'midori' to gendā gyappu" [The History-making Appearance of Housewife Power: "Green" and the Gender Gap], *Gendai no riron* 210 (1985): 68–77; Yamazaki Tetsuya, "Shufu no seikyō undō to ishiki henyō" [The Housewives' Co-op Movement and Their Changing Consciousness], *Toshi mondai* 79.6 (1988): 34. Those who work on Japanese politics in English, however, have yet to admit that housewives make up the body of a successful grassroots effort. For a powerful example of this, compare Aoki's short study of Zushi's city assembly recall movement (cited earlier) with Purnendra C. Jain, "Green Politics and Citizen Power in Japan: The Zushi Movement," *Asian Survey* 31 (June 1991): 559–575.

11. The Japanese language is full of such ambiguous uses. For example, I was taught by one of my Japanese-language professors that it was better to turn down an invitation with the word *chotto* (a little . . .), implying that the situation was a little inconvenient for me, than to offer a complete sentence stating that I did not want to attend the event to which I had been invited.

12. I am borrowing this translation of the Japanese *dairinin undō* from Iwao, *The Japanese Woman*, 248. The word *dairinin* might also be translated as "representative," but Iwao points out that there is another Japanese word for "representative," *daihyō*, connoting a sense of vertical rank. She uses the word "proxy" to emphasize the Netto's concern that its elected officials are acting as voices of their organization and are supposed to enjoy neither higher rank than

non-office-holding members nor independence from the Netto when making decisions in official capacities.

13. *"Shōhi seikatsu kyōdō kumiai hō"* [Consumers' Lifestyle Cooperatives Law], Shōwa Year 23, No. 200.

14. Satō Yoshiyuki, ed., *Josei tachi no seikatsu nettowāku: seikatsu kurabu ni tsudou hitobito* [Women's Daily Life Network: The People Who Gather at the Seikatsu Club] (Tokyo: Bunshindō, 1988), 161–166.

15. Iwane Kunio, *Atarashii shakai undō no yohanseki: seikatsu kurabu-dairinin undō* [The Quarter-Century of the New Social Movement: The Seikatsu Club and the Proxy Movement] (Tokyo: Kyōdō tosho kabushiki kaisha, 1993), 10.

16. Ibid., 8.

17. Ibid., 45–46.

18. Ibid., and see also Satō Yoshiyuki, *Seikatsu seikai to taiwa no riron* [The Lifeworld and the Logic of Communication] (Tokyo: Bunshindō, 1991).

19. See Mario Diani, "The Concept of Social Movement," *Sociological Review* 40.1 (1992): 1–25; Russell J. Dalton, "The Challenge of New Movements," in *Challenging the Political Order: New Social and Political Movements in Western Democracies*, ed. Russell J. Dalton and Manfred Kuechler (New York: Oxford University Press, 1990), 3–20. NSM theory has been applied to the case of Japanese women's anti-nuclear power movements by Hasegawa Koichi.

20. Iwane, *Atarashii shakai undō no yohanseki*, 148–150.

21. Ibid., 155: *"tada tanni dokoka no undō ni sanka suru no de wa naku . . ."*

22. Ibid., 145–158.

23. Ikeda Tetsu, "Dairinin undō zenkoku rentai no igi" [The Meaning of National Proxy Movement Solidarity], *Shakai undō* 150 (1992): 10–19.

24. Satō Yoshiyuki, *Seikatsu seika to taiwa no riron*.

25. Ronald Inglehart, "Values, Ideology, and Cognitive Mobilization in New Social Movements," in *Challenging the Political Order: New Social and Political Movements in Western Democracies*, ed. Russell J. Dalton and Manfred Kuechler (New York: Oxford University Press, 1990), 43–66.

26. Lee Ann Banaszak, *Why Movements Succeed or Fail: Opportunity, Culture, and the Struggle for Woman Suffrage* (Princeton, N.J.: Princeton University Press, 1996), 31.

27. Ibid.

28. This information was presented in materials prepared for the Ōizumi branch committee meeting of January 8, 1993. The way blocks are designed has changed since I obtained this figure, but I have encountered no new evidence that would indicate that rates of organization are substantially different.

29. Satō, *Josei tachi no seikatsu nettowāku*, 114–119.

30. "Shōhi seikatsu kyōdō kumia hō" [Consumers' Lifestyle Cooperatives Law].

31. Satō, *Josei tachi no seikatsu nettowāku*, 1–79.

32. Yamazaki, "Shufu no seikyō undō to ishiki henyō"; also Kunihiro, "Chiiki ni okeru 'shufu' no seiji teki shutaika," and Kunihiro, "Josei no seiji sanka no nyūwēbu" [The New Wave of Women's Political Participation], in *Toshi to josei no shakaigaku*, ed. Yazawa Sumiko (Tokyo: Saiensu-sha, 1993), 217–254.

33. Satō Yoshiyuki, "Seikatsu kyōdō kumiai to feminizumu" [The Seikatsu Cooperative and Feminism], *Shakai kagaku tokyū* 38.3 (1993): 873–903.

34. Amano Masako, " 'Seikatsu-sha' gainen no keifu to tenbō" [The Genealogy and Possibilities of the "Seikatsu-sha" Concept], in *Josei tachi no seikatsu-sha undō*, ed. Satō Yoshiyuki, Amano Masako, and Nasu Hisashi (Tokyo: Maruju-sha, 1995), 17–69.

35. Amano Masako has traced the evolution of the word since it first found its way into Japanese political thought under militarism until its present usage in Netto politics. Her history of the word supports my interpretation of it, although the original source of my interpretation is not her scholarship (which postdates much of my fieldwork) but the definitions I obtained when I asked women in the movement to explain how they understood the word. What seems to be obvious is that, even though they are not aware of the history of the term, Seikatsu Club women do understand the larger social context in which it is employed.

36. Amano, " 'Seikatsu-sha' gainen no keifu to tenbō," 52–53.

37. Ibid., 58–60; and Kunihiro, "Chiiki ni okeru 'shufu' no seiji teki shutaika," 138.

38. Yamazaki, "Shufu no seikyō undō to ishiki henyō," 38.

39. Nemoto Michiko, "Seikyō no nakama" [My Co-op Companions], *Bungei shiki* 26 (1992): 10–13.

40. The other is a member of the Japan Communist Party, also elected for the first time in 1995. Mizusawa is the base of Ōzawa Ichirō, a powerful conservative politician, formerly of the Takeshita Faction of the LDP, which may account, in a large part, for the strength of Mizusawa's conservatives.

41. The organization could not provide statistics, but even the staff member who had worked with other branches of the Seikatsu argued that few members' families could economically afford for women to be full-time housewives.

42. Joann Martin, "Motherhood and Power: The Production of a Woman's Culture of Politics in a Mexican Community," *American Ethnologist* 17 (1990): 477.

43. Ibid., 480–482.

44. Kunihiro, "Chiiki ni okeru 'shufu' no seiji teki shutaika," 132.

45. Sheldon Garon, "Women's Groups and the Japanese State: Contending Approaches to Political Integration, 1890–1945," *Journal of Japanese Studies* 19 (1993): 5–41.

46. *Nerima Seikatsu-sha Nettowāku Nyūsu*, "Deatta. Katatta. Kore ga honban!" [We Met. We Talked. This Is the Real Thing!], 52.6 (1995).

Chapter Six. The Ono Campaign

1. One of the most lucid explanations of this system can be found in Abe Hitoshi, Muneyuki Shindo, and Sadafumi Kawato, *The Government and Politics of Japan*, trans. James W. White (Tokyo: University of Tokyo Press, 1994), 143–144.

2. I have discussed Ueno's views in Chapter 4 as well. For a general history of how the housewife image has been viewed by Japanese feminists see Kanda

Michiko, "Shufu ronso" [The Housewife Debate], in *Shufu ronsō wo yomu* [Reading the Housewife Debates], ed. Ueno Chizuko, vol. 2 (Tokyo: Keisō Shobō, 1990), 214–230; also Ueno, "Shufu ronsō wo kaidoku suru" [Interpreting the Housewife Debates], in *Shufu ronsō wo yomu*, 246–274.

3. Yagi Kimiko, "Bosei ideorogī keiseishiron: Kindai nihon ni okeru chūkan shūdan to no kakawari" [An Essay on the Establishment of Motherhood Ideology: Its Relationship to Mediating Collectives in Modern Japan], in *Josei gaku nenpō* 1989: 184–194.

4. The motto was in English; it was exactly "Keep to Smile." When I explained to campaign organizers that the motto sounded grammatically awkward, they pointed out that the Japanese population for whom the motto was designed would not notice the awkwardness. On the contrary, the words made sense to Japanese with a rudimentary introduction to English, reflecting Ono's healthy attitude and her forward-looking internationalism. It is also worth noting that clothing items displaying English words that sound odd to native speakers but seem trendy to Japanese are very popular with Japanese consumers of all types.

5. At these events I was able to have a chair and take full notes, unlike many other campaign events, where I was too busy.

6. Gerald L. Curtis, *Election Campaigning Japanese Style* (New York: Kodansha, 1971).

7. Unaligned voters total nearly a third of all voters. Takabatake Michitoshi, "The Shift to Political Corporatism," *Japan Quarterly* 33 (April–June 1986): 118–124; Kobayashi Yoshiaki, *Gendai nihon no senkyo* [Modern Japanese Elections] (Tokyo: Tokyo Daigaku Shuppankai, 1991), 48–49.

8. J. A. A. Stockwin, "Political Parties and Political Opposition," in *Democracy in Japan*, ed. Takeshi Ishida and Ellis S. Krauss (Pittsburgh: University of Pittsburgh Press, 1989), 89–111.

9. Curtis, *Election Campaigning Japanese Style*, especially chap. 1.

10. Stockwin, "Political Parties and Political Opposition." See also Ronald J. Hrebenar, "The Money Base of Japanese Politics," in *The Japanese Party System: From One-Party Rule to Coalition Government*, ed. Ronald J. Hrebenar (Boulder, Colo.: Westview Press, 1986), 55–79; Kishimoto Kōichi, *Gendai seiji kenkyū: "nagatachō" no ayumi to mekanizumu* [Modern Political Research: The Mechanism and Movement of "Nagatachō"] (Tokyo: Gyōken, 1989), 179–190.

11. Factions, long believed to have been a part of the puzzle of Japanese corruption, have been officially dissolved. However, as of this writing, the current LDP cabinet arrangement still reflects a distribution of power among representatives of former factions.

12. Kishimoto, *Gendai seiji kenkyū*.

13. All candidates are allowed short "statements of opinion" in a controlled format on public television during a campaign period. During the campaign period, candidates may also hang posters of a regulated size on an assigned spot next to those of other candidates on special campaign bulletin boards. The election commission publishes a newsprint election guide in which each candidate may place one notice of regulated size.

14. Curtis, *Election Campaigning Japanese Style*, 126–178.

15. The idea of a core constituency was developed for American legislators

in Richard F. Fenno, *Home Style: House Members in Their Districts* (Boston: Little, Brown, 1978).

16. Curtis, *Election Campaigning Japanese Style*, 153–178.

17. I, too, had *aisatsu* to make. When Ono formally agreed to allow me to participate in her campaign, the secretary from Kakizawa's office who had introduced me to her told me to call Kakizawa's little sister and thank her for her assistance. Nervously, I did. I will not pretend to have a complete grasp of how and when and to whom *aisatsu* must be delivered. At the end of the campaign I made a bitter mistake that I will never forget. When Ono won, I returned home exhausted and slept the next few days off. I got a call from the wife of the professor of the university where I met the young man whose mother had introduced me to Kakizawa's secretary. I had forgotten to call this young man's mother and thank her for "my candidate's" victory. The son had called his professor in dismay.

18. Hrebenar, "The Money Base of Japanese Politics." One reason running campaigns is expensive must be labor costs. Ono's office was low tech. Only a few word processors existed. Previous year ballot statistics and expected vote counts were written out by hand from records and tallied with a hand calculator. Envelopes were addressed by hand. Ono's schedule was often handwritten. A fax seemed to be the major concession to modern conveniences. It sped communication between the Diet office building and the Tachikawa branch of the campaign office.

19. The cultural importance of favor and obligation in Japanese society is the thesis of Ruth Benedict's classic, *The Chrysanthemum and the Sword: Patterns of Japanese Culture* (Boston: Houghton Mifflin, 1946).

20. Ono is quoted saying as much in an interview study of female Diet members in Iwai Tomoaki, " 'The Madonna Boom': Women in the Japanese Diet," *Journal of Japanese Studies* 19.1 (1993): 103–120; see especially 115. This article is a good summary of some of the common problems and images associated with female Diet members, including Ono.

Conclusion

1. Kurihara Nobuaki, Tanaka Toshiyuki, and Nagumo Takashi, "Saihen no ashi moto 2: Sanin sen, kawaru ōen dantai atarashii pātonā wo mōsaku" [The Basis of Restructuring 2: The House of Councilors Election, Changing Support Groups Seek New Partners], *Asahi shinbun* (Tokyo) 17 June 1995, 7.

2. Anne Phillips, "Democracy and Difference: Some Problems for Feminist Theory," *Political Quarterly* 63.1 (1992): 79–90; Iris Marion Young, "Polity and Group Difference: A Critique of the Ideal of Universal Citizenship," in *Feminism and Political Theory*, ed. Cass R. Sunstein (Chicago: University of Chicago Press, 1990), 117–141.

3. Phillips, "Democracy and Difference"; Young, "Polity and Group Difference"; Will Kymlicka, *Multicultural Citizenship: A Liberal Theory of Minority Rights* (Oxford: Clarendon Press, 1995); Chantal Mouffe, *The Return of the Political* (London: Verso, 1993).

4. For a good example, examine Chantal Mouffe's attempt to marry liberalism and communitarianism in her "radical democracy." She hopes for a more humane public space generated by the more equal representation of more diverse interests. But representation of interest is still her ultimate goal. She does not suggest that the conception of the political sphere be altered in order to permit conversations about when and how some "interests" ought to be submitted to less selfish concerns. Mouffe, *The Return of the Political*.

5. Consider the overwhelming interest in Japanese women and paid work and paid work-related information in three recent English-language texts. Sumiko Iwao has two chapters directly involving work and a third in which work plays an important role (see Iwao, *The Japanese Woman: Traditional Image and Changing Reality* [New York: Free Press, 1993]). In *Japanese Women Working* (ed. Janet Hunter [New York: Routledge, 1993]), only one of ten chapters deals with women's unpaid work in the home. See also Glenda S. Roberts, *Staying on the Line: Blue-Collar Women in Contemporary Japan* (Honolulu: University of Hawaii Press, 1994).

References

Abe Hitoshi, Muneyuki Shindo, and Sadafumi Kawato. *The Government and Politics of Japan*. Trans. James W. White. Tokyo: University of Tokyo Press, 1994.

Allinson, Gary D. "Citizenship, Fragmentation and the Negotiated Polity." *Political Dynamics in Contemporary Japan*, ed. Gary Allinson and Yasunori Sone. Ithaca, N.Y.: Cornell University Press, 1993. 17–49.

―――. "Politics in Contemporary Japan: Pluralist Scholarship in the Conservative Era—A Review Article." *Journal of Asian Studies* 48.2 (1989): 324–333.

Allison, Anne. "Producing Mothers." *Re-imaging Japanese Women*, ed. Anne Imamura. Berkeley: University of California Press, 1996. 135–155.

Almond, Gabriel, and Sidney Verba. *The Civic Culture: Political Attitudes and Democracy in Five Nations*. Newbury Park, Calif.: Sage Publications, 1989.

Amano Masako. " 'Seikatsu-sha' gainen no keifu to tenbō" [The Genealogy and Possibilities of the "Seikatsu-sha" Concept]. *Josei tachi no seikatsu-sha undō*, ed. Satō Yoshiyuki, Amano Masako, and Nasu Hishashi. Tokyo: Maruju-sha, 1995. 17–69.

Aoki Taiko. "Shufu pawā no rekishiteki tōjō: 'midori' to gendā gyappu" [The History-making Appearance of Housewife Power: "Green" and the Gender Gap]. *Gendai no riron* 210 (1985): 68–77.

―――. *Yoron minshushugi—Josei to seiji* [Public Opinion Democracy—Women and Politics]. Tokyo: Waseda Daigaku Shuppanbu, 1991.

Azumi, Koya. "Voluntary Organizations in Japan." *Voluntary Action Research, 1974: The Nature of Voluntary Action around the World*, ed. David Horton Smith. Lexington, Mass.: D. C. Lexington Books, 1974. 15–26.

Babchuk, Nicholas, and Alan Booth. "Voluntary Association Membership: A Longitudinal Analysis." *American Sociological Review* 34 (1969): 31–45.

Bachnik, Jane M. "Introduction: *Uchi/Soto:* Challenging Our Conceptualizations of Self, Social Order, and Language." *Situated Meaning: Inside and Outside in Japanese Self, Society and Language,* ed. Jane M. Bachnik and Charles J. Quinn, Jr. Princeton, N.J.: Princeton University Press, 1994. 3–37.

Banaszak, Lee Ann. *Why Movements Succeed or Fail: Opportunity, Culture, and the Struggle for Woman Suffrage.* Princeton, N.J.: Princeton University Press, 1996.

Barber, Benjamin. *Strong Democracy: Participatory Politics for a New Age.* Berkeley: University of California Press, 1984.

Baumgartner, Frank, and Jack Walker. "Survey Research and Membership in Voluntary Associations." *American Journal of Political Science* 32 (1988): 908–927.

Bellah, Robert. *The Good Society.* New York: Alfred A. Knopf, 1991.

Bellah, Robert, Richard Madsen, William M. Sullivan, Ann Swidler, and Steven M. Tipton. *Habits of the Heart: Individualism and Commitment in American Life.* New York: Harper and Row, 1985.

Benedict, Ruth. *The Chrysanthemum and the Sword: Patterns of Japanese Culture.* Boston: Houghton Mifflin, 1946.

Bestor, Theodore C. *Neighborhood Tokyo.* Stanford, Calif.: Stanford University Press, 1989.

Boling, Patricia. "The Democratic Potential of Mothering." *Political Theory* 19 (Nov. 1991): 606–625.

Booth, Alan. "Sex and Social Participation." *American Sociological Review* 37 (1972): 183–193.

Borantia no machizukuri wo mezashite: Nerima-ku ni okeru borantia katsudō suishin no teigen [Aiming for a Volunteer City: Suggestions for the Promotion of Volunteer Activity in Nerima]. Tokyo: Nerima-ku Shakai Fukushi Kyōgikai, 1989.

Buckley, Sandra. "Altered States: The Body Politics of 'Being Woman.'" *Postwar Japan as History,* ed. Andrew Gordon. Berkeley: University of California Press, 1993. 347–372.

Calder, Kent. *Crisis and Compensation: Public Policy and Political Stability in Japan: 1949–1986.* Princeton, N.J.: Princeton University Press, 1988.

Christensen, Raymond. "The New Japanese Electoral System." *Pacific Affairs* 69.1 (1996): 49–70.

Clifford, James. *The Predicament of Culture: Twentieth Century Ethnography, Literature and Art.* Cambridge, Mass.: Harvard University Press, 1988.

Condon, Jane. *Half Step Behind: Japanese Women of the '80s.* New York: Dodd, Mead, 1985.

Conover, Pamela Johnston. "The Role of Social Groups in Political Thinking." *British Journal of Political Science* 18 (1988): 51–76.

Cordilla, Ann, and Kazuko Ohta. "Central in the Family and Marginal in the Work Force: Women's Place in Japanese Society." *Women's Work and Women's Lives: The Continuing Struggle Worldwide,* ed. Hilda Kahne and Janet Z. Giele. Boulder, Colo.: Westview Press, 1992.

Curtis, Gerald L. *Election Campaigning Japanese Style.* New York: Kodansha, 1971.

Curtis, James E. "Voluntary Association Joining: A Cross-National Comparative Note." *American Sociological Review* 36 (1971): 872–880.

Curtis, James E., Edward G. Grabb, and Douglas E. Baer. "Voluntary Association Membership in Fifteen Countries: A Comparative Analysis." *American Sociological Review* 57.2 (1992): 139–152.

Cutler, Stephen. "Voluntary Association Membership and the Theory of Mass Society." *Bonds of Pluralism: The Form and Substance of Urban Social Networks*, ed. Edward O. Laumann. New York: John Wiley, 1973. 133–159.

Dairinin Undō Kōryū Sentā. "Senkyo kekka" [Elections Results]. *Dairinin undō* 9.6 (1995): 21.

"Dairinin undō: sono 14 nen no seika" [Proxy Movement: The Results of 14 Years]. *Shakai undō* 134 (1991): 2–5.

Dalton, Russell J. "The Challenge of New Movements." *Challenging the Political Order: New Social and Political Movements in Western Democracies*, ed. Russell J. Dalton and Manfred Kuechler. New York: Oxford University Press, 1990. 3–20.

Daniels, Arlene Kaplan. *Invisible Careers: Women Civic Leaders from the Volunteer World*. Chicago: University of Chicago Press, 1988.

Devine, Fiona. "Social Identities, Class Identity and Political Perspectives." *Sociological Review* 40 (1992): 229–252.

Diani, Mario. "The Concept of Social Movement." *Sociological Review* 40 (1992): 1–25.

Dietz, Mary G. "Citizenship with a Feminist Face: The Problem with Maternal Thinking." *Political Theory* 13 (Feb. 1985): 19–37.

Doi, Takeo. *The Anatomy of Self: The Individual Versus Society*. Trans. Mark A. Harbison. Tokyo: Kodansha, 1986.

Easton, David. "The New Revolution in Political Science." *American Political Science Review* 63 (December 1969): 1051–1061.

Ehara Yumiko. "Feminizumu seijigaku no kanōsei" [The Possibility of a Feminist Political Science]. *Revaiasan* 8 (spring 1991): 7–23.

Elshtain, Jean Bethke. *Public Man, Private Woman: Women in Social and Political Thought*. Princeton, N.J.: Princeton University Press, 1981.

Fenno, Richard F. *Home Style: House Members in Their Districts*. Boston: Little, Brown, 1978.

Flanagan, Scott. "The Genesis of Variant Political Cultures: Contemporary Citizen Orientations in Japan, America, Britain and Italy." *The Citizen and Politics: A Comparative Perspective*, ed. Sidney Verba and Lucian W. Pye. Stamford, Conn.: Greylock Publishers, 1978. 127–165.

Flanagan, Scott, Bradley M. Richardson, Joji Watanuki, Ichiro Miyake, and Shinsaku Kohei. *The Japanese Voter*. New Haven: Yale University Press, 1991.

Fujimura-Fanselow, Kumiko, and Atsuko Kameda, eds. *Japanese Women: New Feminist Perspectives on the Past, Present, and Future*. New York: City University of New York Press, 1995.

Fukutake Tadashi. *The Japanese Social Structure: Its Evolution in the Modern Century*. 2d ed., trans. Ronald P. Dore. Tokyo: University of Tokyo Press, 1989.

Fukuyama, Francis. *The End of History and the Last Man.* London: Penguin Books, 1992.

Garon, Sheldon. "Women's Groups and the Japanese State: Contending Approaches to Political Integration, 1890–1945." *Journal of Japanese Studies* 19.1 (1993): 5–41.

"Genron no jiyū ga nainoka shushō" [Prime Minister, Don't You Have Freedom of Expression?]. *Asahi shinbun* (Tokyo) 21 Oct. 1992, 15.

Gold, Doris. "Women and Voluntarism." *Women in a Sexist Society,* ed. Vivian Gornick and Barbara Moran. New York: Basic Books, 1971. 384–400.

Gordon, Andrew, ed. *Postwar Japan as History.* Berkeley: University of California Press, 1993.

Hardy-Fanta, Carol. *Latina Politics/Latino Politics: Gender, Culture, and Political Participation in Boston.* Philadelphia: Temple University Press, 1993.

Hasegawa Kōichi. "Han genshiryoku undō ni okeru josei no ichi: posuto-cherunobuiri no 'atarashī shakai undō' " [Women of the Anti-Nuclear Energy Movement: A Post Chernobyl New Social Movement in Japan]. *Revaiasan* 8 (1991): 41–58.

Hastings, Sally Ann. "Women Legislators in the Postwar Diet." *Re-imaging Japanese Women,* ed. Anne Imamura. Berkeley: University of California Press, 1996. 271–300.

Hawkesworth, Mary E. "Feminist Epistemology: A Survey of the Field." *Women and Politics* 7 (1987): 115–127.

Hekman, Susan. "The Feminization of Epistemology: Gender and the Social Sciences." *Women and Politics* 7 (1987): 65–83.

Hendry, Joy. "Humidity, Hygiene, or Ritual Care: Some Thoughts on Wrapping as a Social Phenomenon." *Unwrapping Japan: Society and Culture in Anthropological Perspective,* ed. Eyal Ben-Ari, Brian Moeran, and James Valentine. Honolulu: University of Hawaii Press, 1990. 18–35.

———. "The Role of the Professional Housewife." *Japanese Women Working,* ed. Janet Hunter. New York: Routledge, 1993. 224–241.

Hertzke, Allen D. *Echoes of Discontent: Jesse Jackson, Pat Robertson, and the Resurgence of Populism.* Washington, D.C.: C. Q. Press, 1993.

"Hitori-hitori ga yūki wo dashite" [One by One, Show Some Courage]. *Asahi shinbun* (Tokyo) 8 Oct. 1992, 15.

Hrebenar, Ronald J. "The Money Base of Japanese Politics." *The Japanese Party System: From One-Party Rule to Coalition Government,* ed. Ronald J. Hrebenar. Boulder, Colo.: Westview Press, 1986. 55–79.

Hunter, Janet, ed. *Japanese Women Working.* New York: Routledge, 1993.

Hyman, Herbert. "Introduction." *Readings in Reference Group Theory and Research,* ed. H. Hyman and E. Singer. New York: Free Press, 1968.

Ikeda Tetsu. "Dairinin undō zenkoku rentai no igi" [The Meaning of National Proxy Movement Solidarity]. *Shakai undō* 150 (1992): 10–19.

"Ikinokori kakeru fujin sōgō zasshi" [General Women's Magazine Gambles on Survival]. *Asahi shinbun* (Tokyo) 18 Jan. 1993, 13.

Imai Yasuko. "The Emergence of the Japanese *Shufu:* Why a *Shufu* Is More

Than a 'Housewife.' " *US-Japan Women's Journal English Supplement*, 6 (March 1994): 44–65.

Imamura, Anne E. "The Japanese Urban Housewife: Tradition and Modern Social Participation." *Social Science Journal* 24 (1984): 139–156.

————. *Urban Japanese Housewives: At Home in the Community.* Honolulu: University of Hawaii Press, 1987.

————, ed. *Re-imaging Japanese Women.* Berkeley: University of California Press, 1996.

Inglehart, Ronald. "Values, Ideology, and Cognitive Mobilization in New Social Movements." *Challenging the Political Order: New Social and Political Movements in Western Democracies*, ed. Russell J. Dalton and Manfred Kuechler. New York: Oxford University Press, 1990. 43–66.

Inoue Teruko and Ehara Yumiko, eds. *Josei no dēta bukku* [Women's Data Book]. Tokyo: Yuhikaku, 1991.

Inuzuka Susumu. "Toshika to danchi seikatsu: 'danchi toshi' no sangyō shakai kōsei" [Urbanization and *Danchi* Lifestyle: The Structure of Industrial Society in a *Danchi* City]. *Chiiki shakai to seiji bunka: shimin jichi wo meguru jichitai to jūmin*, ed. Moriya Takahiko and Furuki Toshiaki. Tokyo: Yūshindō, 1984. 26–37.

Iwai Tomoaki. " 'The Madonna Boom': Women in the Japanese Diet." *Journal of Japanese Studies* 19.1 (1993): 103–120.

Iwane Kunio. *Atarashii shakai undō no yohanseki: seikatsu kurabu-dairinin undō* [The Quarter-Century of the New Social Movement: The Seikatsu Club and the Proxy Movement]. Tokyo: Kyōdō tosho kabushiki kaisha, 1993.

Iwao, Sumiko. *The Japanese Woman: Traditional Image and Changing Reality.* New York: Free Press, 1993.

Jain, Purnendra C. "Green Politics and Citizen Power in Japan: The Zushi Movement." *Asian Survey* 31 (June 1993): 559–575.

Jay, John, Alexander Hamilton, and James Madison. *The Federalist: A Commentary on the Constitution of the United States.* New York: Random House, 1937.

Johnson, Chalmers. "Puppets and Puppeteers: Japanese Political Reform." *Japan: Who Governs, The Rise of the Developmental State.* New York: W. W. Norton, 1995. 212–231.

Jones, Kathleen B. *Compassionate Authority: Democracy and the Representation of Women.* New York: Routledge, 1993.

Josei no genjō to shisaku [The Current Condition of Women's Lives and Women's Policy]. Tokyo: Gyōsei, 1992.

Kabashima Ikuo. *Seiji sanka* [Political Participation]. Tokyo: Tokyo Daigaku Shuppankai, 1988.

Kaminer, Wendy. *Women Volunteering: The Pleasure, Pain and Politics of Unpaid Work from 1830 to the Present.* Garden City, N.Y.: Anchor Press, 1984.

Kanda Michiko. "Shufu ronsō" [The Housewife Debate]. *Shufu ronsō wo yomu* [Reading the Housewife Debates], ed. Ueno Chizuko, vol. 2. Tokyo: Keisō Shobō, 1990. 214–230.

Kelly, Rita Mae, Bernard Ronan, and Margaret E. Cawley. "Liberal Positivistic Epistemology and Research on Women and Politics." *Women and Politics* 7 (1987): 11–28.

Kishimoto Kōichi. *Gendai seiji kenkyū: "nagatachō" no ayumi to mekanizumu* [Modern Political Research: The Mechanism and Movement of "Nagatachō"]. Tokyo: Gyōken, 1989.

Kobayashi Yoshiaki. *Gendai nihon no senkyo* [Modern Japanese Elections]. Tokyo: Tokyo Daigaku Shuppankai, 1991.

Kondo, Dorinne. *Crafting Selves: Power, Gender and Discourses of Identity in a Japanese Workplace.* Chicago: University of Chicago Press, 1989.

Kunihiro Yōko. "Chiiki ni okeru 'shufu' no seiji teki shutaika: dairinin undō sanka-sha no aidentitī bunseki kara" [The Development of a Political Subjectivity in the Local "Housewife": From an Analysis of the Identity of Participants in the *Dairinin Undō*]. *Chiiki shakai gakkai nenpō dai nana shū: chiiki shakaigaku no shin sōten* 7 (1995): 121–148.

———. "Josei no seiji sanka no nyūwēbu" [The New Wave of Women's Political Participation]. *Toshi to josei no shakaigaku,* ed. Yazawa Sumiko. Tokyo: Saiensu-sha, 1993. 217–254.

———. "Shufu to iu kategorī: Kōgakureki josei no shufu ishiki to shutai keisei" [The Category of "Housewife": The Housewife Consciousness and Subject Development of Women with Higher Education]. Master's thesis, Keio University, 1991.

———. "Toshi no seikatsu sekai to josei no shufu ishiki" [The Lifeworld of the City and Women's Housewife Consciousness]. *Toshi to josei no shakaigaku: sei yakuwari no yuragi wo koete* [The Sociology of Women in the City: Moving beyond the Breakdown in Sex Roles], ed. Yazawa Sumiko. Tokyo: Saiensu-sha, 1993. 69–106.

Kurihara Nobuaki, Tanaka Toshiyuki, and Nagumo Takashi. "Saihen no ashi moto 2: Sanin sen, kawaru ōen dantai atarashii pātonā wo mōsaku" [The Basis of Restructuring 2: The House of Councilors Election, Changing Support Groups Seek New Partners] *Asahi shinbun* (Tokyo) 17 June 1995, 7.

Kymlicka, Will. *Multicultural Citizenship: A Liberal Theory of Minority Rights.* Oxford: Clarendon Press, 1995.

Lebra, Takie Sugiyama. "Self in Japanese Culture." *Japanese Sense of Self,* ed. Nancy R. Rosenberger. New York: Cambridge University Press, 1992. 105–120.

Locke, John. *The Second Treatise of Government.* Indianapolis: Bobbs-Merrill, 1952.

Loeser, Herta. *Women, Work, and Volunteering.* Boston: Beacon Press, 1974.

Martin, Curtis H. *Politics East and West: A Comparison of Japanese and British Political Culture.* Armonk, N.Y.: M. E. Sharpe, 1992.

Martin, Joann. "Motherhood and Power: The Production of a Woman's Culture of Politics in a Mexican Community." *American Ethnologist* 17 (1990): 470–490.

Matsumura Naoko. "Seikatsu no gendaiteki tokuchō to shufu yakuwari" [The Characteristics of Modern Lifestyles and the Housewife's Role]. *Josei seikatsu shi dai go kan: gendai,* ed. Itō Yasuko. Tokyo: Tokyo Daigaku Shuppankai, 1990. 235–268.

McCarthy, Kathleen D. "Parallel Power Structures: Women and the Voluntary Sphere." *Lady Bountiful Revisited: Women, Philanthropy, and Power*, ed. Kathleen McCarthy. New Brunswick, N.J.: Rutgers University Press, 1990. 1–31.

McKean, Margaret. "State Strength and the Public Interest." *Political Dynamics in Contemporary Japan*, ed. Gary Allinson and Yasunori Sone. Ithaca, N.Y.: Cornell University Press, 1993. 72–104.

McKillop, Kevin, Michael Berzonsky, and Barry Schlenker. "The Impact of Self-Presentations on Self-Beliefs: Effects of Social Identity and Self-Presentational Context." *Journal of Personality* 60 (1992): 789–808.

McNelly, Theodore. " 'Woman Power' in Japan's 1989 Upper House Election." *Electoral Systems in Comparative Perspective: Their Impact on Women and Minorities*, ed. Wilma Rule and Joseph F. Zimmerman. Westport, Conn.: Greenwood Press, 1994. 149–159.

McPherson, J. Miller. "A Dynamic Model of Voluntary Affiliation." *Social Forces* 59 (March 1981): 705–727.

McPherson, J. Miller, and Lynn Smith-Lovin. "Women and Weak Ties: Differences by Sex in the Size of Voluntary Organizations." *American Journal of Sociology* 87 (1982): 883–904.

Mouffe, Chantal. "Feminism, Citizenship and Radical Democratic Politics." *Feminists Theorize the Political,* ed. Judith Butler and Joan W. Scott. New York: Routledge, 1992. 369–384.

———. *The Return of the Political.* London: Verso, 1993.

Neal, David, and Brenda Phillips. "Female-dominated Local Social Movement Organizations in Disaster-Threat Situations." *Women and Social Protest,* ed. Guida West and Rhoda Lois Blumberg. New York: Oxford University Press, 1990. 252–253.

Nemoto Michiko. "Seikyō no nakama" [My Co-op Companions]. *Bungei shiki* 26 (1992): 10–13.

Nerima Kusei Gaiyō [Outline of the Nerima Ward Administration]. Tokyo: Wada Insatsu, 1992.

Nerima Seikatsu-sha Nettowāku Nyūsu. "Deatta. Katatta. Kore ga honban!" [We Met. We Talked. This Is the Real Thing!] 52.6 (1995).

Nietzsche, Friedrich. *Beyond Good and Evil: Prelude to a Philosophy of the Future.* Trans. Walter Kaufmann. New York: Vintage, 1966.

Nihon Fujin Dantai Rengō Kai. *Fujin hakusho 1992: Konnichi no kazoku mondai* [Women's White Paper 1992: Today's Family Problems]. Tokyo: Horupu shuppan, 1992.

Nihon Fujin Kaigi. *Onna tachi wa seiji wo kaeru* [Women Change Politics]. Tokyo: Emu kikaku insatsu, 1994.

"Nisei giin: sannin ni hitori shidai mo suzukunoka" [Second-generation Legislators: One Out of Three Are from the Next Generation]. *Asahi shinbun* (Tokyo), international satellite ed., 15 March 1994, 9.

Noguchi, Mary Goebel. "The Rise of the Housewife Activist." *Japan Quarterly* 39 (July–Sept. 1992): 339–352.

Nolte, Sharon H., and Sally Ann Hastings. "The Meiji State's Policy toward Women, 1890–1910." *Recreating Japanese Women,* ed. Gail Lee Bernstein. Berkeley: University of California Press, 1991. 151–174.

Ōgai Tokuko. "Sanjūkyū nin no dai ikki fujin daigishi: minshū kaikaku no hoshitachi" [Stars of Democracy: The First Thirty-Nine Female Members of the Japanese Diet]. *U.S.-Japan Women's Journal* 20 (1996): 31–55.

Ōtake Hideo. "Forces for Political Reform: The Liberal Democratic Party's Young Reformers and Ōzawa Ichirō." *Journal of Japanese Studies* 22 (1996): 269–294.

Owen, Diana, and Linda M. G. Zerilli. "Gender and Citizenship." *Society* 28 (July–Aug. 1991): 27–34.

Pangle, Thomas. *The Ennobling of Democracy: The Challenge of the Postmodern Era*. Baltimore: Johns Hopkins University Press, 1992.

Pateman, Carole. *The Disorder of Women*. New York: Routledge, 1989.

———. *The Sexual Contract*. Stanford, Calif.: Stanford University Press, 1988.

Pharr, Susan J. *Political Women in Japan: The Search for a Place in Political Life*. Berkeley: University of California Press, 1981.

Phillips, Anne. "Democracy and Difference: Some Problems for Feminist Theory." *Political Quarterly* 63.1 (1992): 79–90.

———. *Engendering Democracy*. University Park, Pa.: Pennsylvania State University Press, 1991.

Plumwood, Val. "Women, Humanity and Nature." *Socialism, Feminism, and Philosophy: A Radical Philosophy Reader,* ed. Sean Sayers and Peter Osborne. New York: Routledge, 1990. 211–234.

Prime Minister's Office. *Josei no genjō to shisaku* [The Present Condition of Women's Lives and Women's Policy]. Tokyo: Gyōsei, 1992.

Pye, Lucian, and Mary W. Pye. *Asian Power and Politics: The Cultural Dimensions of Authority*. Cambridge, Mass.: Belknap Press of Harvard University Press, 1985.

Rauch, Jonathan. *The Outnation: A Search for the Soul of Japan*. Boston: Harvard Business School Press, 1992.

Rinehart, Sue Tolleson. *Gender Consciousness and Politics*. University Park, Pa.: Pennsylvania State University Press, 1992.

Roberts, Glenda S. *Staying on the Line: Blue-Collar Women in Contemporary Japan*. Honolulu: University of Hawaii Press, 1994.

Rose, Gillian. *Feminism and Geography: The Limits of Geographical Knowledge*. Minneapolis: University of Minnesota Press, 1993.

Rosenberger, Nancy R, ed. *Japanese Sense of Self*. New York: Cambridge University Press, 1992.

Rousseau, Jean-Jacques. *The First and Second Discourses*, ed. Roger Masters, trans. Roger Masters and Judith Masters. New York: St. Martin's Press, 1964.

Ruddick, Sara. "Maternal Thinking." *Mothering: Essays in Feminist Theory,* ed. Joyce Trebilcot. Totowa, N.J.: Rowan and Allanheld, 1983. 213–262.

Sapiro, Virginia. *The Political Integration of Women: Roles, Socialization, and Politics*. Urbana, Ill.: University of Illinois Press, 1983.

Sasakura Naoko. "Ikiyoi wa toroenakatta josei no shinshitsu" [The Unrelenting Vigor of the Women's Political Advancement]. *Ekonomisto* 21 May 1991, 86–89.

Saso, Mary. *Women in the Japanese Workplace*. London: Hilary Shipman, 1990.

Satō Susumu. *Nihon no jichi bunka* [The Culture of Japanese Self-Government]. Tokyo: Gyōsei, 1991.

Satō Yoshiyuki. "Seikatsu kyōdō kumiai to feminizumu" [The Seikatsu Cooperative and Feminism]. *Shakai kagaku tokyū* 38 (1993): 873–903.

————. *Seikatsu seikai to taiwa no riron* [The Lifeworld and the Logic of Communication]. Tokyo: Bunshindō, 1991.

————, ed. *Josei tachi no seikatsu nettowāku: seikatsu kurabu ni tsudou hitobito* [Women's Daily Life Network: The People Who Gather at the Seikatsu Club]. Tokyo: Bunshindō, 1988.

Scalapino, Robert. *Democracy and the Party Movement in Prewar Japan.* Berkeley: University of California Press, 1953.

Schmitt, Raymond. *The Reference Other Orientation: An Extension of the Reference Group Concept.* Carbondale: Southern Illinois University Press, 1972.

Scott, Joan Wallach. "Experience." *Feminists Theorize the Political,* ed. Judith Butler and Joan W. Scott. New York: Routledge, 1992. 22–40.

————. *Gender and the Politics of History.* New York: Columbia University Press, 1988.

"*Shōhi seikatsu kyōdō kumiai hō*" [Consumers' Lifestyle Cooperatives Law]. Shōwa Year 23 (1948), No. 200.

Simcock, Bradford L., and Ellis S. Krauss. "Citizens' Movement: The Growth and Impact of Environmental Protest in Japan." *Political Opposition and Local Politics in Japan,* ed. Kurt Steiner, Ellis S. Krauss, and Scott C. Flanagan. Princeton, N.J.: Princeton University Press, 1980.

Smith, David Horton. "Research and Communication Needs in Voluntary Action." *Volunteerism: An Emerging Profession,* ed. John G. Cull and Richard E. Hardy. Springfield, Ill.: Charles C. Thomas, 1974. 111–186.

Smith, J. Robert. *Japanese Society: Tradition, Self and the Social Order.* New York: Cambridge University Press, 1983.

Smith, Tom W. "Trends in Group Membership: Comments on Baumgartner and Walker." *American Journal of Political Science* 34 (1990): 646–661.

Spivak, Gayatri Chakravorty. "Can the Subaltern Speak?" *Marxism and the Interpretation of Culture.* Urbana: University of Illinois Press, 1988.

Steiner, Kurt, Ellis S. Krauss, and Scott C. Flanagan. *Political Opposition and Local Politics in Japan.* Princeton, N.J.: Princeton University Press, 1980.

Stockwin, J. A. A. "Political Parties and Political Opposition." *Democracy in Japan,* ed. Takeshi Ishida and Ellis S. Krauss. Pittsburgh: University of Pittsburgh Press, 1989. 89–111.

Sugawara Kazuko. "Chihō josei giin ōryō shinshutsu no igi to kadai" [The Significance and Problems of the Large Increases in Local Female Legislators]. *Jichi no naka no onnatachi, Jichitai gaku nenpō* 5 (1992): 27–41.

Taira, Koji. "Dialectics of Economic Growth, National Power, and Distributive Struggles." *Postwar Japan as History,* ed. Andrew Gordon. Berkeley: University of California Press, 1993. 181–183.

Takabatake Michitoshi. *Nihon seiji no kōzō tenkan* [Structural Shifts in Japanese Politics]. Tokyo: Sanichi Shobō, 1994.

————. *Seiji no hakken* [The Discovery of Politics]. Tokyo: Sanichi Shobō, 1983.

————. "The Shift to Political Corporatism." *Japan Quarterly* 33 (April–June 1986): 118–124.

Takami Kuwayama. "The Reference Other Orientation." *Japanese Sense of Self*, ed. Nancy R. Rosenberger. New York: Cambridge University Press, 1992.

Tanaka Aiji. " 'Seitō shiji nushi' sō noishiki kōzō : seitō shiji gainen saikentō no shiron" [Attitudinal Structure of Independent Voters: Rethinking Measurement and Conceptualization of Partisanship]. *Revaiasan* 20 (1997): 101–129.

Tanaka Yasumasa. "Tokai no shufu to chihō no shufu" [Changing Japanese Housewives in Urban and Rural Areas]. *Gakushūin Daigaku Hōgakubu Kenkyū Nenpō* 25 (1990): 1–90.

Tocqueville, Alexis de. *Democracy in America*. Ed. J. P. Mayer, trans. George Lawrence. New York: Harper and Row, 1969.

Tōroku borantia no jittai to ishiki ni kansuru chōsa hōkokusho [A Report on the Survey of the Nature and Consciousness of Registered Volunteers]. Tokyo: Nerima-ku Shakai Fukushi Kyōgikai, March 1990.

Tronto, Joan C. "Politics and Revision: The Feminist Project to Change the Boundaries of American Political Science." *Revolutions in Knowledge: Feminism in the Social Sciences,* ed. Sue Rosenberg Zalk and Janice Gordon-Kelter. Boulder, Colo.: Westview Press, 1992. 91–110.

Ueda Miho. *Tōkyō shufu monogatari* [The Tale of a Tokyo Housewife]. Tokyo: Geibunsha, 1992.

Ueno Chizuko. *Kapuchōsei to shihonsei* [Capitalism and Patriarchy]. Tokyo: Iwanami Shoten, 1990.

————. "Shufu ronsō wo kaidoku suru" [Interpreting the Housewife Debates]. *Shufu ronsō wo yomu* [Reading the Housewife Debates], ed. Ueno Chizuko, vol 2. Tokyo: Keisō Shobō, 1990. 246–274.

Uno, Kathleen S. "The Death of the 'Good Wife, Wise Mother'?" *Postwar Japan as History*, ed. Andrew Gordon. Berkeley: University of California Press, 1993. 293–322.

————. "Women and Changes in the Household Division of Labor." *Recreating Japanese Women,* ed. Gail Lee Bernstein. Berkeley: University of California Press, 1991. 17–41.

Van Wolferen, Karel. *The Enigma of Japanese Power: People and Politics in a Stateless Nation.* New York: Alfred A. Knopf, 1989.

Verba, Sidney, Kay Lehman Schlozman, and Henry E. Brady. *Voice and Equality: Civic Voluntarism in American Politics*. Cambridge, Mass.: Harvard University Press, 1995.

Ward, Robert E. "Japan: The Continuity of Modernization." *Political Culture and Political Development,* ed. Lucian W. Pye and Sidney Verba. Princeton, N.J.: Princeton University Press, 1965. 27–82.

"Watakushi ga shiji wo yametta riyū" [The Reason I Gave Up Supporting (a Party)]. *Asahi shinbun* 9 June 1995, 12th ed., 6.

Watanuki Jōji. "Yūken-sha to shite no josei" [Women as Voters]. *Revaiasan* 8 (1991): 23–40.

Wilson, John. " 'Public' Work and Social Participation: The Case of Farm Women." *Sociological Quarterly* 31 (1990): 107–121.

Wuthnow, Robert. "The Voluntary Sector: Legacy of the Past, Hope for the Future?" *Between States and Markets: The Voluntary Sector in Comparative Perspective*, ed. Robert Wuthnow. Princeton, N.J.: Princeton University Press, 1991. 3–29.

Yagi Kimiko. "Bosei ideorogī keiseishiron: Kindai nihon ni okeru chūkan shūdan to no kakawari" [An Essay on the Establishment of Motherhood Ideology: Its Relationship to Mediating Collectives in Modern Japan]. *Josei gaku nenpō* [Women's Studies Yearbook] 1989: 184–194.

Yamazaki Tetsuya. "Shufu no seikyō undō to ishiki henyō" [The Housewives' Co-op Movement and Their Changing Consciousness]. *Toshi mondai* 79.6 (1988): 34.

Yazawa Sumiko. "Toshi ni ikiru josei" [Women in Urban Areas]. *Toshi to josei no shakaigaku: seiyakuwari no yuragi wo koete* [The Sociology of Women in the City: Moving beyond the Breakdown in Sex Roles]. Tokyo: Saiensusha, 1993.

Yoshinaga Michiko. "Seikatsu-sha gawa ni tatteinai: dakkara yominikui" [You Don't Stand on the Side of the Ordinary Person, That's Why You're Hard to Read]. *Asahi shinbun* (Tokyo) 26 Sept. 1992.

Young, Iris Marion. "Polity and Group Difference: A Critique of the Ideal of Universal Citizenship." *Feminism and Political Theory*, ed. Cass R. Sunstein. Chicago: University of Chicago Press, 1990. 117–141.

Index

academic perspectives: Ph.D. Kenkyūkai, 22; United States–Japan Educational Commission, 22; on women's roles, 59
advisory board, 79–80
aging parents: limits on housewives' freedom, 56–58; Seikatsu Co-op participation and, 152–153
aisatsu: author's experience with, 225n17; defined, 171; Ono campaign and, 180, 186
amateur politicians, 149–162

Banaszak, Lee Ann, 131
Bellah, Robert, 13
Bestor, Theodore, 211n10
bicycle citizenship: anti-democratic aspects of, 202; bicycling in Ōizumi and, 1–2; concept summarized, 3, 24, 25; contrasted with classical citizenship, 201; contrasted with interest representation, 65, 198; endangered in politics, 197; men and, 25; obligation as component of, 199, 200
Boling, Patricia, 12
Booth, Alan, 94–95
borantia: defined, 97–98
Buckley, Sandra, 121–122

campaign announcers: Japanese term for, 61
chiiki: defined, 137
chōnaikai: defined, discussed, 76

citizenship: American rhetoric concerning, 212n16; classical vision of, 201; defined, 63–64, 214n4; essentializing gender roles and, 12; motherhood as challenge to, 10–12; opportunities for ignored, 62; univocality and, 10–12
classical citizenship, 201
cooperative: compared with Sagyōsho, 123; feminism and, 147–148; founding of, 127–130; *han* explained, 134, 152; Hikari-ga-oka branch, 156–158; housewife identity and membership in, 140–145, 151, 154–155, 158; Iki-iki Matsuri, 121, 124–126, 139; Iwate branch, 145; leadership selection, 158; Netto and, 123–127, 135–137, 146–150, 158–163; Ōizumi branch, 133–134, 152, 155–156; organizational structure of, 134–135; reluctance to participate in Netto, 153; *seikatsu-sha* and, 138–140; *shutai* and, 130, 138; study session conflict, 155–157
Curtis, Gerald, 175

dairinin undō: defined, translation explained, 221n12
data collection, 16, 19
Dietz, Mary, 12
distance as description of politics, 74–78

Ehara, Yumiko, 14–16
elections: House of Councilors (1989), 4–5; House of Councilors (1992), 166–

elections *(continued)*
168, 174–177; Mizusawa City assembly, 145; Nerima Ward assembly, 153; Netto 1993 failures, 123; Netto 1995 successes, 195; Tokyo assembly 158
elite bias in research, 7, 66, 206n22
Elshtain, Jean Bethke, 12
essentialism, 12
ethic: *gyōsei* and *yaruki* and, 110–114; of housewife, 54–55, 150–151; of volunteer, 103–112
ethnography, 14–16

feminism/feminists: political science and, 14, 163, 206n8; Seikatsu rhetoric and, 147–148; use of male texts by, 13

gender structures: constraints within, 15; essentializing, 12; Netto rhetoric and, 151, 163; *seikatsu-sha* and, 143; voluntarism and, 93–96
geography: bicycle methodology as, 26–27; mapping of consciousness, 17, 26–27; mapping of research site, xii
globalization, xi, xiv
Gold, Doris, 95–96
"good wife, wise mother," 31, 68; Japanese term for, 68
gyōsei: defined, compared with *yaruki*, 110–112; effect on Sagyōsho atmosphere, 118, 115; volunteer seminar and, 114

han, 134, 151–153, 156–157
Hardy-Fanta, Carol, 209n35
Hashimoto-san (conservative in neighborhood), 37
Hertzke, Allen, 9, 13
Hikari-ga-oka branch, 145
Hobbes, Thomas, 11
House of Councilors: elections explained, 166; 1989 election, 4–5; 1992 election, 166–168, 174–177
housewife identity: ambivalence about, 43–46, 51; constraint on political participation and, 86, 122; contrasted with classical citizenship, 201; ethic of, 54–55; "good wife, wise mother" and, 31, 68; Japanese terms for, 29–30; in media, 30–31; in neighborhood, 18, 148; Netto's rhetorical use of, 124, 126, 146, 148–149; Ono's rhetorical use of, 89, 165–173, 191–193; other housewives and, 53–54, 58;

political action and, ix, 64; privatization and, 67–69, 73–74, 78; PTA and, 37; public quality of, 28, 42, 54, 60, 69; Seikatsu Co-op membership and, 138, 140–142, 151, 154–155, 158; *seikatsu-sha* and, 140, 143, 145; social status and, 26, 32, 53; specialist quality of, 29; work's uncertain status and, 31, 45–47, 51–53, 213n27

Iida Tsuneko (Taito Ward Assembly speaker, leader of Ono's Pure Bell Association), 172, 185–186
Iki-iki Matsuri: explained, 121, 124–125; compared to Ono campaign, 126; connection to *seikatsu-sha* explained, 139
interest representation, 65, 198
Iwane Kunio: founding Seikatsu Cooperative, 127–132
Iwao, Sumiko, 68
Iwate branch, 145

Japan New Party, 174
Japanese Voter, The, 7
Jones, Kathleen, 11

Kakizawa, Kōji (House of Representatives member), 177, 181–182, 188
Kameda-san: explaining political distance, 75, 77–78
Kanagawa Netto, 162
Katano Reiko (Nerima Ward elected representative, Netto connection), 77, 137
Kawashima-san: with aging parents, 56–58; as progressive volunteer, 38
Keiko: with mother, 49–50; as new wife, 38–40
kōenkai: defined, 167; Kakizawa Kōji's, 181–82, 188; Ono Kiyoko's, 167, 177–180
Kunihiro, Yōko, 31, 42, 148

Lebra, Takie, 40–42
liberal democracy: contrasted with bicycle citizenship, 198; end of Cold War and, 4; individualism and, 9; motherhood as a challenge to, 10–12; non-Western examples of, ix; *seken* and, 41; universal citizenship and, 10–12, 208n30; West and, 13
Liberal Democratic Party: factional competition in, 175–176; Japanese political system and, 18; 1989 election and, 5;

1992 election and, 174–178; 1993 split and, 195; Ono Kiyoko's campaign organization and, 81, 174–175, 188; unaligned electorate and, 5; volunteer activity and, 90; women and, 188–191
Locke, John, 10
Loesser, Herta, 96

Madonna Boom: 1989 election and, 6, 82
mapping: consciousness, 17, 26–27; research site, xii
Martin, Joann, 148
meibō: defined, 185
membership drive, 154
men: as absent husbands, 49; advisory board membership and, 79–80; bicycle citizenship and, 25; dominance of, in politics, 80–82; dominance of, in PTA, 79; Iwane Kunio (founder of Seikatsu Co-op), 127–132; in Ono campaign, 179, 184; voluntarism and, 93–98
methodology: bicycles in, 3, 14, 17, 19–23, 26–27; data collection, 16, 19; elite bias in, 7, 66, 206n22; ethnography, ix, 14–16, 208n31; participant observation, x; political participation research and, 66; sampling, 19; taxi research in, 13, 14, 16
mijika: defined, 74; political consciousness and, 74, 77, 201; politicians' unacceptable version of, 87
Miura-san (Seikatsu Co-op activist), 140–141
Miyazawa Kiichi (former prime minister), 186
Morita Itsuko (Setagaya Ward representative, Netto affiliated), 150, 162
Morita Kensaku (House of Councilors candidate), 168
motherhood: citizenship and, 12; Netto rhetoric and, 149; political actors and, xiii, 148
Motō Ryō (candidate for ward chief), 113–114
Mouffe, Chantal, 208n30, 226n4

Nakasone Yasuhiro (former prime minister), 176, 179, 186
neighborhood association: Japanese term for, discussed 76
Nerima: advisory board for disaster preparedness, 79–80; author's entry to, 17; Hikari-ga-oka neighborhood, 61; urban

qualities, 32–33; voluntarism in, 99–100, ward assembly elections, 153; ward of Tokyo, 2; Welfare Council and, 99, 105
Netto (Nettowāku): explained, 123; feminism and, 147; Kanagawa Netto, 162; Katano Reiko and, 137; members as neighborhood housewives, 148; Morita Itsuko, 150, 162; Nerima branch conflict with organization, 159; Nerima Ward assembly election, 153; 1995 election and, 195; Okawahara-san, 162; organizational structure, 135–136; reluctant participation by Seikatsu Co-op members, 153; rhetorical use of housewife identity by, 124, 126, 146, 149, 151, 161; Takada Chieko and, 137, 146–149, 158–161; Tokyo Assembly and, 158
New Social Movement theory, 129–132
"Not in My Backyard" problem, 109

obligation, 199–200
Ogura Motoi (House of Councilors candidate), 166, 175–176
Ōizumi: author's entry to, 17, 19; neighborhood in Nerima, Tokyo, 2; urban qualities, 32–33, 34–35; voluntarism in, 99
Okawahara-san (Tokyo Assembly representative, Netto affiliated), 162–163
Ono Kiyoko, 18; *aisatsu* and, 171, 180–181, 186; bicycle methodology and, 19–21; campaign staff and, 177, 182–185; Ginza appearance by, 164; Hikari-ga-oka speech by, 61–62; housewife rhetoric, use of, 89, 165, 167–170, 173, 191–193; Kakizawa Kōji and, 177, 181–182, 188; *kōenkai* and, 167, 177–180; *meibō* and, 185; 1992 campaign photo collection and, 61; organization of campaign and, 100–101, 172, 175, 177–178, 185–191; poster problem and, 188; supporters' discussion of, 171–172; as talent legislator, 167–168; as taxi politician, 165
organization: advisory board, 79–80; *chōnaikai,* 76–77; housewife identity and, 149, 155–156, 159; Japan New Party and, 174; *kōenkai,* 167, 177–182, 188; Liberal Democratic Party and, 81, 174–175, 188; Netto and, 135–136; Ono's campaign and, 100–101, 172, 175, 177–178, 185–191; political power and, 77, 81–

organization *(continued)*
83, 87, 150; Seikatsu Cooperative, 135–
134; Sagyōsho, 100–101; study session
conflict and, 155–157; types of volunteer, 94–99

Pateman, Carole, 10–11
Pharr, Susan, 8
Ph.D. Kenkyūkai, 22
political culture: spectator citizenship, 5;
study of women in, 8
political participation: elite focus of existing research, 66, 206n22; historical pattern of women's, 67; housewife duties,
constraint of, 80, 86; housewives' new
form of *(shufu pawā)*, 67, 122; perception of political distance and, 75–77;
privatization and, 67–69, 73–74, 78;
Seikatsu Cooperative Netto movement
and, 123–124, 136, 146–147, 153;
women's underreporting of, 84;
women volunteers, rate of, 98
political pedigree, 177, 182–184
political science, 6; bicycle methodology,
3, 14, 17, 19–23, 26–27; data collection,
16; elite bias in, 7, 66, 206n22; elite focus of existing research, 66, 206n22;
ethnography, ix, 14–16, 208n31; participant observation, x; political participation research and, 66; sampling
method, 19; taxi research, 13, 14, 16
politics: closed quality of, 82; conflicts
with housewife identity, 64; contrasted
with voluntarism, 91, 114; corruption
and, 83; defined by housewives, 63, 85;
distance as description of consciousness
about, 74–78; Japanese terms for, 63;
male dominance and, 80–82; *mijika*,
74, 77, 87; organization and money in,
83; separation from public world, 84;
talk about, 63, 69–73; volunteers' rejection of, 112–113
privatization, 67–69, 73–74, 78, 84, 163
professional politicians, 161–162
PTA: networks built in, 36, 48; housewife identity and, 37; male dominance
in, 79; talk about politics in, 69, 70, 77;
women presidents of, 79, 215n18
public-private dichotomy, 68, 74
Pure Bell Association: Iida Tsuneko,
leader of, 172, 185, 186; *meibō* of, 185;
Ono campaign appearances and, 172,

187; organization of, 178, 187; strategy,
190

rhetorical use of housewife: by Netto,
124, 126, 146, 149, 151, 161; in Ono
campaign, 89, 165, 167–170, 173, 191–
193
Rousseau, Jean-Jacques, 209n39
ryōsai kenbo: defined, 68

Sagyōsho: Christmas Party, 116; community ties and, 109; compared with Seikatsu Co-op, 123; ethic of, 103, 108, 112;
expansion to Clubhouse, 115, 117; *gyōsei*
and, 110–115, 118; introduced, 91; making friends at, 106; members, 108;
Motō Ryō and, 113–114; "Not in My
Backyard" problem and, 109; organizational structure contrasted with Ono
campaign, 100–101; politics and, 112;
staff, 106; *yaruki* and, 110–114
Sasaki-san: advising daughter, 38, 49–50;
changing representation of housewife
identity and, 23, 46–48, 50; work and,
51–52
Satō-san: Sagyōsho and, 101–102, 119–120;
work and, 46
Satō Yoshiyuki, 131
Scott, Joan, 209n31
second-generation politicians, 82
seiji: defined, 63
seikatsu/seikatsu-sha: connection to housewife identity, 140–143; defined, 138–139;
feminism and, 147–148; politics and,
142; usage defined, 85; young mother's
worries about, 85
Seikatsu Cooperative: compared with Sagyōsho, 123; feminism and, 147–148;
founding of, 127–130; *han*, 134, 151–153,
156–157; Hikari-ga-oka branch, 156–158;
housewife identity and membership in,
140–145, 151, 154–155, 158; Iki-iki Matsuri, 121, 124–126, 139; Iwate branch,
145; leadership selection, 158; membership drive, 154; Netto and, 123–127, 135–
137, 146–150, 158–162; Ōizumi branch,
133–134, 152, 155–156; organizational
structure of, 134–135; reluctance to participate in Netto, 153; *seikatsu-sha* and,
138–140; *shutai* and, 130, 138; study session conflict, 155–157
seken: defined, 41

self, sense of: relational quality of, 39–40; *seken* and, 41

Setagaya Ward Assembly, 150, 162

shakaijin: defined, 111

shikaku shakai: defined, 150

shufu: translation discussed, 29–30

shufu pawā: defined, 67

Shufuren, 128

shutai: defined, 130–131; gender and, 138

social status, 26, 32, 53

Spivak, Gayatri Chakravorty, 209n31

study session conflict, 155–157

Takada Chieko (Nerima Ward representative, Netto affiliated), 137, 146–147, 149, 158–161

"talent" legislator, 167–168

Tanaka Kakuei (former prime minister), 81

Tanaka-san: with aging parents, 58; as full-time housewife, 48; volunteering, 90, 104–106

taxi citizenship: concept summarized, 24

taxi politician, 165, 201

Tocqueville, Alexis de: purpose in studying America, 8; volunteer activity and, 91–92

Tokyo Assembly elections, 158

Tsubokawa-san (Seikatsu Co-op activist), 156

Ueda-san: wife of field study sponsor, 17, 37; Sagyōsho and, 102; survey of Seikatsu Cooperative members, 137

Ueno Chizuko, 167

Ueno-san: PTA president, 79; discussing leadership, 80–81

uguisu-jo: defined, 61, 168; in Ono campaign, 184, 186

unaligned electorate, 5

United States–Japan Educational Commission, 22

universal citizenship, 10–12, 208n30

univocality, 10–12

Voice and Equality, 94

voluntarism: contrasted with politics, 91,

114; ethic of, 103–112; *gyōsei* and, 110–114; housewife duties and, 107; housewife rhetoric and, 89; inclusiveness and, 107; Indian women and, xiii; instrumental-expressive dichotomy, 94; Japanese term for, 97–98; structure of, in Nerima and Ōizumi 99–100; politics and, 112–113; specialization within, 107; study of, 92–93, 216n6, 216n8, n9; study of, sexism and, 93–96, 220n26; Welfare Council and, 99, 105; *yaruki* and, 110–114

volunteer seminar, 114

Watanabe Michio (former minister of foreign affairs), 177, 186

women and work: exclusion and, 65, 122; "good wife, wise mother" image and, 31; housewife identity and uncertain status of, 45–47, 51–53, 213n27; "M"-curve in employment and, 31; statistics on, 211n12, n13

women in politics: clean politicians and, 83; as elected representatives, statistics on, 220n16; harassment of assemblywomen, 150; Iida Tsuneko, 172, 185–186; Katano Reiko, 77, 137; Liberal Democratic Party and, 188–191; Madonna Boom, 6, 82; Morita Itsuko, 150; Motō Ryō, 113–114; Okawahara-san, 162–163; Ono campaign staff and, 184; Ono Kiyoko, 18–21, 61–62, 89, 100–101, 165–172, 177–191; Pure Bell Association and, 172, 178, 185–186, 190; Seikatsu Cooperative Netto movement and, 6, 123–124, 146–150, 153, 158; studied in political science, 8, 66; Takada Chieko, 137, 146–147, 149, 158–161; taxi politician and, 165, 201

Yamamoto-san (Seikatsu Co-op member), 143–144

yaruki: defined, compared with *gyōsei*, 110–112; volunteer seminar and, 114

Young, Iris Marion, 11, 13

yūzei: defined, examples of, 166, 192

STUDIES OF THE EAST ASIAN INSTITUTE
Selected Titles

Japan's Total Empire: Manchuria and the Culture of Wartime Imperialism, by
Louise Young. Berkeley: University of California Press, 1997.
Troubled Industries: Confronting Economic Change in Japan, by Robert Uriu.
Ithaca: Cornell University Press, 1996.
*Tokugawa Confucian Education: The Kangien Academy of Hirose Tansō (1782–
1856),* by Marleen Kassel. Albany, N.Y.: State University of New York
Press, 1996.
The Dilemma of the Modern in Japanese Fiction, by Dennis C. Washburn.
New Haven: Yale University Press, 1995.
The Final Confrontation: Japan's Negotiations with the United States, 1941, ed-
ited by James W. Morley. New York: Columbia University Press, 1994.
Landownership under Colonial Rule: Korea's Japanese Experience, 1900–1935, by
Edwin H. Gragert. Honolulu: University of Hawaii Press, 1994.
Japan's Foreign Policy after the Cold War: Coping with Change, edited by Ger-
ald L. Curtis, Armonk, N.Y.: M. E. Sharpe, 1993.
The Writings of Kōda Aya, a Japanese Literary Daughter, by Alan Tansman.
New Haven: Yale University Press, 1993.
The Poetry and Poetics of Nishiwaki Junzaburō: Modernism in Translation, by
Hosea Hirata, Princeton: Princeton University Press, 1993.
Social Mobility in Contemporary Japan, by Hiroshi Ishida. Stanford: Stanford
University Press, 1993.
Sowing the Seeds of Change: Chinese Students, Japanese Teachers, 1895–1905, by
Paula S. Harrell. Stanford: Stanford University Press, 1992.
*Explaining Economic Policy Failure: Japan and the 1969–1971 International Mone-
tary Crisis,* by Robert Angel. New York: Columbia University Press, 1991.
Suicidal Narrative in Modern Japan: The Case of Dazai Osamu, by Alan
Wolfe. Princeton: Princeton University Press, 1990.
Financial Politics in Contemporary Japan, by Frances Rosenbluth. Ithaca: Cor-
nell University Press, 1989.
Education in Japan, by Richard Rubinger and Edward Beauchamp. New
York: Garland Publishing, 1989.
Neighborhood Tokyo, by Theodore C. Bestor. Stanford: Stanford University
Press, 1989.
Aftermath of War: Americans and the Remaking of Japan, 1945–1952, by How-
ard B. Schonberger. Kent, Ohio: Kent State University Press, 1989.
*Japan and the World, 1853–1952: A Bibliographic Guide to Recent Scholarship in
Japanese Foreign Relations,* by Sadao Asada. New York: Columbia Univer-
sity Press, 1988.
Remaking Japan: The American Occupation as New Deal, by Theodore Cohen,
edited by Herbert Passin. New York: Free Press, 1987.
The Japanese Way of Politics, by Gerald L. Curtis. New York: Columbia University Press, 1988.
Urban Japanese Housewives: At Home and in the Community, by Anne E. Ima-
mura. Honolulu: University of Hawaii Press, 1987.

Japan's Modern Myths: Ideology in the Late Meiji Period, by Carol Gluck. Princeton: Princeton University Press, 1985.

Japanese Culture, third edition, revised, by H. Paul Varley. Honolulu: University of Hawaii Press, 1984.

Japan Erupts: The London Naval Conference and the Manchurian Incident, edited by James W. Morley. New York: Columbia University Press, 1984.

State and Diplomacy in Early Modern Japan, by Ronald Toby. Princeton: Princeton University Press, 1983 (hardcover); Stanford: Stanford University Press, 1991 (paperback).

Private Academies of Tokugawa Japan, by Richard Rubinger. Princeton: Princeton University Press, 1982.

Tanaka Giichi and Japan's China Policy, by William F. Morton. Folkestone, England: Dawson, 1980; New York: St. Martin's Press, 1980.

The Fateful Choice: Japan's Advance into Southeast Asia, edited by James W. Morley. New York: Columbia University Press, 1980.

Patterns of Japanese Policymaking: Experiences from Higher Education, by T. J. Pempel. Boulder, Colo.: Westview Press, 1978.

Contemporary Japanese Budget Politics, by John Creighton Campbell. Berkeley: University of California Press, 1977.

Japanese International Negotiating Style, by Michael Blaker. New York: Columbia University Press, 1977.

Insei: Abdicated Sovereigns in the Politics of Late Heian Japan, by G. Cameron Hurst. New York: Columbia University Press, 1975.

Shiba Kōkan: Artist, Innovator, and Pioneer in the Westernization of Japan, by Calvin L. French. Tokyo: Weatherhill, 1974.

Composition: Binghamton Valley Composition
Text: 10/13 Galliard
Display: Galliard
Printing and binding: Maple-Vail Book Manufacturing Group